Therapy in the Age o

Therapy in the Age of Neuroscience: A Guide for Counsellors and Therapists is an essential guide to key areas of neuroscience that inform the theory underlying psychotherapy, and how they can be applied to practice. Laying out the science clearly and accessibly, it outlines what therapists need to know about the human nervous system in order to be able to engage with the subject.

Chapters cover the neuroscience underlying key aspects of therapy such as relationships, emotion, anxiety, trauma and dissociation, the mind-body connection, and the processes which enable therapists to engage deeper aspects of mind and psyche. This book responds to the need for counsellors and therapists to have an accessible and comprehensive guide to how contemporary neuroscience views mind and body.

Therapy in the Age of Neuroscience will appeal to psychotherapists, counsellors and other mental health professionals who wish to learn more about how to integrate neuroscience into their work.

Peter Afford has worked as a counsellor and therapist in private practice and in organisations for over 25 years. He has developed and taught courses in neuroscience for therapists since 2007 and has been a Focusing teacher since the 1980s.

"In *Therapy in the Age of Neuroscience*, psychotherapist Peter Afford boldly integrates the voices of contemporary neuroscientists into a therapist-relevant narrative that interlaces psychological constructs including diagnostic features with a knowledge of the relevant role that specific neural structures play in movements, thoughts and feelings. Through the lens of a therapist, the reader is informed how a knowledge of neuroscience can inform, support and at times transform treatment models relevant to mental health."

Stephen W Porges, PhD, Distinguished University Scientist, Indiana University, Professor of Psychiatry, University of North Carolina, and author of *The Pocket Guide to the Polyvagal Theory: The Transformative Power of Feeling Safe*.

"This book is a useful compendium of recent thinking on the emotional brain. Written in a clear, readable style, it will help psychotherapists to digest neuroscientific knowledge and integrate it with the practice of psychotherapy."

Sue Gerhardt, author of *Why Love Matters*.

Therapy in the Age of Neuroscience

A Guide for Counsellors and Therapists

Peter Afford

LONDON AND NEW YORK

First published 2020
by Routledge
2 Park Square, Milton Park, Abingdon, Oxon OX14 4RN

and by Routledge
52 Vanderbilt Avenue, New York, NY 10017

Routledge is an imprint of the Taylor & Francis Group, an informa business

British Library Cataloguing-in-Publication Data
A catalogue record for this book is available from the British Library

Library of Congress Cataloging-in-Publication Data
A catalog record has been requested for this book

ISBN: 978-1-138-67934-4 (hbk)
ISBN: 978-1-138-67935-1 (pbk)
ISBN: 978-1-315-51273-0 (ebk)

Typeset in Times New Roman
by Swales & Willis, Exeter, Devon, UK

To the memory of Eugene Gendlin, a philosopher who disliked science, but whose bio-philosophical thinking, with a practice to accompany it, helped me understand enough neuroscience to be able to write this book.

Contents

Figures

Tables

Acknowledgements

For offering their time to talk with me, my thanks to Iain McGilchrist and Daniel Glaser.

For responding to questions, my thanks to Stephen Porges, Jaak Panksepp (before his death in 2017), Robert Sapolsky, Susan Greenfield, Allan Schore, Louis Cozolino and Sue Gerhardt.

For engaging in many helpful discussions over the years, my thanks to Dale Mathers.

For commenting on draft chapters, my thanks to Richard Kradin, Tony Cook, Stella Law, Francis Atkinson, Camilla Sim, Keith Silvester, Em Farrell and Michael Soth.

My thanks to everyone who's participated in my neuroscience seminars and discussion groups, helping me develop my understanding of the subject, especially Jacky Selwyn-Smith and Maria White (before her untimely death in 2017) for their sustained enthusiasm.

And, of course, my thanks to everyone who's ever walked into my consulting room and demonstrated the many realities of the human psyche.

Finally, my thanks to Sue for her patient support and for being far more realistic than I was about how long it would take to write this book – and for solving my problem of procuring bespoke brain diagrams by drawing them herself.

Introduction

A long time ago, in a previous century, I was in a bookshop one lunchtime when a tome entitled *The Feeling of What Happens* fell off a shelf into my hands, as books sometimes do. Having searched for my feelings over many years of immersion in therapy, focusing and bodywork, the title drew me in. Written by an eloquent neuroscientist, Antonio Damasio, I understood enough to find it stimulating. I'm a therapist, not a neuroscientist, but my interest in the subject was sparked.

Since then, I've read many neuroscience books and attended many neuroscience talks. Come the new millennium, I began giving short seminars on the subject and have now done over 100 day-long seminars to groups of therapists, in which I've faced many questions and the occasional brickbat. In 2011, I put my head above the parapet and launched a nine-day course for qualified therapists, spread over a year. Having run it five times, the obvious next step was to transform the course material into a book.

Much of this book is a round-up of what prominent people in this area have to say. I'm happy to align with the rough consensus developing amongst other psychotherapists writing about neuroscience, in particular the Californian triumvirate of Allan Schore, Lou Cozolino and Dan Siegel. I add my own perspective so, whilst offering a summary of what's already out there, I hope to break some new ground.

I draw on the work of two camps of writers: neuroscientists, who generally know little about therapy, and other therapists who've delved into neuroscience. Wherever possible, I refer to the first camp to explain the science. Neuroscientists have interesting things to say, and some of them say it very well. But in matters psychological, the therapists are needed.

Neuroscience isn't a monolith. It's a mosaic of contributions from many individuals, each with their own voice. "Everything said is said by someone," say Chilean biologists Humberto Maturana and Francisco Varela (1987: 26). So I'll introduce my cast of characters and let them speak. This requires inserting a lot of references, and I try to minimise the disruption it causes by keeping to one voice per paragraph wherever possible; the science that follows a reference is the same voice speaking, sometimes with my own commentary.

Books on this subject often rely heavily on journal articles reporting research results, but I rely on books and lecture material. Research articles provide data, whilst books are the outcome of expert minds, better qualified than mine, that have digested and reflected on such data. This modus operandi helps keep my head above water amidst a subject constantly threatening to overwhelm with detail.

But surely neuroscience is evolving rapidly, and anyone writing about it should be up on the latest research? At the overview level relevant to therapists, I'm not persuaded. Although new research is reported all the time, progress in making sense of it moves slowly as even experts need time to absorb findings and consider their meaning. I'm interested in the big picture view that allows non-scientists to see the wood as the trees proliferate. I include some recent offerings from the big beasts of the neuroscience jungle – and sometimes I find that their earlier work packed a bigger punch and return to that.

Neuroscience is a scarily complicated subject. My aim is to go deep enough that you can think for yourself about the science and be equipped to read neuroscience books without succumbing to neural meltdown. But not too deep. Some technical terms are unavoidable, but I keep them to a minimum (promise!). There's a glossary at the end to look them up whenever you want, and I've relegated some technical points to notes at the end of chapters.

A nice thing about neuroscience is that it's about you and me, as we all have one of the items under discussion lodged within us. A problem with it is that it stirs curiosity about an alarmingly wide range of topics. I cover many here, but some I've left out as they won't all fit into one book. Examples are love and sex (sorry), which are surprisingly tricky topics.

There are no case studies since I don't think they illustrate neuroscience well. The gap between the principles of the subject and the detail of clinical work is wide. Neuroscience is a body of knowledge, not a system of psychological thinking, and it needs interpreting to be useful to therapists. I find it better to discuss neuroscience angles on case material in small supervision and training groups. Here I simply illustrate the science with personal or clinical examples of a general nature.

A writer's choice of language can raise hackles, so let me come clean on my use thereof.

First, neuroscientists love electronic analogies – circuits, wiring, coding, information processing, and so forth. But brains are the work of nature, and I resist likening my brain to my computer – it's not hard to tell the difference. I prefer nature analogies, such as pathways and forests, wherever possible.

Second, I rarely make gender distinctions. Please read gender specific words as covering all genders. Simply for simplicity's sake, I normally refer to the therapist as 'she' and to the client as 'he'. Also, to the child as 'he'.

Third, I write about mothers, fathers and parents, not about 'primary caregivers', a term that's functional rather than poetic. Life starts with mother and hopefully father too, and these words connect us with the psychological archetypes and our evolutionary past. When I refer to 'mother', for example, I mean a person in a mothering role who may or may not be the biological mother.

Speaking of which, mothers in particular can get a hard time in discussions about child development, and sometimes they do here. I can't see how to avoid this if we're to stand up for the child, which as therapists we must. So let's bear context in mind. Mothers have the most demanding job, one they can only fulfil with the support of partners, families and communities – and one that politicians and business leaders, usually men, sometimes make much harder.

Fourth, there's a tendency for writers to make up their own terminology to add to the profusion of existing neuroscience and psychotherapy terms, which I don't always find helpful. However, I'm guilty of doing so myself because I made up 'right brain-body ensemble', 'foreground mind' and 'background bodymind' whilst writing this book – but have otherwise endeavoured to keep to standard terminology to minimise confusion.

To illustrate the brain, diagrams are needed to complement the words. I include some basic ones, but the brain is a complex three-dimensional thing, whereas diagrams are two-dimensional. I recommend you equip a portable computer screen with an application that shows a three-dimensional brain, in colour, that you can rotate.

I take an integrative view of therapy in this book, and write for the profession and its close relations: counselling, psychoanalysis, clinical psychology and so forth. By therapy, I mean all of these disciplines where two people face each other in a room. I like to seek common ground amongst the tribes of the therapy world.

Nevertheless, we all have our bias, so I'll be transparent about 'where I'm coming from'. I was originally drawn into psychology by reading Jung, and he's accompanied me ever since. My first training was a year of biodynamic therapy (Gerda Boyesen), so I'm into the body. Then I learnt Focusing (Eugene Gendlin) and started teaching it because 'you teach best what you most need to learn', so the 'felt sense' is often mentioned. Later, I did my professional training in psychosynthesis and imbibed its sensible, warm-hearted and transpersonal ambience. For years I've had a psychoanalytic supervisor of a Jungian persuasion who's influenced my thinking. Jung and Gendlin are my pre-eminent guides, Jung for understanding the nature of the psyche and Gendlin for understanding the process of psychological change and how to work with it. My liking for working dialogically and experientially will be evident.

Fools rush in where angels fear to tread, and given the complexity of neuroscience I'm a complete fool. I've repeatedly faced down my inner critic by reminding myself that my wide reading of the rock stars of neuroscience, allied to my long experience of therapy (occupying both chairs and having crossed the 10,000 hours rubicon in the therapist's chair some years ago) gives me a particular, somewhat unique, perspective.

I've had the annoying habit of wanting to know how things work since I was a young child. My parents assumed I'd become an engineer. However, I was hopeless at maths, but liked stories and wondering what made people tick – and what was wrong with me, because I often felt quite inadequate. After meandering through the world during my 20s and 30s, I became a psychotherapist, but I never lost my interest in what goes on underneath bonnets. Hence, perhaps, my enthusiasm for neuroscience.

Neuroscience provides insights into many topics that arise in the therapy room. But more than this, it gives us a map of the nervous system underlying our psychology. I believe this makes a pragmatic starting point for thinking about the psychological phenomena therapists encounter. Whilst you can use this book as a reference for the various topics covered, you need to read the first seven chapters to appreciate the map as a whole.

Chapter 1

Therapy meets neuroscience

Introduction

Human encounters in the therapy room are a world apart from neuroscience with its hi-tech wizardry for peering into people's brains. Yet both disciplines explore the human nervous system, and they share common ground. Both accept the formative power of early experience and the potential for changing mature brains. Both know that the brain can't be seen in isolation from the rest of the body. And both recognise that our cognitive capacities are frequently trumped by our affective ones.

Their meeting has history, since Freud began his career as a neurologist and speculated about the future for psychology:

> Biology is truly a land of unlimited possibilities. We may expect it to give us the most surprising information, and we cannot guess what answers it may return in a few dozen years ... They may be of a kind which will blow away the whole of our artificial structure of hypotheses.
>
> (cited in Solms & Turnbull 2002: 298)

Have those hypotheses been blown away yet? I suspect not. But perhaps there's a steady process of erosion and re-sculpting happening whereby some go, some remain and others are revised. I hope this book is a useful contribution to the discussion underpinning such a process.

However you feel about neuroscience, it's increasingly hard to avoid. Trainers and speakers at gatherings of therapists love to include morsels of neuroscience. So should therapists study neuroscience, and if so, which aspects of it? How deeply into the technical details should we go? Does neuroscience require us to change what we do? What strikes me is how the morsels are handed out without much contextual understanding of the subject. Trees are sprouting, but we lack a wood.

Objections to neuroscience

Not all therapists are sold on neuroscience, so I'll start by examining some arguments against embracing the subject.

Why learn about the hypothalamus? A colleague in a peer supervision group once said she couldn't see how it would help her to know about the hypothalamus. She had a point: isolated facts are useless, and potentially misleading. But an understanding of the stress response, in which the hypothalamus plays a key role, is clearly pertinent to therapy. Detail belongs in context.

Science has no place in a healing human encounter. A more vehement objection is that science should be kept apart from the art of therapy; the dialogue could be diminished by technicalities, the human soul lost. For example, clinical psychologist Richard House wrote a while back: "forgive me, but what conceivable relevance can neuroscience have to a client and me when we're sitting in a room together, trying to co-create a healing encounter?" (2013: 42). Fair enough, but behind the therapist's role in that encounter lie her theories guiding her interventions, and neuroscience gives her a new perspective on the client's difficulties and what may be needed to resolve them.

Science is reductionist. A related argument is that neuroscience is reductionist ('this is merely that'), deterministic (your biology determines your behaviour) and materialistic (soul and spirit are banished) and therefore philosophically opposed to therapy. But these supposed evils of human thinking concern the way science is done, while we can consider the results without being reductionist. Cannot science be combined with art – or craft? Also, I'm sometimes astonished how ascribing anything to the brain can be called reductionist when it's the most complex known object in the universe!

A little knowledge is a dangerous thing. This argument carries weight, since neuroscience is an alarmingly complicated subject. Would prudence dictate that we steer clear of it? Certainly, we should beware getting too excited about individual findings and jumping to unwarranted conclusions. But however complex a subject is, it's always possible to distil detail into a high-level summary that offers understanding without sacrificing facts.

Therapists don't need neuroscience to do good therapy. This is true – therapists gain an intuitive understanding of how brains work from examining their own psyches (hopefully) and spending their days encountering other people's psyches. Nevertheless, if another perspective on the human psyche brings fresh insights, why dismiss it? It can be combined with intuition, experience and psychological theory.

Good reasons for embracing neuroscience

Clients present for therapy because their brains don't function as they wish, and therapists use *their* brains to help them function better. So what are the arguments in favour of therapists embracing neuroscience?

Our psychology is rooted in our biology. Psychology and neurobiology can't be separated without straying into dualism, the separation of mind from body for which Descartes is endlessly berated. We needn't wonder which comes first, like chickens and eggs, for we can dance with both. Biology offers another perspective.

Neuroscience makes the implicit explicit. Everyone has an implicit understanding of how minds work, their own and others' – we've been figuring them out from day one. Therapists are meant to have a particularly well developed implicit understanding, informed by self-reflection and psychological theory. If we say we rely on intuition rather than theory, we're probably guided by implicit principles that could be called 'theories of human nature'. Neuroscience makes the implicit a tad more explicit, allowing us to wonder what effect our interventions might have on our clients' nervous systems. We can cross-refer between implicit understanding and an appreciation of the nervous system.

Neuroscience provides a check on psychological thinking. Psychological thinking usually starts with experience and observation, and then we build theoretical edifices on top. Now we can test the validity of these edifices against neuroscience. A good example is trauma and dissociation: with what's now known about the nervous system, our understanding of these important topics is, I think, considerably clearer (the proof of the pudding lies in Chapter 7).

Neuroscience has an integrative influence. The therapy world is divided into many camps. Neuroscience studies the human nervous system that applies to everyone, individual variations notwithstanding, and it gives us pointers that therapists of all persuasions can use. It provides a shared knowledge base to refer to. It's also integrative in that it encompasses the body as well as the brain, since the nervous system reaches everywhere inside. And although cognitive neuroscience has dominated the field, there's affective neuroscience as well. So I'll address body as well as mind, and feeling as well as thinking.

Neuroscience can normalise the problem. Explaining something a person struggles with, and feels shame around, in neurobiological terms can help them accept themselves as they are ("oh! that makes sense – I thought there was something wrong with me").

Neuroscience is interesting! I think this is the best argument for embracing neuroscience. Here are revelations, not about a faraway universe, but about what goes on in our own heads, minds and bodies – under the bonnet.

The nature of the beast

It's easy to imagine neuroscience is something that it isn't. Some caveats are in order.

Beware seeking certainty. I'm often asked questions that assume that neuroscience has the answer to everything (and that I know a lot more than I do). It doesn't. It offers a body of knowledge (of which I know only a fraction) that complements psychology. Even brain scanning is not as exact a method as you might imagine. The reality is that neuroscience hasn't discovered the holy grail of human nature, and we don't know exactly what's happening in people's brains in the therapy room. Your clients may not want to put their head in a brain scanner, or even sit with a hairnet of electrodes wiring them to a machine. Instead, neuroscience provides a framework that allows you to reflect on *might* be happening.

Anything you do will change the brain. Enthusiastic proponents of newfangled therapeutic techniques often claim that they 'change the brain' (as distinct from those that don't!). But our brains are changing all the time anyway, so on its own this statement doesn't mean much. The question to ponder is "what sort of effect *might* this technique have on my client's brain?". Then you can follow a line of thought. And when someone's brain does change, which we can deduce from their changed behaviour and experience, we can speculate about its nature. One day, people may have routine brain scans at the beginning and end of therapy, but that day is in the future.

Don't reduce, associate. Learning about the brain can tempt us into the dreaded reductionism. For example, hearing that mystical experiences involve the right temporal lobe might lead you to think that such experiences are merely the result of activity in this part of the brain. But there's no need to state things in such bald terms, and anyway such a conclusion isn't warranted. What we can say is that there's an *association* between mystical experiences and activity in the right temporal lobe, and be curious about it. Then we open the discussion up, rather than use science to close it down.

Correlation usually beats causation. We can also be tempted into thinking in simplistic causal terms. For example, depression involves chemical imbalance in the brain, so you might think the imbalance causes the depression. But neuroscience doesn't say that chemical imbalance causes depression, it says the two are correlated: a depressed brain is one with different neurochemistry from a healthy brain. This may tell us something about depression and about the role antidepressants can play in alleviating it.

Beware the fatal attractions of pop psychology. Our minds can run off with neuro-nuggets we hear about. It takes discipline to be patient and not rush to conclusions. An example of pop psychology causing trouble is the left and right hemispheres business. When new insights arose from split-brain research in the 1960s, pop psychology ideas took hold: some people (logical thinking types) were 'left-brained' and others (intuitive creative types) were 'right-brained'. This is an over-simplification, and the real differences between the hemispheres are subtler and much more interesting (Chapter 3).

Neuroscience doesn't explain everything. There are some things people bring to therapy that lie beyond the scope of neuroscience – such as synchronicity, subtle energies, chakras, telepathy. But there are plenty of other things that regularly come to therapy about which it has much to say, including memory, 'the unconscious', stress, anxiety, trauma and dissociation – all subjects I'll address.

We need contextual understanding. Writers and speakers love to dispense morsels of neuroscience as if everyone knew enough to appreciate their significance. For example, I just read in Daniel Levitin's *The Organised Mind,* a book written for a general audience, about "neurons with nicotinic receptors located in a part of the brain called the substantia innominata" (2015: 47). A nice example of the impressive Latin names given to brain areas, but who's heard of this area (I haven't)? And who understands how nicotinic receptors work – is this about smoking? Similar statements about the details of brain areas that are entirely opaque to the layperson abound these days.

So let's first have a wood before we inspect the trees, an overview to help us make sense of the detail. It makes the whole subject more interesting, because you can do more with it.

Neuroscience enters therapy

So what should therapists do with neuroscience?

Some people now claim that their therapeutic methods are 'neuroscience-based', but I'm sceptical. It seems more likely that they've devised their techniques and then looked for some neuroscience to validate them. If you started out only with neuroscience, you could soon be lost in seeking new directions for therapeutic interventions – we need psychological ideas to find our way around.

Here's my perspective on the question.

We don't need neuroscience to validate what we do. Psychotherapy has been practiced for a long time, and we can be confident that how we work is grounded in theory and affirmed by our experience in the therapy room. If we needed validation from neuroscience and brain scanners, rather than from clients' feedback and our own observations, we'd be in deep trouble.

Neuroscience doesn't tell you how to do therapy. I'm sometimes asked, in effect, "can you skip the technical detail Peter and just tell us what we should be doing differently?" No, I can't! If you imagine that neuroscience is able to do this, you're much mistaken – it's a jungle lacking clearly marked paths through it. We need to bone up on neuroscience and then discuss its bearing on how we work.

Don't try to apply neuroscience – absorb it. Looking for quick ways to apply neuroscience in the therapy room is, I think, a mistake. Neuroscience can't be reduced to bullet points for therapists to follow. Rather, I recommend growing your understanding and allowing it to influence your thinking about what your clients bring and how you might respond to them.

Your learning curve will be more rewarding. And discussing neuroscience with supervisors and colleagues before 'applying' it in the room will give you more confidence.

Neuroscience doesn't replace psychological theory. It's a different kind of theory, and we can have both alongside each other, dancing between them to see what neuroscience can add to what we already know. We can hypothesise and speculate, reflecting on our experience in the light of the science. Perhaps some of it will make more sense than some psychological concepts do, since it's rooted in our biology – which we can find in our experience.

Neuroscience is a different kettle of fish. We can adopt psychological theories that resonate with us and adapt them in creative ways, but we can't play with scientific concepts in the same way. They've grown via a different route so that if you want, for example, to argue with Panksepp about his list of fundamental emotions (Chapter 5), you need to do your own lab research into neural pathways and neurochemicals. We have to take neuroscience as it is – we don't have the luxury of believing whatever we want to believe.

Don't let neuroscience dictate. People sometimes ask if neuroscience says that the brain of someone suffering a condition can change. This is putting the cart before the horse. First, we should engage with our clients to get a sense of whether they might change, and *then* we can cross-refer with neuroscience. If the person changes, their brain changes. If neuroscience were pessimistic about a particular condition, we might be stopped from trying; and if it were optimistic, it would be talking about an average brain, whereas we work with individual brains. Brains can't be examined for diagnosis and repair.

Talking neuroscience to clients. Having learnt some neuroscience, the extent to which you share it with your clients is up to you. You can keep your new knowledge to yourself if you prefer. Technical talk doesn't really belong in the therapy room – clients don't generally want to share their pain with experts, they prefer compassionate human beings. When I say something neuroscientific, I like to keep it to one sentence and allow my client to respond – which tells me how it goes down with them.

On the other hand, neuroscience ideas sometimes make more sense to people than psychological ones. The power of addictions, for example, and some of the weirder experiences in body and mind that can happen with trauma and dissociation. A little neuroscience may validate their experience and stop them thinking they're the only person on earth suffering it.

Jung said we should leave theory outside the therapy room so we can meet the client unencumbered with preconceived ideas in our head (1995). We can do the same with neuroscience. First we should meet the client, and *then* refer to neuroscience if we think it might help. Sometimes a bit of neuroscience may creep in during the session in response to something.

The rest of the time, it can be a resource for reflecting on a case after sessions, and in supervision.

Some of the diagrams in this book, such as the window of tolerance (Chapter 5), usually make sense to clients. You can draw them spontaneously or have them ready-prepared for when it feels right to use them.

Conclusion

Instead of exciting recipes for new therapeutic interventions, neuroscience provides a map of the psyche based on our biology and evolutionary history. Actually, a series of maps: it shows how mind and body are interlinked, how the brain comes in layers with emotion arising from below and cognition descending from above, and how the brain comprises two minds, one more united with the body, the other able to stand aside from it. Neuroscience sheds valuable light on the nature of memory and 'the unconscious', and on the inner turmoil of trauma and dissociation.

Like it or not, neuroscience is here to stay, but that's not itself a reason to embrace it. The proof will be in the pudding: can this complex science help us unravel the mysteries of the inner world and the self-destructive nature of much human behaviour? The challenge is also for neuroscience: to explain the human mind in a way that's useful in the therapy room. It's time to bring biology and psychology together. Schore thinks there's an "urgent need for an overarching theoretical perspective that can … make meaning out of the … massive amount of data the mental health and life sciences are now generating" (2012: 10). I hope that what follows contributes to the development of such a perspective.

If we stay grounded in our experience and honour the psychological theories that work for us in the therapy room, the third perspective that neuroscience provides can act as a catalyst for developing our work. I think neuroscience supports working long-term (as well as short-term), working experientially with emotion, images and the body, and working with the therapeutic relationship. Given my background and training, I would say this, wouldn't I? but I'll explain why.

We need the big picture view of the nervous system so we can go beyond dispensing morsels of neuroscience to serving a meal. The jigsaw pieces are here, and it's time to put them together and see the picture they reveal. Let's begin with the wood, then the trees will make more sense. Let's keep our minds open, and not just look for what we want to hear.

Chapter 2

The brain is a nervous system

Introduction

The human brain is "the most complicated material object in the known universe," says Edelman (2005: 14). Let's not allow this to discourage us: with a little effort, complex subjects can be summarised into a comprehensible outline. I'll begin at the beginning and explain the brain with the aim of painting a contextual picture to underpin the rest of the book. Some technical terms are unavoidable, but I'll aim to strike a balance and avoid unnecessary ones.

You may already know some of what follows, but I recommend reading it anyway so you can follow my reasoning in later chapters.

Nervous systems: the overall framework

That the brain is a nervous system need not surprise therapists accustomed to encountering their clients' anxieties, not to mention their own. And by describing it as a nervous system, the body is included from the outset. If you were to remove a brain from its skull, it would come with the spinal cord and a lengthy tangle of nerve endings attached. To have just the brain that sits in the head, you'd need a sharp knife to separate it from what sits below in the body. Evolution found it practical to keep the main lump of neural jelly safely encased in its protective skull, close to eyes and ears and well away from everything else sloshing around in the body. So really the brain is a part of the nervous system, which sub-divides into constituent elements as follows (see Figure 2.1).

The *central nervous system* is the brain itself plus the spinal cord – one whole thing. Most images of the brain are therefore misleading, as the brain is effectively in the body as well as in the head.

The *peripheral nervous system* is the tangle of nerves that run from the spinal cord and the brainstem at the top (the bottom of the brain) to every nook and cranny in the body. Every single blood vessel, however small, has a nerve attached.

The *autonomic nervous system* is the part of the peripheral (and the central that links with it) that regulates the inner life of the body, and that's not under

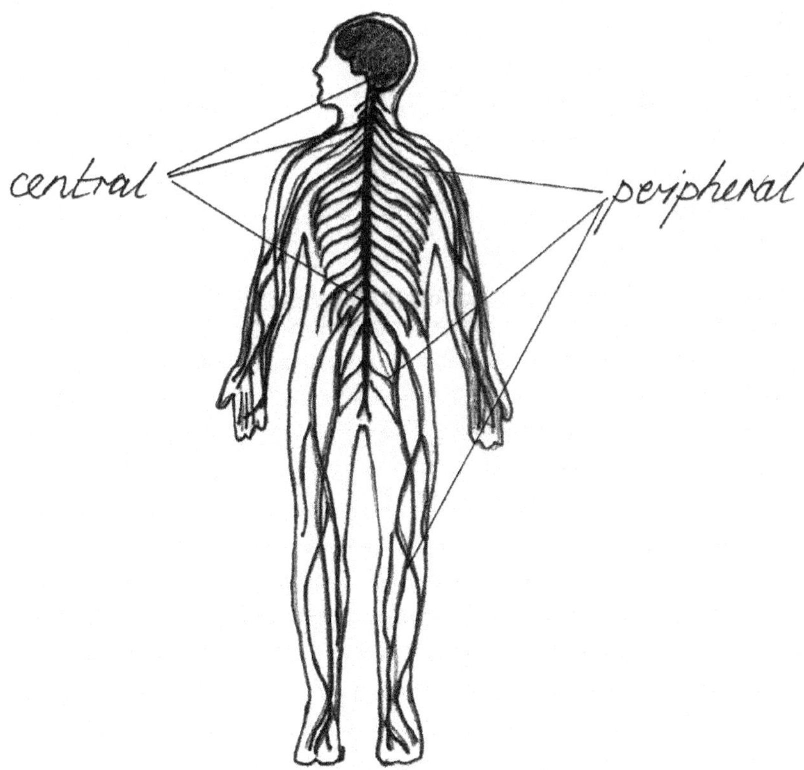

Figure 2.1 Nervous systems: the central nervous system consists of the brain and spinal cord, the peripheral nervous system extends to every nook and cranny of the body

conscious control. It does its own thing, such as when *you* want to go to sleep, but *it* keeps you awake. There's more signalling in the autonomic nervous system from body to brain than vice versa because the brain needs a detailed picture of what's happening in the body, whereas the instructions it sends to the body to change something are relatively simple.

The autonomic nervous system sub-divides into two branches. The *sympathetic nervous system* does arousal, such as waking you up in the morning and mobilising energy for life's battles. It's 'sympathetic' because it was once thought that the thinking brain sympathised with the emotional viscera in the body (Sapolsky 2004). The *parasympathetic nervous system* does the opposite, relaxing you and putting you to sleep: 'rest and digest', instead of 'fight or flight'. It's 'parasympathetic' simply because 'para' means alongside and its pathways sit alongside sympathetic ones. Sympathetic arousal and parasympathetic calming frequently overlap by degrees, but the brain generally doesn't allow both to be full on simultaneously.

Neurons and synapses: the building blocks

Brain cells are called *neurons*, and we have plenty of them, around 100 billion to be roughly precise, an astronomically large number.[1] Think of them as like trees, for reasons I'll come to (see Figure 2.2). Unlike other sorts of cells, neurons don't get replaced. You're pretty much born with your 100 billion and that's it for life. There are exceptions (as there are to everything in biology), but it's generally a good idea to hang onto those you're born with.

Everything your brain does involves neurons. LeDoux says brain cells "participate in myriad activities, from seeing and hearing to thinking and feeling, from awareness of self to the incomprehension of infinity" (2003: 39). Note the word 'participate' here: there's an endless philosophical debate as to whether neurons cause experience or experience causes neurons. Take your pick, but LeDoux wisely hedges his bets.

Axons and dendrites

Neurons are born networkers that sprout nerve fibres to communicate with other neurons. If neurons are trees, these fibres are the roots and branches, the roots being *axons* and the branches *dendrites.* Axons and dendrites seek each other out to connect via a *synapse.* Neurons typically sprout a

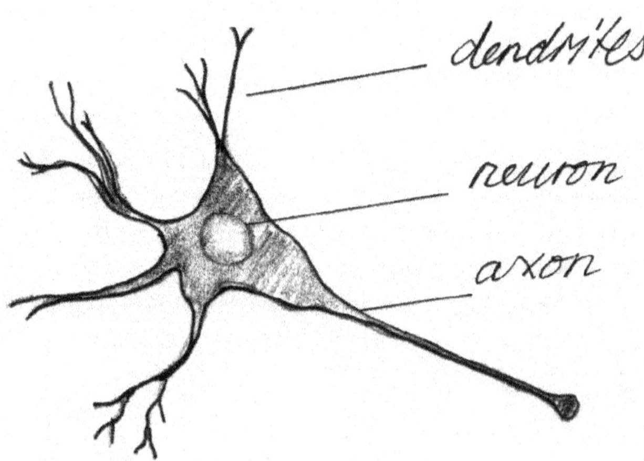

Figure 2.2 A neuron, very simplified, illustrating its cell body, branching dendrites and long axon

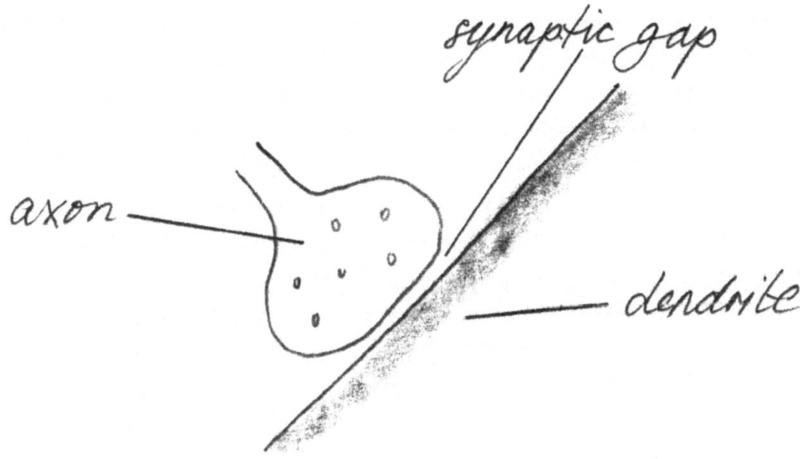

Figure 2.3 A synapse, very simplified, illustrating the tiny synaptic gap between the axon of one neuron and a dendrite of another.

single axon which branches at the end to form a few hundred synapses that send signals, and a bush of dendrites studded with thousands of synapses to receive signals (Kandel 2007). Axons can be short to link with neighbouring neurons, or long to link with distant ones in other brain regions or the spinal cord.

What matters is how well-connected neurons are. At birth, there are few connections amongst the 100 billion, so the newborn's brain is limited in what it can do. All learning in life involves new or altered connections between neurons, and the capacity to grow and change these connections continues until we die.

A synapse (from the Greek for clasping) is the point of connection between the axon of one neuron and the dendrite of another (see Figure 2.3). It's actually a small *synaptic gap* one-thousandth of a millimetre across. We have trillions of them. They enable neurons to communicate "like lips whispering very close to an ear", says Kandel (2007: 65).

Firing

Neurons communicate by 'firing' across synapses. A minute electrical charge called an *action potential* zaps down the axon and triggers the release of neurochemicals that cross the synapse to the adjoining dendrite in milliseconds. If a neuron is bombarded with sufficient chemicals from other neurons to become highly charged itself, it also fires and passes the signal on to more neurons. The overall effect of what firing across the brain might look like if we could watch it is described by cognitive scientist Guy Claxton as "flickering chains of fairy lights, and if you were able to slow it down, you would see a continuous unfolding of one pattern into the next" (2005: 254).

So neurons signal each other electro-chemically and, at any moment, billions of synapses are firing away. "Electrochemical conversations between neurons make possible all of the wondrous (and sometimes dreadful) accomplishments of human minds", says LeDoux (2003: 48).

What determines which neurons have synapses with which other neurons in the first place? The principle is that 'neurons that fire together, wire together'. If something causes neurons to fire at exactly the same moment, they tend to grow synaptic connections so that their future collaboration is more efficient. Therefore, what neurons do depends on their history. And from this, all neural and psychological development unfolds.

Grey matter and white matter

Brains get called 'grey matter', but a living brain is pink (were you ever to set eyes on one). Scientifically, grey matter refers to neurons and their short axons to neighbouring neurons, whereas white matter refers to long-distance axons from one region of the brain to another.

To speed up the action potentials that travel afar, some long axons are coated in white fatty tissue called *myelin*, rather like the insulation around electric wires. Hence myelinated pathways appear white and are fast, long-distance ones. Not all long axons are myelinated, since fast signalling is a recent evolutionary development; evolutionarily older axons are not myelinated.

Neural pathways: networking locally and afar

Axons, dendrites and synapses enable connections between neurons. Each neuron can make anywhere up to 10,000 links with other neurons, so the whole brain is a living network of many trillions (Ramachandran 2011). Here's a measure of the unimaginable complexity of the human brain.

However, "the brain is not a bowl of random spaghetti with its wires randomly spreading and slithering around with each toss of the chef", Gazzaniga points out, even if it looks like one (2016: 337). Each connection is meaningful, with its own history and biological purpose. LeDoux elucidates: "by way of these connections, communities of cells that work together to achieve a particular goal can be formed across space and time in the brain" (2003: 40); and the result is that your synapses "are who you are" (2003: 324).

Neurons, like trees, network together in their millions to form local, purpose-built jungles. And these jungles link with other jungles, so the brain is really a jungle of jungles. Neurons talk to neurons in their local jungle and to neurons in other jungles, some neighbouring and others distant. Neuroscientists refer to jungles as *regions* and *nuclei*. The outcome is that, in Damasio's words:

> Mind and behaviour are the moment-to-moment results of the operation of galaxies of nuclei ... If the galaxies are well organised and work harmoniously, the owner makes poetry. If not, madness ensues.
>
> (2010: 312)

When enough synapses in a jungle fire, that area is said to 'light up'. Whenever you think or feel something, "one neural neighbourhood influences the firing patterns of others, and those neighbourhoods in turn influence the firing patterns of others, and so on, in a tide of information that washes over the entire brain in less than half a second", says Lewis (2012: 23).

The pathways linking jungles are bunches of axons forming *nerve bundles* and *fibre tracts*. Signalling along nerves and across synapses is one-way, but receiving neurons talk back to sending ones along pathways in the reverse direction. Such feedback loops get called *circuits*. A circuit complex enough to enable, for example, seeing or hearing, is called a *system*.

The specific pathways amongst the jungles of our brains make us who we are. Our individuality lies in the particular networks of pathways that grow and in the precise details of the synapses that lie along them. LeDoux says "the key to individuality ... is not to be found in the overall organisation of the brain, but rather in the fine-tuning of the underlying networks" (2003: 36).

The connections in an individual brain are now known as the *connectome*, a term inspired by the genome (Seung 2013). Unlike your genome, your connectome, shaped by both genes and experience, changes throughout your life. Seung says that "in the same way that the water of the stream slowly shapes the bed, neural activity changes the connectome" over time (2013: xix).

To keep things simple, I'll generally refer to pathways and networks, and sometimes to systems.

Neurochemistry: making nervous systems work in diverse ways

Brain activity means neurons communicating, and this involves cascades of chemicals being released across synapses. LeDoux describes it well:

> Chemicals are oozing and sparks flying constantly, during wakefulness and during sleep, during thoughtfulness and during boredom. At any one moment, billions of synapses are active.
>
> (2003: 49)

Think of the synaptic gap as a river, and the chemicals as beach balls flung across to the other side, where they slot into *receptors* on dendrites to deliver their message. Then they return whence they came to be recycled. A neuron secretes the same small set of chemicals, or even just one, at all of its synapses (Seung 2013). And the same chemical may perform different functions in different places.[2]

Neurotransmitters

These are the beach balls that whizz across synapses. The two big ones are:

- *glutamate* (related to its culinary namesake) 'excites' the next neuron into firing
- *GABA* (its full name is extremely long) 'inhibits' the next neuron from firing

Glutamate and GABA act quickly in milliseconds and are found all over the brain.

Other neurotransmitters are sometimes referred to as *neuromodulators*. They float across synapses too, but act more slowly in receptors to modulate the effect of glutamate and GABA. They come in three categories: monoamines, neuropeptides and hormones, and are found in particular brain regions. There are probably hundreds of them (Sapolsky 2004).

While glutamate and GABA in particular pathways signify specific stimuli, *monoamines* change the overall state of many areas simultaneously so that stimuli have different effects. For example, they can bring on a state of high arousal to deal with danger, or a state of low arousal when you go to sleep. Some well-known monoamines and their associations are:

- *dopamine*: motivation and anticipating rewards
- *serotonin*: dampens emotional arousal
- *acetylcholine*: attention and learning
- *noradrenaline*: physical and mental arousal (*norepinephrine* in American).

These neurochemicals follow specific pathways to change your brain state, so there are, for example, *serotonergic* pathways and *dopaminergic* ones.

Neuropeptides affect our emotional states. Released with neurotransmitters, they stay around long enough to modulate their effect. The best known are *endorphins*, a contraction of endogenous (originating in the body) and morphine, so they're often referred to as 'endogenous opioids'. Like opiate drugs, they reduce pain and stress and promote feelings of calm and well-being. Endorphin release can be triggered by exercise, meditation, music and hanging out with friends. Neuropeptides are also released in the body.

Unlike other neurochemicals, *hormones* are mainly produced in the body by organs such as the adrenal glands. They're released into the bloodstream and thereby float into the brain, crossing the *blood-brain barrier*, that keeps harmful toxins out of the brain, in the process. Hormones act like lubricants for particular mental and physiological states. Two well-known ones and their associations:

- *oxytocin*: emotional bonding and feeling good[3]
- *cortisol*: mobilising energy and stress

Other 'neuromodulators' are alcohol and recreational drugs; they achieve their effects by altering the behaviour of glutamate and GABA.

Overall, neurochemistry is complex (try reading a textbook on the subject). For one thing, these chemicals get involved in different things as LeDoux explains:

> the same basic transmitters, modulators, and hormones can be involved in very different functions. Our abilities to see, hear, remember, fear danger, and desire happiness all involve excitatory (glutamate) synaptic transmission regulated by inhibitory (GABA) synapses and modulated by peptides, amines, and hormones.
>
> (2003: 61)

And Damasio warns that "knowing that a substance is working on certain systems, in certain circuits and receptors, and in certain neurons, does not explain why you feel happy or sad" (1996: 160). We must beware the temptation to equate emotional states with particular chemistries.

Neuroplasticity: brains keep changing until they die

It's in the nature of nervous systems to be plastic – i.e. changeable. This enables them to adapt to different environments and experiences. Our brains are always changing, from before birth and right up to death. If they didn't, we would learn nothing and be unable to remember what happened yesterday. All areas of the brain display plasticity, some more than others.

Neuroplasticity means that neurons, axons, dendrites and synapses can both grow and wither, but most of the time it means that what happens at synapses can be altered by experience (LeDoux 2003). *Synaptogenesis* is the growth of new synapses when neurons sprout new dendrites. *Neurogenesis*, the birth of new neurons, is less common because in general we don't acquire new ones as life proceeds. If you want to change your brain, your best bet lies with your synapses.

Let's examine plasticity across the lifespan by exploring the stages of neural development. More than half our genes are thought to be in the brain, but there aren't enough to account for our personal connectome, so the nature–nurture debate is really about how pathways get built during development (LeDoux 2003).

In the womb

The nervous system begins with the ectoderm which becomes the skin. Some cells in it fold inwards to form the *neural tube*, which becomes the spinal cord (Siegel 2007). Most of our 100 billion neurons grow in the neural tube and then migrate to their genetically ordained place in the brain. Up to 250,000 are generated every minute at the peak of production – there's a lot going on during pregnancy (LeDoux 2003).

The baby's developing brain is affected by the chemistry of the *uterine environment*, which links with mother's body chemistry via the placenta. Embryos can't make the amino acids needed for the proteins that fuel the body growth of body and brain, so they get them from mother who in turn gets them from what she eats (LeDoux 2003). Mother's quality of nutrition, and her stress and anxiety levels, all affect the baby's developing brain (Sapolsky 2017).

At birth

We're born with some synapses already formed, thanks to our genes and environmental influences (Damasio 2010). They're mainly lower in the brain, closer to the spinal cord, while neurons further up bide their time before linking up. Enough synapses exist for the brain to be a unique, individual brain – even the brains of identical twins are different (Carter 2000). Nature follows patterns, and then creates variations.

As newborns, our neural pathways allow us to see, hear, move and regulate autonomic functions. We have over 20 involuntary reflexes controlled by the brainstem at the top of the spinal cord (Cozolino 2010). These enable us to suck, swallow, reach out and grasp with our hands, orient our eyes to mother's eyes, and more. Within two days, we can stick our tongue out to imitate adults, and tell the difference between their different facial expressions.

Infancy

In the early years, neurons sprout an over-abundance of synapses – the technical term is *exuberance* (who says science is dry and boring?). The greatest number is reached around 2 years old, with different areas peaking at different times (LeDoux 2003). Many will get pruned away, but in the meantime infants surprise and delight their parents who conclude that their child is especially gifted.

Some development is *experience-expectant*: exuberance happens in areas genetically primed for experiences the infant is born to expect, such as touch, gaze and voice in response to parental attachment behaviour. This is when we first learn what to do with our feelings (Gerhardt 2015). The early years are critical, not because what's learnt cannot be learnt later on so much as what's learnt becomes a springboard for learning more (LeDoux 2003). A sort of snowball effect.

Attachment relationships are the main driver of neural development in infancy (Schore 2012). Pleasure experienced with mother grows the neural capacity to experience pleasure later in life, whereas a lack of maternal attunement grows the neural capacity to experience shame. These variations are all enabled by the infant brain's plasticity. The influence of other people on us is strongest in early life, which is why parents loom large in the therapy room (Gerhardt 2015).

Childhood

The child's experience determines which synapses survive and which are pruned. The axons of synapses that survive become more complex as their activity develops (LeDoux 2003). The brain acquires its individual shape, a process known as *sculpting*. Early-forming synapses undergo *long-term potentiation*: the repetition of similar stimuli stabilises neural pathways which are less amenable to change later in life. This is especially true of areas lower in the brain, and fortunately the frontal lobes higher up are the most plastic and have the power to over-rule problematic pathways lower down.

Adapting to experiences that are not genetically planned for (e.g. languages, counting) is called *experience-dependent* development. The synapses that grow enable the child to learn, but this also implies a vulnerability to harmful experiences as the brain develops. Young mammalian brains need to play if they are to develop properly, for play organises the child's brain (Panksepp 2012).

A concept in childhood neural development is that of *sensitive* or *critical periods* when particular functions are genetically primed to develop, so that if you miss them you'll struggle to catch up later on. But it's somewhat controversial, thanks to the scope for neuroplasticity throughout life.

Adolescence

Adolescence is all about the frontal lobes, the final brain region to mature, and they only reach maturity around age 25 (Sapolsky 2017). Neural maturity equals psychological maturity, so this is a significant point. Sapolsky summarises the adolescent predicament:

> If by adolescence limbic, autonomic, and endocrine systems are going full blast while the frontal cortex is still working out the assembly instructions, we've just explained why adolescents are so frustrating, great, asinine, impulsive, inspiring, destructive, self-destructive, selfless, selfish, impossible, and world changing.
>
> (2017: 155)

Axons in the frontal lobes become myelinated during adolescence to make them better connected and the brain as a whole more efficient. There's a steady improvement in their ability to inhibit other areas of the brain – to get control of emotional and hormonal impulses. And a gradual increase in their owner's attention span.

The frontal lobes are the least subject to genetic control, which makes adolescents impressionable and open to influence (Sapolsky 2017). The long time they take to mature may be so that, despite the challenges en route to maturity, the end result is the best brain possible. If all goes well.

Adulthood

Neuroplasticity means that the adult brain can change, though not as effortlessly as before. Neurons may die and synapses may wither on the 'use it or lose it' principle, and there is inevitable cognitive decline. But the important pathways formed by personal experience endure. So you may forget what you went upstairs to fetch, but you may also benefit from past experience for guidance, and your emotional reactivity may decline as you mellow.

By adulthood, the number of synapses is down to 60% of its peak when we were toddlers (Seung 2013). New synapses are created, others eliminated, as we make our way through life, but the total number remains fairly constant.

All brain areas exhibit plasticity, but it's the plasticity of the frontal lobes we appeal to most in the therapy room. The frontal lobes are large and contain a lot of synapses to work on.

Old age

Neuroplasticity continues into old age and may even be present in brains suffering from Alzheimer's (Goldberg 2009). At the same time, there is cognitive decline thanks to the "gradual degeneration of dendrites, neurons, and the biochemical mechanisms that support neural health and plasticity", says Cozolino (2010: 329).

Conclusion

Neuroplasticity enables people to recover, at least to some extent, from strokes and brain injuries. It also enables people to change in therapy, and this has much to do with the frontal lobes, the most plastic area of the adult brain. We should also remember that plasticity enables brains to change outside the therapy room – "life is the best therapist" as one of my biodynamic trainers liked to say. This raises the question of what's special about the therapy room, and what can happen there that doesn't happen in the rest of the client's life.

Neural architecture: evolution across three axes

How on earth did the brain, with all its weirdly shaped bits, get to look as it does? The answer must lie in its evolutionary history. Brains have evolved from the bottom up, with new bits added as needed, and old bits conserved and continuing to evolve. With over a thousand distinguishable areas in the human brain, how can we make sense of it as a whole? One way is to explore the brain's architecture along three axes: the vertical from top to bottom, the horizontal from front to back, and the horizontal from left to right.

Another way to make sense of the brain is to consider its three most striking anatomical features. One is its wrinkly walnut-like appearance, another is the collection of odd-looking bits that sit below and within the main wrinkly bit, and the third is the clear division through most of it between left and right sides. These can all be explained.

The top-bottom axis: cortex and subcortex

The bottom half of the brain, which came earlier in evolution, is the *subcortex*, while the top half that evolved later is the *cortex*. The cortex is the wrinkly stuff that looks like a walnut; it's Latin for bark and, like bark, it covers the subcortical areas that lie within and below (see Figure 2.4).

A popular way to describe this vertical arrangement is the idea of the *triune brain* which slices the brain three ways into two layers of subcortex, the 'reptilian' and 'mammalian' brains, plus the 'human' cortex (MacLean 1990). This three-way division isn't great science as reptiles have some mammalian areas and mammals have some human ones. I'll generally keep to the two-way slicing of cortex and subcortex, though even here the dividing line is debatable, such is the ability of the brain that's studied to defy the brain that studies it. But the triune brain is a good starting place for getting your head around what's inside it.

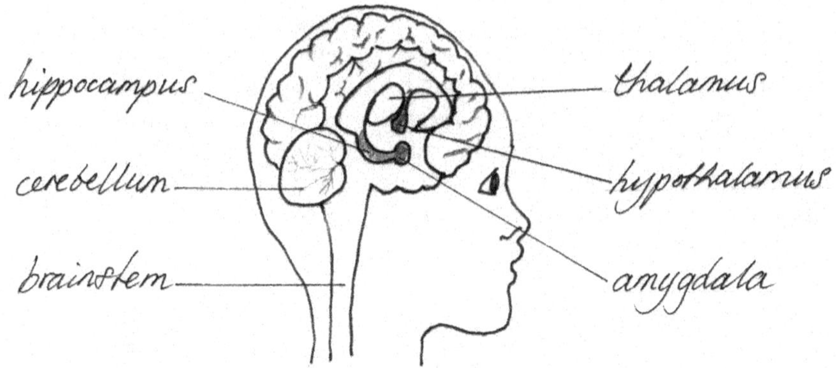

Figure 2.4 Subcortical brain areas: brainstem, cerebellum, hippocampus, thalamus, hypothalamus and amygdala.

The so-called *reptilian brain* sits at the bottom. Reptiles can be aggressive, catch prey, mate and defend their territory. We can do all these things too, some people particularly well (they may be described as 'reptilian'). The reptilian brain comprises two big areas at the top of the spinal cord:

- the *brainstem* holds the rest of the brain up "like fruit on a stalk" (Seung 2013: 7) – it looks after bodily arousal including breathing and heartbeat, puts you to sleep and wakes you up
- the *cerebellum* co-ordinates movement, balance and posture

This arrangement led Morrison to describe the brain as being "like an old farmhouse, a crude patchwork of lean-tos and other extensions that conceal entirely the ancient amphibian-reptilian toolshed at its core" (cited in Gerhardt 2015: 51).

The *mammalian brain* also gets called the *limbic system*. This part of the brain evolved so that mammals could improve on reptiles by taking care of their offspring, playing with each other and generally having a richer emotional life. It plays an important role in our emotions, appetites and urges, and includes some well-known brain areas:

- the *amygdala* is associated with stress, anxiety, fear and aggression (the word is Latin for almond, which it resembles)
- the *hippocampus* is associated with narrative and spatial memory (Latin for seahorse, which this area resembles in cross-section)
- the *hypothalamus* constantly adjusts the chemistry of body and brain
- the *thalamus* relays sensory signals around the brain

There are two of each of these, one on the left and one on the right, but they're usually referred to in the singular.

Cortex and *neocortex* (neo for new), interchangeable terms for our purposes, sit on top of the subcortical areas below. The cortex is the size and thickness of a large table napkin (Edelman 2005). Such is the size of the human cortex, evolution had to crumple it up to fit into the skull, hence its wrinkly walnut appearance. The napkin is thick enough to be made up of six layers of tissue, each of which is composed of *cortical columns* arranged vertically: you need a ridiculously powerful microscope to see any of this.

The cortex enables faculties that don't concern other creatures, such as abstract cognition, philosophy, and remembering where your car keys are (Sapolsky 2004). To which we can add imagination, empathy and thoughtfulness. Lewis describes the result as "a super-network of ... babbling neurons" that "constitute the physical substrate of who we are, what we think, what we do, what we experience" (2012: 22).

The top-bottom axis reflects the difference between generating possible actions on one hand (bottom), and sifting and choosing the best one on the other (top). It's the difference between the basic things of life, such as survival reactions, and more evolved capacitics that enable learning and change. Subcortical reactions tend to be fast, whereas cortical responses need time. The subcortex does what it does, whereas the cortex simulates and predicts (Glaser 2017). *Bottom-up* means the subcortex is in charge, *top-down* means the cortex is – as it should be most of the time.

The front-back axis: frontal and posterior lobes

Amidst its wrinkles, the cortex has several hundred distinct areas, each of which plays a particular role. It also has a primary anatomical division into four cortical *lobes* (times two, as there's a left and a right of each) (see Figure 2.5):

- the *occipital* lobes are at the back, signals from the eyes arrive here, so they handle vision
- the *parietal* lobes sit in front of the occipital, signals from the body arrive here to be combined with signals from the senses
- the *temporal* lobes are below the parietal at the side of the brain (think temples), signals from the ears arrive here, so they deal with sound and speech
- the *frontal* lobes are where their name implies: massively expanded in the human brain to enable so-called *executive functions* such as planning and problem solving.

The first three are the *posterior lobes* and receive sensory signals from the environment and the body, whereas the frontal lobes receive only what

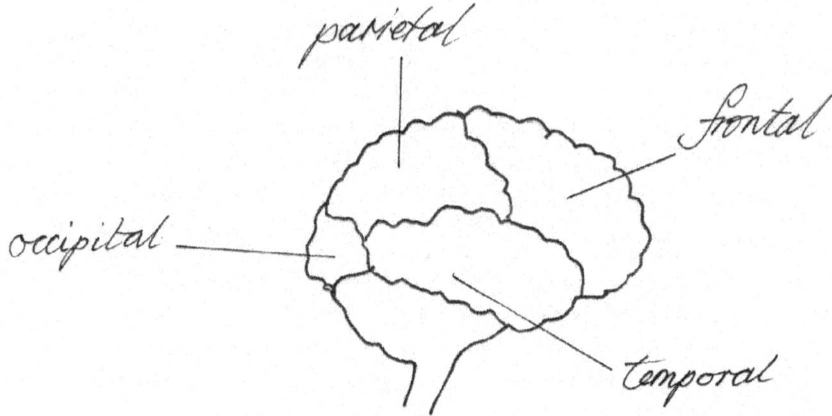

Figure 2.5 The four cortical lobes, viewed from the right side of the head: occipital, parietal, temporal and frontal.

other areas of the brain, including the posterior lobes, choose to pass on to them. They integrate what they're sent into a 'higher order' picture of the whole brain and what it's doing at any moment.

The front part of the frontal lobes, the larger part, is called *prefrontal.* For our purposes, frontal and prefrontal are generally interchangeable terms. Frontal lobes and frontal cortex are interchangeable terms for everyone, neuroscientists included.

The frontal lobes achieve their purposes largely by inhibiting the posterior lobes, allowing the brain as a whole to respond in more finely judged ways (McGilchrist 2009). They enable us to do many wonderful things: to reflect on our decisions, stop ourselves from doing things we might later regret, imagine another person's inner world, liberate ourselves from the past and dream about the future. Without them, psychotherapy wouldn't be possible. McGilchrist thinks they've made us "the most powerful and destructive of animals", but also "the 'social animal'... with a spiritual dimension" (2009: 22).

A good way to characterise the front-back axis is to contrast reflective responses (frontal lobes) with habitual ones (posterior lobes).

The left-right axis: the cerebral hemispheres

The brain seen from above is clearly split down the middle (cerebral and cortical are interchangeable terms). The division of the cortex into two hemispheres gives rise to *lateralisation,* some things on one side, some on the other, and to *hemispheric specialisation, dominance* or *bias*: the idea that a certain function (language, for example) may be the preserve of one hemisphere more than the other.

Why is the cortex divided in this way? The answer for now is that the whole of the brain is anatomically lateralised, even the brainstem where the divide isn't evident (Porges 2012). Everything else comes in visible two's: amygdalae, hippocampi, hypothalami and so forth, though you might never glean this from reading neuroscience books.

Left-right overlaps with top-bottom because the right hemisphere has richer connectivity with subcortical areas than the left has. This means we can talk about the 'right brain', embracing both cortex and subcortex, whereas the 'left brain' is more confined to the cortex. The left hemisphere is something of an ivory castle standing apart. Another consequence of this aspect of neural anatomy is that the right hemisphere can be said to form an ensemble with the body, a key idea in this book. This feature of neural architecture looks to be of such significance to therapy that it gets its own chapter (the next one) (see Figure 2.6).

Brain areas in general

Although areas of the brain are specialised for different things, anything that brains do requires many regions to work together. With all its many areas, the brain is really a seamless network of pathways in which

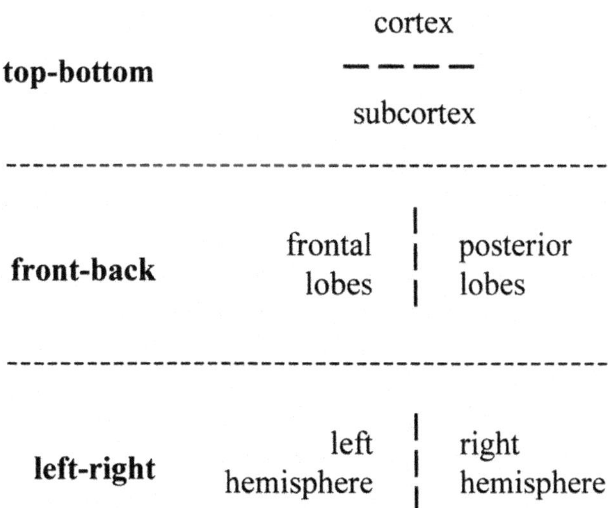

Figure 2.6 The three axes of neural architecture, one vertical and two horizontal.

particular areas 'play a key role in' or 'help mediate' a behaviour (Sapolsky 2017). The function of a particular area is embedded in the context of its connections with other areas.

How brains work: not like computers

Brains have no central processor, no memory stored faithfully on a neural hard drive, and they never stop firing, even when we sleep. They are said to 'compute', 'information' and 'data' sent along nerves to be 'processed' – but these are poor analogies. Nervous systems represent stimuli by virtue of which pathways fire.

Excitation and inhibition

Signalling across synapses either excites or inhibits the next neuron in the chain. Some synapses are excitatory (releasing glutamate), while others are inhibitory (releasing GABA). The balance of all the excitatory and inhibitory signals arriving in a neuron determines whether it fires too, either exciting or inhibiting the neurons *it* links to (LeDoux 2003). To move my leg, speak a word or write a sentence requires specific neurons to fire and specific pathways to become excited, others inhibited.

Overall, there's more inhibition than excitation in the brain. It likes to turn most of itself off, so that excited pathways can do their job without interference. Neural inhibition is different from psychological inhibition; a lack of it can lead to unwanted experiences such as epileptic seizures and psychosis.

Mapping

The brain combines signals from different sources such as eyes and ears and makes a 'map', mimicking what's going on outside with its firing patterns inside (Damasio 2010). Neural maps are also made as we recall events and people from memory. Mapping is going on all the time.

Unlike human maps, these maps are not static. The lines in a neural map result from the momentary firing of certain neurons. They change from moment to moment to reflect changes in the body and in the world around us, like an electronic billboard displaying moving images. Mapping happens with *every* sensory pattern the brain constructs, including sights, sounds, touches, smells, tastes, pains and pleasures. The idea that observing firing patterns in someone's brain (if you could do this) can tell you what they're thinking about is fanciful – for now at any rate.

Neural maps don't have to come into our awareness for them to influence our thinking and behaviour. Sometimes they're referred to as 'images'

– but I'll generally stick to 'maps' or 'mapping' to avoid confusion with visual images.

Anticipation

As brains perceive what's happening, they anticipate what they think is happening, accurately or otherwise. They search for patterns to recognise, and make guesses based on past experience. Perception is a two-way process of matching between sensory signals triggered by stimuli and remembered patterns. This is why witnesses to the same accident tend to give different accounts of it, and why taking your time to make judgements and assessments is a good idea.

Anticipation implies that psychological projection is in the nature of how brains work. It makes many things possible, such as returning a tennis ball coming at you at 100 miles an hour or, on a longer timescale, feeling hopeful about going to see a therapist.

Resolving ambiguity

The brain is "the ambiguity-resolving machine par excellence!" says Kandel (2007: 297). It tries to resolve ambiguities in the sensory signals it receives by deciding which remembered pattern it's recognising, constructing a perception from little information. Something must be something. From its viewpoint, it's better to make a quick guess about an apparent danger than wait to be sure and risk disaster. Sometimes we need to train our frontal lobes to pause this process, bring it into awareness and reflect, for example, whether another person really is a threat to our well-being.

Neural signalling is two-way

Signalling along individual nerves is one-way, but when an area of the brain signals another the traffic goes both ways. The receiving area is prone to signalling in the reverse direction to modulate the signals heading its way, either to amplify those signals ('give me more') or to inhibit them ('OK, that's enough'). This is why neuroscience deals in 'circuits' – everything goes back and forth in a loop. For example, the brainstem triggers dopamine release in the frontal lobes to motivate the whole brain, while the frontal lobes regulate the triggering and therefore the amount released.

If we think in terms of natural processes rather than mechanical ones, all this may seem, well, more natural. The scientific term for it is *reverberative.*[4]

Binding

With zillions of pathways and networks firing at any given moment in response to all the different things happening around us and within us, how do we manage to have a unified conscious experience of anything (on a good day anyway)? There's no little person in our head (a *homunculus*) knitting all the mapping in different areas into one perception. For example, the visual cortex breaks down into over 30 areas for the different aspects of vision (edges, motion, colour etc.), yet the end result is the experience of seeing a single image.

The answer is unclear, and Rose considers the "binding problem" to be "the central theoretical problem for twenty-first-century neuroscience" (2006: 157).

Background processing

The brain is always active, with more or less firing in any particular area. If an area is said to fire when X happens, it means that the firing rate exceeds a threshold, enough to register on a brain scanner. As our experience changes, so does brain activity.

There's background processing all the time, even if most areas aren't doing much. Ongoing experience continually modifies activity in neural networks, knowledge is represented by chains of associations linking local and distant areas, and networks are always interacting with other networks (Claxton 2005). The brain doesn't store things in neural filing cabinets for looking up later on; instead, it's constantly changing. On this therapy depends: something will always come along.

If we could see all this firing, it might be like watching a firework display, with old patterns forever subsiding and new ones constellating. One display might be in our awareness, many others continuing outside awareness (Damasio 2010).

Switching metaphors, we could think of neural activity as being like the movement of water in the ocean. Claxton elaborates: "what we are aware of, in any moment, are the 'breakers' of our brain activity, behind each of which lies a partly or completely invisible groundswell of less strongly activated memories and predictions" (2005: 378). Underneath the waves breaking on the surface are currents we don't see and hidden depths, but aspects of these may rise to the surface sometimes and form new waves.

Fortunately for us, most neural processing stays outside awareness. For example, the brain's interactions with the body. If we were aware of all the signalling that changes our heart rate and breathing, and all the body's signalling feedback of its inner state, we'd go nuts. Happily, our brains do all this for us in the background.

Another illustration of background processing lies in the illusion that we're instantly aware of stimuli that come along, and that we act after we've become aware of whatever it is (Cozolino 2010). In fact, the brain reacts within a tenth of a second to a stimulus, whereas it takes around half a second to come into awareness. During the gap, the brain is shaping our perception and deciding how to respond. Hence we can react to things in ways we later regret. But when we have time, which we do in therapy, to hold something in awareness, we can ponder how best to respond using our frontal lobes and their capacity for inhibiting subcortical and posterior lobe reactions.

What brains do: the need for a nervous system

We may equate brains with our human proclivity for thinking and reasoning, but there are more fundamental reasons for having them. We need to think about what nervous systems originally evolved to do.

Sensing and moving

To find its way around, a creature needs senses so it knows what's out there, and muscles so its body can move. Even a worm needs a nervous system to get around, whereas plants stay put, so they don't need one. The brain evolved so we could move, and movement is at the root of everything else it does, including our cognitive abilities (Gallese 2014). And even before we move, we sense. "The job of a brain is to turn sensations into behaviour", says McCrone (1999: 194). Our sensory nerves connect us with reality, and the brain combines signals from senses to make maps of the world around it.

Babies practise moving long before they head down the birth canal. Having completed the enormous movement out into the world, they reach out their arms towards mother. The way a client moves as they enter our therapy room, confidently or hesitantly, may tell us something about them. Trauma can make it hard for people to move in easy flowing ways.

Everything in the nervous system that concerns moving is called *motor*: motor cortex, motor nerves and so forth. The direction of travel is from brain to body. And everything that concerns sensing is called *sensory* – sensory nerves, sensory areas. The direction of travel is the opposite, from body to brain. Sensory and motor are intimately linked, so there is *sensorimotor cortex* (and now 'sensorimotor therapy').

Sensing and moving concern more than external senses and limb movements. The brain senses the body itself, including the viscera, and triggers changes (movement) in organs – raising or lowering heart rate, speeding or slowing breathing, starting and stopping digestion, and so forth. Neuroscience sheds light on the inner world of body and feeling we work with in therapy.

Perception

Brains perceive what's going on around them, and the act of perception is a creative one (Kandel 2007). Because the brain needs to know what's out there as soon as possible, even with little sensory input, it refashions sensory signals according to its own assumptions based on previous experience. So perception involves interpretation and judgement. This means that we first see something as a whole, and only afterwards turn our attention to specific features (McGilchrist 2009).

The rapidity of recognising patterns and resolving ambiguity suggests that, as Ramachandran says, it's almost as if "each of us is hallucinating all the time and what we call perception involves merely selecting the one hallucination that best matches the current input" (2011: 57). The hidden assumptions in people's perceptions that underlie their projections are grist for the mill in the therapy room.

Memory and learning

Nervous systems don't want to waste energy re-inventing the wheel every day, so they learn from experience and remember what they've learnt when similar patterns of firing evoke past experiences. Eric Kandel, who won a Nobel prize for deciphering the nervous systems of sea slugs in order to understand memory, says "learning is the process by which we acquire new knowledge, and memory is the process by which we retain that knowledge over time" (Kandel & Hawkins 1999: 140). Knowledge is not only facts that you learn explicitly, it's also experiences and impressions you absorb implicitly, such as your mother's facial expression, voice tone and how she responds to you when you arrive in the world.

Memory is a 'system property' of nervous systems (Edelman 2005). Although certain brain areas, such as the hippocampus, are particularly linked to memory, synapses and pathways and networks everywhere hold aspects of memory. It's more an adaptation to experiencing life than a fixed representation of something. 'Laying down' memory involves changing the strength of certain synapses. Emotional arousal strengthens memories, but if the arousal is strong and the person stressed, memory is impaired (LeDoux 2003).

Remembering is essentially reconstructive (Damasio 1996). Recalling a memory is to some degree an act of imagination (Edelman & Tononi 2000). Memories are reconstructed each time with a fresh constellation of firing patterns, which makes them durable but not necessarily accurate. Synapses change in the act of remembering.

When we talk about our 'memories', we mean *explicit memory*. But we begin life with *implicit memory*, the knowing of how we are and how others are and how the world is. We can't explain it and we may fail even to recognise it. Early learning about attachment and affect regulation is implicit: the brain extracts the underlying patterns in repeated experiences which later feed our intuitive knowing, outside awareness.

Much of therapy concerns implicit memory. It lasts better in old age than explicit memories do – 'you never forget how to ride a bike'. Implicit memory based in feeling tends to endure, but we can only bring into awareness feelings, sensations and the typical reactions of others, not what actually happened.

Conscious memories are only possible from around age 2 or 3 because the hippocampus is needed to lay down *autobiographical* (or *narrative* or *episodic*) memory for later recall, and it's not sufficiently developed until then. If you believe you have explicit memories from an earlier age, they may be fantasies from later on about your infancy that you remember, or something you were told (or neuroscience has got it wrong).

There are other kinds of memory. *Semantic* memory is of words and facts, *procedural* memory is of skills and habits (such as riding a bike), and *working* memory is what you can hold in your mind at any one time (generally not very much, phone numbers over ten digits long pose a problem).

Language

Many things human brains do are discussed in later chapters: relationships, feelings, sleeping, dreaming and so forth. But language is worth considering now as it's intrinsic to relationships and talking therapy.

Language gets neuroscientists excited. LeDoux thinks the emergence of language in the human brain "involved a revolution rather than an evolution of function" (2003: 198). It changed the way the brain works, enabling it to experience and think about events in ways other brains can't. For Greenfield (2001), the ability to construct sentences enables us to associate anything with anything else, thereby endowing us with creative imagination:

> once we established language and were able to escape the immediate here and now, then not only were we able to plan for the future and remember the past, but to indulge in scenarios that have never been, to imagine magical entities and mystical, mythical scenarios.
>
> (2001: 75)

Language is an embodied skill and an expression of emotion that evolved from music and gestural communication, enabling us to connect with ourselves and others (McGilchrist 2009). Its foundations lie in the body and in lived experience, but we can also use it to distance ourselves from the body and other people. The reasons for this paradox are discussed in Chapter 3. The psychoanalyst Daniel Stern expresses the ambiguous possibilities of language in child development very well:

> with its emergence, infants become estranged from direct contact with their personal experience. Language forces a space between interpersonal experience as lived and as represented. And it is exactly across this space that the ... associations that constitute neurotic behaviour may form. But also with language, infants for the first time can share their personal experience of the world with others.
>
> (1998: 182)

Nervous systems in the therapy room

How can we make practical use of this picture of nervous systems in therapy?

Stimulating neuroplasticity with the frontal lobes

Stimulating neuroplasticity is what therapists do (Cozolino 2017). All psychological techniques can change the brain in some way, so the question is: what sort of change do we want to bring about?

Progress in therapy leans heavily on the plasticity of the frontal lobes, the most plastic area of the human brain. They're capable of getting a better grip on what happens elsewhere in the brain, such as the amygdala generating stress and anxiety. Their capacity for reflection and holding thoughts and feelings in awareness can be exploited in the room. To make the most of this, the therapist can encourage fresh experiencing – new feelings and thoughts. If therapy goes around in circles or allows the client to avoid addressing self-defeating behaviours, there's probably less neural change. The therapist needs to get the client's neuroplasticity working, which may mean pointing his attention to emotionally uncomfortable places.

Encouraging integration across the three axes of neural architecture

Neural architecture maps the territory of the nervous system that we explore in therapy. We can't know what neurochemicals are floating around in someone's brain, but we can do something with the brain's structure. The three axes enable us to think about the problems with psychological integration clients bring into the room, and on how to overcome them.

Neural integration is a multi-faceted topic in neuroscience but essentially means that since our conscious experience can't be subdivided in the moment into independent elements, the underlying neural processes must be integrated (Edelman & Tononi 2000). Psychologically, 'conscious experience' includes things we're aware of and things we aren't. A mild lack of integration involves keeping certain feelings and thoughts out of awareness, while a more severe form involves old trauma fragments erupting from seemingly nowhere. Cozolino believes that "on an experiential level, integration is the ability to feel, think, and live life, love, and work, with a minimum of defensiveness" (2017: 27), and stimulating integration is what therapists do. Neural integration translates into psychological integration.

Poor top-bottom integration might be reflected in uncontrolled emotions and traumatic re-enactments, poor front-back integration in a lack of self-awareness and thoughtfulness, and poor left-right integration in all manner of things, but most obviously in defensiveness and difficulties engaging with one's inner world. The nature of healthy integration across each neural axis might be characterised as follows:

- *Top-bottom*: the cortex sifts subcortical reactions to triggers and chooses effective ones, as opposed to relinquishing control, emotional turmoil and acting out. The work in therapy is to integrate old trauma fragments that erupt so they can be regulated by the cortex.
- *Front-back*: the frontal lobes reflect on situations and decide on the best response, as opposed to allowing the habitual responses of the posterior lobes to continue outside awareness. The work is to heal old emotional wounds and encourage undeveloped aspects of the personality.
- *Left-right*: both hemispheres contribute to an experience and feelings can be expressed, as opposed to the left inhibiting the right defensively, or the right taking over with overwhelming emotions or dissociative fragmentation. The work involves reflection and exploring the inner world of feelings, images and the body.

It may be that most psychological difficulties include aspects of all three axes, and all transformative moments in therapy see changes across all three. "Restoring neural integration requires the simultaneous reregulation of networks on both vertical and horizontal planes", says Cozolino (2017: 30). Working across all three axes enables problems to change as well as be explained, and catharsis that brings realisation in its wake. Nevertheless, the left-right axis is at the centre of therapeutic work, and it leads naturally to the other two axes when required.

Reconstructing memory

Since explicit memories are reconstructive and involve imagination, we can approach them as we would dreams and images, taking them seriously but not necessarily literally. Of course, sometimes this isn't enough: the client who thinks they remember being abused in childhood may want to know whether or not this is a true memory. But even here it helps to have a good understanding of how memory works, and in my experience what I say in response can be a delicate matter. The client may need both to perceive the therapist's neutrality and to feel that his story is believed.

We shouldn't go digging for buried memories; we should allow memories that have been forgotten to surface of their own accord in the process of therapy – which they do, sometimes at least. No one needs to *try* to remember what happened in childhood, and therapy is more productive if the client learns to trust an unfolding process that includes memory recall.

Neuroscience gives grounds for accepting the reality of both 'false' and 'recovered' memories. Research has demonstrated that a memory can be 'implanted' such that someone becomes convinced that a false memory actually occurred (Cozolino 2010). Furthermore, the brain cannot reliably distinguish between memories of lived experience and of internal fantasy – everything arises from neural maps in pathways and networks. Reliable memories tend to return in stages over time, rather than all at once, and often come with a sense of 'I'd forgotten about that'.

The evidence from brain scanning is that false memories originate in the left hemisphere, whereas true autobiographical memories originate in the right (Kandel & Hawkins 1999). We should therefore be able to *sense* the difference.

Talking therapy that connects

Language is a double-edged sword in the therapy room. It can trap us into merely 'talking about' and going nowhere meaningful. One of the main complaints I've heard repeatedly over the years from clients is that they talked about their problems and childhoods at length in therapy, but that was it, nothing changed. *Merely* talking is clearly not enough for transformation to *really* happen.

But dialogue can also free clients to express things they carry inside they haven't previously articulated. It's not that we should stop them talking and get them to draw and paint and move, though these other mediums of self-expression work well. Rather, the talking needs to reach the deeper, more meaningful and sometimes more emotionally difficult places that they haven't spoken from before.

The ambiguous nature of language discussed above is also present in the therapy room. While language can become an obstacle, it can also facilitate the bridging of inner and outer worlds, and can help to integrate the different areas of the brain (Cozolino 2010).

'Unconscious' as an adjective rather than a noun

It may be time to bury the idea of 'the unconscious' as a walled-off compartment of the mind crying out for illumination. As Claxton says:

> not only are "the gods and spirits" non-existent ... but the unconscious is dead too. We may choose to continue using it as a metaphorical or poetic way of talking, but thar ain't no such animal.
>
> (2015: 12)

Instead ... if we continue with the ocean metaphor discussed earlier, then the ocean depths are what's meant by 'the unconscious', while the surface is our field of awareness. During therapy, new currents may rise to the surface, and new sorts of waves may break. And the therapist may be able to point the client's attention to waves he hasn't noticed before that break further away. What confuses this issue is that many clients come with dissociated fragments of memory and emotion left over from unresolved trauma. We may call these 'unconscious' contents, but they're not complete experiences waiting in a dark forgotten 'unconscious mind'.

For example, recalling a core memory of childhood abuse in therapy can trigger remembering other instances of abuse, as the ocean currents get stirred. Pointing out aspects of experience that escape the client's attention – body language, feelings he suppresses the moment they arise, the likely implications of the story he tells – broadens his field of awareness to include what's at the edge.

Gazillions of unconscious processes underscore whatever is in our awareness at any moment, and as Gazzaniga says "you don't even know that they exist unless you follow what's going on in brain research" (2016: 339). Very little brain activity reaches consciousness, "certainly less than 5%, and probably less than 1%", reports McGilchrist (2009: 187). Our brains make decisions, solve problems and make judgements without the need for conscious anything. However, the results can enter awareness, especially if someone else points them out to us. The triggering of an emotional state happens outside consciousness, but the resulting body and brain states needn't remain 'unconscious'.

So a thought or a feeling can be 'unconscious' in that we're unaware of it, but there's no 'unconscious' as a place to visit in therapy.

Conclusion

The brain starts with the whole nervous system that extends throughout the body as well, and then leads us into its three architectural axes, one vertical and two horizontal. This gives us an overview for making sense of the biology underlying our psychology. The human brain has evolved to make the most of good circumstances, but when circumstances are less good, such as children growing up in dysfunctional families, it falls back on its evolutionary past, and the result is psychological survival laced with suffering.

A psychologically healthy brain must be one that's well integrated across all three axes. This requires the frontal lobes, at the pinnacle of the brain's evolutionary development, to play their role in integrating cognition and emotion, self and other, mind and body. All these aspects of our experience must be able to enter awareness when needed. When something – a feeling, thought, sensation, memory, for example – lies outside the overall integration and therefore can't come into awareness, psychological problems arise. The aim of therapy is to create a space for such aspects of experience to enter awareness and be integrated in the frontal lobes. They must be felt in the body, experienced in the context of the therapeutic relationship, and reflected on.

The more the whole brain with its diverse capacities is available in an experience, the more it's free to follow a natural course and the better able the person is to respond creatively to situations and to be himself. Neural integration is reflected in psychological integration, allowing the mind to be free from damaging inner conflict. The real test? Integration *feels* better than defensiveness and dissociation. 'Feels better' in this context isn't just a 'feel good' sort of feeling; it's a sense of rightness, even when it brings painful feelings with it.

In the therapy room, we can work with all three forms of integration or the absence thereof, but the one that stands out is the left-right one we can sense in the here-and-now flow of a session. So the next chapter is devoted to the left-right axis.

Notes

1 Neurons are the main building blocks of nervous systems, but they're supported by another sort of cell called *glia*, which supply them with nutrients and of which there are ten times as many.
2 Sapolsky gives an example: "at one synapse, neurotransmitter A sends a message relevant to pancreatic regulation, while at another synapse the same neurotransmitter substance may pertain to adolescent crushes" (2004: 278).
3 Oxytocin is also released in the brain, where it's classified as a neuropeptide.
4 Another term for the two-way reverberative signalling is 're-entry' (Edelman 1992).

Chapter 3

One brain, two minds

Introduction

Brains come in two halves. Viewed from above, the divide down the centre may look familiar, and having two of something is a normal aspect of inhabiting a body. But why has evolution opted for two hemispheres rather than one – and might the idea of a divided psyche have something to do with this arrangement?

Psychology can look to nature in exploring this biological divide, following the principle of 'carving nature at its joints'. Simplistic notions about left and right hemispheres abound, while neuroscientists often have surprisingly little to say about them. So my aim here is to present a summary of the current science, and ponder what it might mean in the therapy room. The differences between the hemispheres sheds light on the idea of 'the unconscious', on what happens in trauma and dissociation, on psychological defences and 'repression', and on the mind-body connection. They also raise questions about the relative emphasis we place on the cognitive and affective aspects of therapy.

Science and pop psychology

The whole business of left and right hemispheres has been common currency since striking findings from research into split-brain patients, who've had the connections between their hemispheres surgically cut, became apparent in the 1960s. Pop psychology latched onto these findings and invented a series of over-simplifications that are more wrong than right, such as logical left hemispheres versus emotional right hemispheres, and people being either left-brained or right-brained. These ideas diverted attention from a complex and evolving scientific picture, and amount to the sort of false dichotomies that appeal to one side of the brain – the left.

Many books by the world's leading neuroscientists scarcely mention this striking anatomical feature of the brain. Is it because the subject becomes personal as you wonder about your own hemispheres? Or because, as Gazzaniga admits, to accept that "*two* minds are coexisting in one cranium, is almost not comprehensible" (2016: 114)? It defies our personal experience.

Whatever the reason, this is a topic with great psychological potential, so it gets a chapter of its own.

Happily, the subject has been transformed with the publication of Iain McGilchrist's *The Master and His Emissary*, a scholarly tome that pulls together a huge number of research articles into a comprehensive account of the two sides of the brain (2009). McGilchrist, a psychiatrist and all-round scholar, has done us a great service with this book, and it's time we got our heads around what it reveals.

The experience of having two hemispheres

Let's first get a feel for the difference between the hemispheres and their respective contributions to our experience. According to McGilchrist, the left hemisphere focuses attention on whatever is foreground, while the right maintains 'global' attention to the background of the world around us and the world within us, the inner life of the body (2009).[1] Our focused attention is more in our awareness than our global attention, hence our tendency to look at everything, including this subject, from a left hemisphere perspective. We're inherently biased.

As you read, your left hemisphere focuses attention on the text, but if someone moves in your peripheral vision, your right hemisphere may divert your attention. Left concentrates on the detail of what you're reading, while right gets the general drift and maps your felt experience, liking it or disliking it, while keeping your heart rate and breathing adjusted for reading. Your felt experience may intrude on your focused attention at some point, as may a pang of hunger from your body.

Nature has organised the complementary contributions of the hemispheres so well that we have no direct sense of having two minds – a good example of binding (Chapter 2). We generally experience ourselves as having one mind, albeit one that moves in and out of different states. There's no experiential exercise you can do that makes the difference between the hemispheres evident. The brain is too tricky for that, and you can't just turn your hemispheres on and off. So we need to reflect on the science in the light of our remembered experience in order to understand it.

I recall a period in my childhood when I *was* aware of having two minds, and I called them 'left' and 'right'. Left was dominant and right was the underdog. I sympathised more with right, but I struggled to let it take the lead. The experience faded as I grew into adolescence – perhaps it just became too familiar to be noticeable.

Two hemispheres are better than one

I recommend using both your hemispheres and resisting the temptation to favour one over the other. Everything we do that's of real value is best done with both. But sometimes we may inadvertently lean too far towards one or the other, and this phenomenon can lead people into therapy.

At the same time, it helps to be aware that we all come to the subject with a left hemisphere bias. We use focused attention to figure it out, we use conceptual language to discuss it, we immerse ourselves in detail – all of which require heavy input from the left – and we live in a modern world constructed largely by the left hemisphere: scientific concepts, computer systems, always in a hurry. The right hemisphere is something completely different from the left, but left tries to understand it in its own terms. The result is misunderstanding. But when we pause, reflect on our experience and allow our intuition in, we can reduce the bias and see more clearly.

I draw extensively on McGilchrist here, but I also follow a rough consensus amongst other therapists who have written about neuroscience, especially the Californian triumvirate of Schore, Cozolino and Siegel.

The strange business of the hemispheres

This is a curiously problematic subject. There's a large elephant in the neuroscience field here, and it's time it got more attention. If neuroscientists accuse non-scientists of misrepresenting the hemispheres (and they do), it would be reasonable to counter that they themselves have failed to present a comprehensive explanation of this rather major aspect of neuroanatomy. McGilchrist, who's worked in brain research, seems to be the first person to attempt to do this.

What neuroscientists do say about the hemispheres

Although neuroscientists may not have attempted a full explanation of the hemispheric divide, some of the key pieces of the jigsaw puzzle come straight from some well-known scientific mouths.

Roger Sperry was a neuroscientist who won a Nobel prize for his studies of 'split-brain' patients who had undergone surgery to cut the corpus callosum that bridges the hemispheres, in order to control severe epilepsy. With their completely separated hemispheres, it was relatively easy to find out what each one did. Sperry concluded that "each surgically disconnected hemisphere appears to have a mind of its own, but each cut off from, and oblivious to, conscious events in the partner hemisphere" (1985: 14–15). This implies that the rest of us are also endowed with two minds, albeit ones that are *not* separated from each other.

Michael Gazzaniga studied with Sperry and continued the work on split-brain patients. He outlined one of the well-known differences between the hemispheres: left is "chock full of speech and language processes" while right is "able to do some fancy visual tasks" (2016: 114). And he introduced the idea of the 'left hemisphere interpreter' which means this hemisphere:

> has a tendency to grasp the gist of a situation, make an inference that fits in well with the general schema of the event, and toss out anything that does not ... The right hemisphere does not do this. It is totally truthful.
>
> (2016: 152)

It's the truthfulness of the right that we seek in therapy.

Jaak Panksepp, a neuroscientist who coined the phrase 'affective neuroscience', thinks the hemispheres "have such different cognitive and emotional perspectives on the world": the left is the one that generally speaks to others and sometimes lies and constructs "a social masquerade", whereas the right is the one that reveals "deep, intimate emotional secrets" (2005: 302). No wonder the psyche is prone to being divided.

From Damasio, we learn a hugely significant aspect of the right hemisphere: that it's specialised for mapping the inside of the body, the viscera. He says right is dominant for our "integrated body sense" whereby the mapping of inner states is woven together with that of limbs and trunk (1996: 66). This point is fundamental: the right hemisphere is more integrated with the body than the left is. He also says right is dominant for mapping emotional processes which, unsurprisingly, are closely related to body sense. Left maps these things too, but "left hemisphere representations are probably partial and not integrated" (1996: 66). In other words, nature didn't decide to put these functions in one hemisphere and not the other, but during evolution one came to do the job rather more efficiently than the other, so the balance tipped in its favour.

V.S. Ramachandran is a neurologist who treats patients with brain injuries and describes the strange effects that strokes and brain damage can have. He thinks the hemispheres are quite different in nature. Whereas left is "a conformist, largely indifferent to discrepancies", right is "the opposite: highly sensitive to perturbation" (2005: 141). You can see the value of this arrangement: one mind attuned to the flux of inner and outer worlds and therefore inherently unstable, the other able to ride out its partner's ups and downs, shut out information it doesn't need and concentrate on the task in hand.

Ramachandran describes clinical cases that illustrate Damasio's point about the right hemisphere mapping the viscera (2011). Strange things can happen to stroke patients, particularly when the stroke is in this hemisphere, such as denying that their left arm belongs to their body ("that's your arm, doctor!"). The reason for this is that their damaged right hemisphere is no longer registering the signals from the viscera within the arm so, although they can see it, they don't sense it from within.

Elkhonon Goldberg is a neuroscientist known for his work on the frontal lobes. He found that the right hemisphere is linked to "cognitive novelty" and the left to "cognitive routines" (2009: 66), a contrast which represents a "paradigm shift in our thinking about the two hemispheres" (2009: 270). So when the mind is doing something new or unfamiliar it needs the right in particular, but when doing something familiar and well-rehearsed it leans more to the left. Right's bias for novelty may be because its different regions are more interlinked than those of the left, so that new connections needed for new mental mapping form more quickly on this side.

Some big beasts of neuroscience therefore provide important pieces of the hemispheric jigsaw puzzle. But it's McGilchrist who's put them together to reveal the all-important big picture.

False dichotomies and over-simplifications

The problematic nature of this subject may have something to do with the human love of reducing the complexities of life into pairs of opposites that become false dichotomies. Two hemispheres present low-hanging fruit for this. Perhaps neuroscientists see the trap and steer clear of it, but miss the interesting stuff in the process.

The left hemisphere is often painted as rational, logical and analytical, and the right as emotional, intuitive and creative. There may be a grain of truth here, but the reality is subtler. We need both hemispheres to think rationally, left can be emotional too, but with different emotions, and if you want your intuition and creativity to bear fruit you need your left as well as your right.

Describing people as either left-brained or right-brained is even worse, and tends to imply that thinking and paying attention to detail is bad, whereas following your intuition is good. The truth is that people sometimes prefer one hemisphere over the other for a particular mental task, so it rather depends on what task they're asked to perform (McGilchrist 2013).

The question we should be asking is: what does each hemisphere contribute to a particular experience? If nature prefers two hemispheres to one, it would be reasonable to imagine that their different contributions might be complementary. We might also think in terms of differing 'left-right constellations' for particular experiences. Instead of asking which hemisphere does X and which does Y, we can hypothesise about the role each plays in a particular experience.

McGilchrist's 'master and emissary' thesis

McGilchrist's work makes a contextual understanding of left and right hemispheres possible for the first time. It's full of solid science, but it also contains a big thesis about the development of western culture over millennia, and it's here that it may be most open to criticism. McGilchrist thinks that the world we inhabit today has lurched far into left hemisphere territory with potentially disastrous consequences, the emissary having forgotten about the master who sent him on his mission. Personally, I find this wider thesis quite convincing, but it's his detailed account of the science of their differences that I draw on here. This is based on some 2,500 research papers and over 20 years of studying the subject. Whatever one's views on the wider thesis, there's no sense in throwing the scientific baby out with the cultural bathwater.

The fact is that McGilchrist has written the most comprehensive account of the hemispheres and the themes that emerge. What I offer here is a summary of a few key points that stand out. The material refers to *The Master and His Emissary* unless otherwise indicated.

The differences between the hemispheres

Let's begin with the neuroanatomy of the hemispheres, and then look at their respective contributions to psychological life. All levels of the brain are lateralised. The anatomical divides are visible above the brainstem, so all other brain areas have a left and a right side. The hemispheres are the 'cerebral hemispheres', i.e. they belong to the cortex (see Figure 3.1).

Why do we have two hemispheres?

I originally assumed we have two hemispheres in order to co-ordinate two legs, arms, eyes and ears. But McGilchrist believes that the need for focused attention to the foreground and global attention to the background lies at the root of our having divided brains (2010).

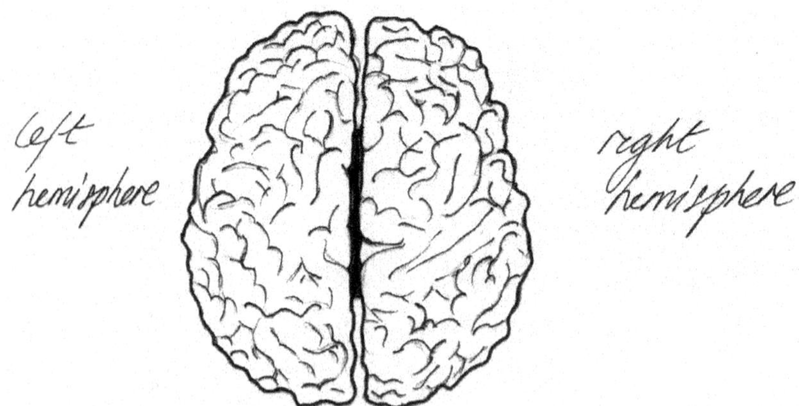

Figure 3.1 The left and right hemispheres shown from above. The dark area joining them is the corpus callosum

Consider a bird pecking in the ground for grains to eat. It focuses attention on the grains to pick them up with its beak, but if it's to stay alive in a competitive world, it must also be alert to predators lest it become someone else's meal. The bird maintains global attention in its peripheral vision so it can change the focus of its attention quickly should danger appear. Having one hemisphere for focused and another for global attention is a neat arrangement, enabling creatures to be predators without becoming prey.

Something similar happens in your brain as you read. Your left hemisphere focuses on words and details while your right hums away in the background ready to spot anything in your surroundings or in your body that needs attention. You may be so engrossed (I hope!) that your left ignores signals from your right, and only later do you realise you're ravenously hungry.

Left-handed people

The picture I'm painting assumes you're right-handed, but what if you're one of the 11% of people who are left-handed? The answer, for our purposes here, is in most cases nothing.

Of left-handed people, 75% follow the same pattern of hemispheric specialisations as right-handed people do, and most of the 25% who don't, simply have the specialisations reversed, which adds up to the same divided brain in the end. A small minority have what are called 'abnormal patterns of lateralisation', and this correlates to some degree with unusual creativity, being on the autistic spectrum, and suffering ADHD and schizophrenia.

Asymmetries

The hemispheres look symmetrical, but nature doesn't do things so tidily. There's a whole raft of small but potentially significant asymmetries between them.

The left hemisphere is wider at the back and extends further backwards, while the right is wider at the front and extends further forward, so that the brain appears slightly twisted about its central axis, as if nature has tweaked it clockwise. The neurochemistry differs on either side, with rather more dopamine (associated with motivation) pathways in the left hemisphere, and rather more noradrenaline (associated with mental energy) ones in the right (Goldberg 2009). There are differences in white matter, the nature of the interconnected pathways in either hemisphere and their connections with subcortical levels, between the hemispheres – all of which are significant as will become clear below. And according to McGilchrist, the relationship between the hemispheres is asymmetrical in that left is "ultimately dependent on" right, because it's the latter that keeps the body attuned to the outer world (2009: 6). We may think we can be permanently happy in our consciously constructed lives and worlds, but sooner or later reality intrudes in the form of unwanted feelings or other people behaving in ways we don't like.

The right hemisphere has richer connections with subcortical areas

This is because there is more myelination of axons in the right hemisphere, giving faster signalling to and from subcortical areas, and because a stimulus in this hemisphere has more diffuse effects than in the left. Subcortical areas include the limbic system and the HPA axis (Chapter 6) that's involved in triggering stress and anxiety in the body, so that affect and somatic regulation are more its province than the left's.

The differences between the hemispheres' connections with subcortical areas need not be very great for them to have a significant impact. If right is marginally more efficient in linking cortical and subcortical activity, then it will tend to dominate in functions that depend on such linking. Affect regulation is one of these, as we'll see.

The right hemisphere has richer connections with the body

As the subcortex lies between the hemispheres and the body, the richer connections between the right hemisphere and subcortical areas mean that it's also better connected with the body. While each hemisphere controls movement in the limbs on the opposite side of the body, the right is dominant for mapping sensory feedback from the viscera and combining it with other aspects of bodily feedback, making it more body-oriented than the left.

The right hemisphere, subcortex and body could be said to form a 'right brain-body ensemble'. This is where we can sense "I *am* my body". But left is one step removed, like an ivory tower, so we say "I *have* a body", one that's attached. Its relative independence from the body may be a reflection of its dependence on right for news of the internal state of the body – and its ability to suppress that news.

Left is better connected within areas, right is better connected between areas

According to Goldberg:

> the left hemisphere is characterised by a slightly greater reliance on short local pathways than is the right. The opposite is true for the right hemisphere: it has a slightly greater reliance on the long inter-regional pathways than does the left.
>
> (2009: 256)

This is reflected in the greater amount of white matter (longer myelinated axons) in the right, and means there's more connectivity *between* its different regions than in the left. The greater preponderance of local pathways *within* regions in the left may enable greater specialisation of functions based in it.

All this makes the right the more interconnected and 'wholistic' hemisphere, the left the more modular hemisphere.

The significance of these neuroanatomical differences

The left hemisphere seems better set up for specialised functions, the prime example being our language abilities, while the right is better set up for integrated ones, such as keeping the inner world of the body (heart rate, breathing etc.) in sync with what's happening around us. So right might be said to provide the foundation for left's specialist skills.

In McGilchrist's view, the right hemisphere lives to 'get' the whole of a situation, while the left lives to manipulate something or someone in that situation (2015). What a brilliant division of labour! Left wants certainty, so it makes our mind up fast, whereas right opens us up to possibilities. Having a balance of both of these seems like a good idea.

The right hemisphere is where we have a 'felt sense' of the present moment, the wholistic feel for a situation that's rooted in the body. Because the inner state of the body constantly changes, the landscape in this hemisphere is always changing too – right is more open to change than left, and is where psychological change begins.

How the hemispheres work separately and together

How does the neuroanatomy of the hemispheres translate into the way they work? We should start from the premise that both are available to their owner at any time. "Both hemispheres are involved in almost all mental processes, and certainly in all mental states", says McGilchrist (2009: 10), and "both hemispheres take part in virtually all 'functions' to some extent, and in reality both are always engaged" (2009: 93). At the same time, one may be dominant for a particular task. If this sounds paradoxical, that's because it is.

Language, for example, is biased to the left hemisphere, but bringing it alive and animating our speech requires the right. Creativity may depend on right's interconnectedness for fresh impulses to arise, but it requires left's participation for us to manifest something meaningful in the world. Reasoning and imagination likewise need both.

The corpus callosum keeps the hemispheres separate

The two hemispheres are linked via the corpus callosum, a bridge of some "300–800 million fibres connecting topologically similar areas in either hemisphere", according to McGilchrist (2009: 17). This is a relatively modest number in neural terms, which means that "only 2% of cortical neurons are connected by this tract" (2009: 17). The other 98% fire without direct contact with their partners on the opposite side. This seems a rather delicate arrangement, so that small variations in the way a person's hemispheres are linked may snowball into significant differences in how they integrate over time – with significant psychological results.

There's constant communication across the bridge, happening in milliseconds, to co-ordinate the hemispheres. Yet the signalling also keeps them separate. Although most signalling is excitatory ("please join in"), some is inhibitory ("please shut up"). Furthermore, excitation may itself lead to inhibition, for "stimulation of neurons in one hemisphere commonly results in ... a prolonged inhibitory arousal, in the other, contralateral, hemisphere" (2009: 18). McGilchrist thinks the corpus callosum's main role may be 'functional inhibition' so that one hemisphere can suppress the other. Whilst enabling the hemispheres to be integrated, the corpus callosum, paradoxically, keeps them separate so they don't interfere with each other. Information is shared between them, but the worlds where that information is handled need to be kept apart since left and right process things differently.

The experiences of split-brain patients illustrate what happens when the corpus callosum is cut and the inhibition and separation stop. One man tried to embrace his wife with one arm only for his other arm to push her away, and a woman who reached into her wardrobe to get something to wear with one hand found that her other hand followed it in and picked something she *didn't* want to wear.

'Winner takes all'

Although each hemisphere may be capable of responding to a situation, "at the level of moment to moment activity the hemispheres may operate a 'winner takes all' system", says McGilchrist (2009: 10). This may happen either because one hemisphere is better suited to a task than the other, or because it gets in first due to the signalling time across the corpus callosum (the twinkling of an eye can be long enough in neural terms). This tendency can work very fast, moment by moment. It doesn't mean that one hemisphere will necessarily dominate for long periods of time – both hemispheres are needed for most things we actually do.

So the corpus callosum may differentiate the hemispheres as much as it integrates them. Evolution has led to greater differentiation between them over time – along with more sophisticated functioning in each hemisphere.

Left inhibits right more than vice versa

Whilst either hemisphere can inhibit the other, left inhibits right more efficiently than vice versa. If the two hemispheres are in conflict (as with the split-brain patient choosing what to wear), one may simply silence the other, and left does this to right more than vice versa (it was her left hand, controlled by her right hemisphere, that picked what she didn't want to wear). It enables left to focus on its task unimpeded, and evolution may have enhanced its capacity to inhibit right.

For example, if left is focusing on a foreground task, ignoring what arises in right's global attention to what's happening inside and outside can enable it to complete the task. On the other hand, if this happens too often for too long, we may fail to appreciate warning signs from our suffering bodies or our suffering partners and pay the price later on.

The nature of right hemisphere functions may mean that this hemisphere doesn't benefit as much by inhibiting the left. But right *is* prone to overwhelming left with emotional arousal in a way that disrupts left's cognitive functions.

Competition and co-operation

Do the two hemispheres co-operate or do they compete? Goldberg thinks "a competitive relationship exists between the two hemispheres, most likely mediated by the inhibitory pathways of the corpus callosum" (2009: 269). McGilchrist, however, thinks the hemispheres undertake tasks that, while conflicting, are nevertheless complementary. Their very incompatibility can permit something new to arise. Apparent competition may lead ultimately to co-operation – which, after all, requires differences. The functional inhibition enabled by the corpus callosum may actually facilitate this co-operation. Each hemisphere has to remain independent, and to some extent ignorant, of what goes on in its counterpart.

There's a paradox: the hemispheres need to stay separate and yet at the same time co-operate. Nature may have reached a pinnacle in its ability to achieve this in the human brain, yet in doing so it may have set up a large vulnerability to things going awry during neural and psychological development. Emotional wounding and traumatic dissociation are likely to upset the delicate balance of hemispheric co-operation.

Right-left-right to synthesise what both hemispheres know

A significant aspect of McGilchrist's thesis is his assertion that only the right hemisphere can synthesise what both hemispheres know into a useable whole. This point fits with the integrative functions of the right. Its synthesising role may be reflected in the fact that it's the source of fresh thoughts and feelings. This implies that if left ignores right too much, it may get carried away with repetitive thinking that, while clever, departs from reality. It's often other people who put us right when this happens. The principle for using our brain well then becomes 'right-left-right': start with what arises in the right hemisphere, allow the left to make its specialist contributions, then send the whole lot back to the right for re-integration into the whole.

Problems arise when the left hemisphere cements what it's articulated into place without allowing time and space for the right to digest and integrate it with everything else. For example: clinging onto theoretical edifices without allowing them to be refreshed over time.

The hemispheres' complementary contributions

What do these differences between the hemispheres amount to in our actual experience? Let's examine some contrasting contributions of each hemisphere that combine to create our experience, but which are also prone to becoming detached. Essentially complementary in nature, they can nevertheless lead to conflict. Those belonging to the left can lose sight of those made by the right, and those belonging to the right can derail those of the left.

The thread that runs through them is that the right hemisphere connects us with our bodies, each other and the world, while the left stands aside from the body and separates one person and one thing from another in order to do something with them or it. Right attends to whatever is 'other', with which it's in relationship, while left attends to a world, one step removed from reality, of language and representations in order to grasp something.

The paired contributions that follow are available all the time in our hemispheres. McGilchrist describes their relationship thus: they "are both vital but are fundamentally incompatible" and therefore they need "neurological sequestration from one another" in either hemisphere (2009: 127).

Foreground – background

Because of the separation of focused and global attention between the hemispheres, the left is concerned with the foreground, the right with the background. What's foreground is what's in our awareness that we're engaging with – such as reading words on a page and trying to grasp their meaning. In the background is our peripheral awareness of our surroundings, so that movements or sounds may divert our attention away from the page. Also in the background is our somatic and emotional state, which may also divert our attention at times.

Take speaking, for example. McCrone explains the hemispheres' contributions:

> matching areas on either side of the cortex actually share the job of speaking; the difference is that the left does the 'foreground' tasks, such as drawing together actual sentences and recognising individual words, while the right cortex deals with 'background' jobs, such as putting the emotional colouring into what we say, or making creative associations between words.
>
> (1999: 174)

There's a hint of conscious and unconscious minds here, but the right hemisphere isn't all in the dark. Its contribution comes at the edge of awareness, such that it may or may not enter consciousness, which isn't the same as it being unconscious. We could talk of *more conscious* and *less conscious* processes. Sometimes it suits us to leave right hemisphere things in the background out of awareness, other times we're stuck until we allow them into awareness, so they become foreground.

Explicit – implicit

What's foreground is explicit – we know what it is. What lies in the background is merely implicit – present but unnoticed. If we can deal with a situation by considering only the explicit things, then all well and good. But often we can't, and then life gets more interesting and we must be open to what's implicit.

McGilchrist thinks it is the left hemisphere's job to "render the implicit explicit" so that we can do something with it (2009: 181). It "forces the implicit into explicitness" by proceeding in a sequential manner, and "brings clarity" to something in our experience (2009: 207).

Detail – context

The left hemisphere focuses on the explicit detail in the foreground, while the right takes care of the context that's implicit in the background – which includes our body, the world we inhabit and other people. Returning to the example of speaking, McCrone describes the contributions of left and right thus:

> on one side of the brain we are focusing in close, getting the detail of the grammar and the choice of words just right, but over on the other we are taking the big picture view, managing the overall tone and picking up on any broader nuances of meaning.
>
> (1999: 174)

Left allows us to zoom in on the detail, right allows us to step back and see the big picture.

Neuroscience itself is full of details, but we have the context of our lived experience of our own nervous systems to make them relevant and meaningful. Even neuroscientists are human and have such a context.

Detail and context provide endless scope for discussion and disagreement. You can be sure of your details, but the moment someone changes the context, you can lose the argument. Everything changes. The context includes inconvenient facts, other people's views, and uncertainty, which isn't always to the left hemisphere's liking.

Known – unknown

The left hemisphere's bias for routine and the right's for novelty leads to left contributing what's known and familiar, and right what's unknown and new. The openness of mind required for new experiences starts in the right hemisphere. McGilchrist says "because the right hemisphere sees things as they are, they are constantly new for it" (2009: 80), so it has an affinity "for all that is 'other', new, unknown, uncertain" (2009: 83). Whereas the left likes to put things into familiar categories based on abstraction, often language-based, so its affinity is for "well-worn familiarity, certainty" (2009: 83).

Purpose – vigilance

Our left hemisphere has aims and goals, something it wants to get or achieve, whereas our right takes life and the world as they are. Left can keep us on track of our intentions, right keeps inner and outer worlds together and lets us know if something doesn't feel right. Left wants to get somewhere, right is on the lookout for threats and discrepancies, and may divert us with the unexpected. So some meditation practices involve having no aim so that we can experience just being.

McGilchrist says "the left hemisphere always has 'an end in view', a purpose or use" (2009: 127), whereas "only the right hemisphere can direct attention to what comes to us from the edges of our awareness" (2009: 40). The left hemisphere is "drawn by its expectations", whereas the right is "vigilant for whatever exists 'out there'", so this is the hemisphere that can "bring us something other than what we already know" (2009: 40) – it notices what we might otherwise miss.

Grasping something – sensing the whole

We need focused attention to grasp objects and manipulate them, so this is a left hemisphere job. Think of this as having started in human evolution with our use of tools, and the same principle now applying to our use of words and ideas. But underlying our ability to grasp something lies the right hemisphere's ability to have a sense of the whole situation and our feeling about it. Our felt sense of how something 'sits' inside helps us find our way around the detail we want to grasp.

We can grasp facts and details until the cows come home, but if we lose touch with our feelings and our sense of how others are reacting to us, we 'lose the plot'. As McGilchrist says, while "the left hemisphere's relationship with the world is one of reaching out to grasp, and therefore to *use* it, the right hemisphere's appears to be one of reaching out – just that" (2009: 127).

Re-presenting – presence

The right hemisphere is present to inner (bodily) and outer (situational) worlds, and is where inner and outer come together in an integrated state of 'presence'. Then the left gets to know about it and 're-presents' the experience, maybe in language and maybe slotting it into a familiar category. Right lives the territory, left maps it.[2] Maps are useful, but we shouldn't mistake them for the territory. McGilchrist thinks these respective contributions are "close to the core of what differentiates the hemispheres" (2009: 50).

Something that happens here is that we may talk about the wonders of 'being present', and then we get caught up in the idea and the words ... and cease to be present. Meditation practices sometimes encourage people to let words and thoughts pass by so they can return to a state of presence.

Categorising – discerning

The right hemisphere identifies individuals, the left recognises categories. The former is based on fine discriminations, the latter on useful classification. McGilchrist says the left hemisphere is "more concerned with abstract categories and types", while the right is "more concerned with the uniqueness and individuality of each existing thing or being" (2009: 51) – and "finer discriminations between things" (2009: 52).

So we recognise faces with our right hemispheres and arrange people into personality types with our left hemispheres. Categorising has the advantage of making sense of complex subjects (such as brain areas), while discerning differences scores on getting it right in particular situations, and noticing when something looks out of place, even if we can't say why.

Certainty – possibility and ambiguity

The left hemisphere, with its categories and representations, is good at tying things down into certainties so that we can get on with what we're doing. It does this even if it gets it wrong, and is prone to confabulating – insisting something is the case even if it clearly isn't. The more open right hemisphere, able to deal with new situations, is relaxed about mere possibilities and ambiguous situations. When we're stuck, we depend on it to get unstuck. But we may need to be patient, tolerating uncertainty, ambiguity and not-knowing for a while before deciding and acting.

McGilchrist elaborates:

> the left hemisphere needs certainty and needs to be right. The right hemisphere makes it possible to hold several ambiguous possibilities in suspension together without premature closure on one outcome.
>
> (2009: 82)

Left enables us to act quickly and decisively when needed. Right enables us to live with contradictions and nuances, and to avoid getting marooned in "I'm right, you're wrong" positions.

Two minds in the therapy room (times two)

The hemispheres play their respective roles in the therapy room and, by reflecting on the scientific picture, their dynamics sometimes become apparent. The hemispheric model may not explain everything that happens in therapy, but it sheds light on much that does. One reason for this is that it explains how psyche is bound up with the body via the right brain-body ensemble, whilst the more conscious mind in the left hemisphere can become detached from it.

Therapy is much about integrating the hemispheres' different contributions. Left and right integrate naturally as we go through life, except when they don't because of emotional wounds and traumatic experiences that keep them apart. Psychological survival may be enabled by stopping the natural process of integration; it works, up to a point, but there's always a price to pay.

Two hemispheres present for therapy

Jung said there are four people in the room – he was including the anima or animus of both client and therapist (1983).[3] Might this have something to do with there also being four hemispheres in the room? And does the most striking divide in neural architecture have something to do with the divided psyche? Some common psychological polarities probably reflect the hemispheric divide: ego and self, head and heart, mind and body, conscious and unconscious.

The hemispheres work together seamlessly in principle, but brains that present for therapy are likely to be beset by some sort of conflict between them. The client's left hemisphere brings a presenting issue and starts speaking, telling a story and going into details. Sometimes it then asks the therapist for the answer to the problem – not an entirely unreasonable request! His left hemisphere has run out of solutions. But if all the therapist does is provide an answer, he's unlikely to be any further forward.

His right hemisphere expresses itself in his manner of greeting at the door, his facial expression, body language and style of communicating. Although it may be in the background, it's central to the therapeutic enterprise. It brings his inner life, and is the source of images and forgotten memories. It's also the home of overwhelming emotions, depression, trauma, dissociation and shame.

A hypothesis: right provides the foundation for left. This foundation takes time to become visible, though hints as to its nature may be immediately apparent. It comprises the client's affect regulation, attachment patterns, mind-body connection and inner life. It's prone to fragmentation, and the problems that arise from this are often those that bring people to therapy.

The hemispheres' complementary contributions in the therapy room

Let's go through the left-right contributions outlined above and see how they might apply in the therapy room.

Foreground – background. Presenting issues, story and content may occupy the foreground, and the client may be immersed in them. The therapist, however, needs to have one foot in the background: the feeling 'in the room', the nonverbal communication and so forth. Therapists are trained to be alert to the background and to interrupt the dialogue with observations about it ("this feels like a lot, let's go slowly").

The right hemisphere's broad attention to background factors breaks up the left's focused attention so that something new can arise. Part of the therapist's job is to draw the client's attention to background processes he may not be aware of – feelings, his body, what happens as he relates and communicates.

Explicit – implicit. Client and therapist work together to make explicit what's implicit. The right hemisphere's world of buried feelings, forgotten childhood memories, attachment patterns and so forth needs to become foreground. It emerges little by little – we have to trust the process. The left hemisphere is needed to unpack what emerges so that something new can unfold ("I wonder what this 'feeling negative' really is . . ."). McGilchrist says "the left hemisphere cannot deliver anything new direct from 'outside', but it can unfold, or 'unpack', what it's given" by the right (2009: 208).

Detail – context. The content may include any amount of detail, and clients often believe the therapist needs a lot. Fortunately, they both share a context which grows as therapy proceeds. It may include the client's childhood, his family system, the themes that emerge during therapy, the dynamics of the therapeutic relationship and much more. The therapist's job is to bear all these in mind whilst attending to the detail, and sometimes to encourage the client to do this as well ("this new story feels like what happened in your family"). Contextual factors tend to be biased to the right hemisphere, and bringing them into awareness can stop the left from going around in circles filling the space with details.

Known – unknown. Clients often enter therapy when their left hemispheres have run out of ways to deal with unwanted feelings. Their usual coping mechanisms – such as eating, sleeping, waiting for the problem to go away – are no longer working, and they need the therapist's help to allow something new to unfold from their right hemisphere to shift the problem.

The therapist must guide the client into unfamiliar places so that transformation can happen. Sometimes the support of the therapeutic relationship enables him to express hidden things ("I've never told anyone this"), sometimes buried childhood memories return in the adult mind ("I'd forgotten that happened"), or maybe fresh potential emerges as he loosens up inside ("I didn't realise it's OK to say 'no'").

Purpose – vigilance. Most clients come to therapy with an aim that fuels their engagement. Their left hemisphere focuses attention on it, but sometimes it gets in the way – such as when the client says "Peter, I need you to make me less anxious". If only I could! – but then he would already have found the fix for himself. What I need to do is keep his left hemisphere onside and wait for his right to appear – vigilance. Sooner or later something unexpected for us both arises from the right. The client feels an inner shift and becomes more trusting of therapy, of me ("I found last week's session very useful") and of himself.

Grasping something – sensing the whole situation. I want to grasp what my client is telling me, whilst also sitting back and letting his story wash over me to get a sense of the whole interaction we're having – the coherence (or lack of it) of the story, the underlying patterns in his experience, my own feelings that arise in response. Does listening to him bring me alive or send me to sleep?

When I have a sense of the whole therapeutic situation, my intuition comes alive and I can find my way forward in the dialogue. The nature of our dialogue may help the client to find a sense of coherence in what at first seems confusing to him.

Re-presenting – presence. My client (re)presents his experience, his story and his dilemma in what he says to me. While he does this, I sense his presence in the room with me, his manner of communicating, his patterns of relating. His (re)presentation and presence may seem incongruent to me: he may minimise his difficulties and hope that six sessions will sort them out, whilst leaving me sensing pain, trauma and disturbance. I may reflect what's implicit, for example, "you're speaking very quickly, you seem to have a lot you want to tell me".

Categorising – discerning differences. The client or the therapist, or maybe both, may find categories to be helpful signposts: attachment styles, character types, enneagram numbers and so forth. At the same time, the therapist can be alert to her sense of the unique individual before her, and encourage him to be discerning ("if we say this about you, does it feel like it fits your experience?").

Certainty – possibility. The client may have fixed beliefs about himself ("I was abused in childhood, I'm not able to have a relationship now"). The therapist can keep an open mind, point out any exceptions to the rule that become apparent, and be explicit about the possibility of change ("maybe one day you'll feel able to manage your emotions sufficiently to allow yourself to get close to someone").

More left-right contrasts in the therapy room

Let's explore some further contrasts in the hemispheric contributions to the therapy process.

Telling a story – telling the story. The client's left hemisphere may tell stories each week, perhaps to fill the space and survive the session. It feels quite different when he trusts the therapist enough to tell *the* story (that needs to be told). This requires both hemispheres, and it starts with autobiographical memory in the right hemisphere. The emotional engagement is felt by both parties.

Rationalising – being rational. The client's left hemisphere may rationalise his behaviour, avoiding a deeper exploration. But he needs both sides of his brain to be rational, which involves marrying thinking with feeling.

Defending – letting go. The client's left hemisphere may defend against uncomfortable experiences anchored in his right – by suppressing emotion, avoiding painful topics, and in extremis denying what he's not ready to face. When he feels safe enough with the therapist, left is able to let go to right, and then a natural healing process begins.

Merely talking about – really feeling it. Left loves to talk about life experiences, especially those for which it thinks the therapist should have a remedy. This may lead nowhere. It's a very different matter to talk about a meaningful experience and really feel it as we do so, left and right co-operating. A common complaint I hear about previous therapies is that "we just talked about my childhood" – something was missing, namely, really feeling it.

Content – process. All the talking about and analysing, even with sophisticated psychoanalytic concepts, may amount to a lot of content and no more, the left hemisphere trapped in the world it's constructed for itself. But somewhere underneath it all there's a process happening in both parties' right hemispheres, and the therapist can point to it ("this must be important but my mind's getting sleepy – I wonder what's really going on . . .").

Explanations – images and symbols. Both parties' left hemispheres may seek explanations for problems, and a good explanation may be a relief. But at some point therapy needs more than explanations. Images and symbols that arise in the right hemisphere (of either client or therapist) imply inner movement and bring something fresh to reflect on. Simply allowing images to emerge may have a transformative effect – explanation may not even be needed.

Theory – intuition. The left-right divide applies to the therapist as well as the client. Theory is a left hemisphere construction, based (hopefully) on someone's personal experience. Therapists have to draw on both their left hemisphere's store of theories and their right's capacity for intuition – that may lead them in a different direction.

Congruence – incongruence. Congruence (of body and speaking, for example) requires both hemispheres. Incongruence (where the feeling evoked doesn't match the words spoken, for example) is a sign of a conflict between the hemispheres. Bessel van der Kolk, a Boston trauma therapist, puts it beautifully:

> while the left half of the brain does all the talking, the right half of the brain carries the music of experience. It communicates through facial expressions and body language and by making the sounds of love and sorrow: by singing, swearing, crying, dancing or mimicking.
>
> (2014: 44)

Psychological defences and dissociation

The hemispheric model allows us to distinguish defences and dissociation which disrupt the integrated working of the hemispheres in different ways. Defences involve the left hemisphere inhibiting the right's contributions; justifying, intellectualising or simply filling the space with talking suggest it's struggling to stay in control and avoiding letting in the right with its uncomfortable states. Dissociation is centred in the right and involves inner and outer worlds coming apart in traumatic overwhelm, integration turning to fragmentation; the foundation that right provides for both hemispheres crumbles, and neither hemisphere functions effectively.

Simply put, defences may be against unwanted feelings or dissociative collapse – in the latter case, with good reason, for whilst painful feelings are simply painful, the inability to function properly, and the shame that accompanies it, is intolerable. Who would want to go there? Defensiveness and dissociation are intertwined.

Both defences and dissociation require a human relationship to overcome them so that the hemispheres can re-integrate. The therapeutic relationship has to make painful feelings bearable, and it needs to provide a solid holding when experience fragments and becomes chaotic.

The right hemisphere's vulnerability to dissociation and fragmentation after trauma, and the left's defence against further dissociation, often lie behind whatever brings people to therapy. Clients defend against dissociation for good reason, yet their defensiveness has become an obstacle to living their life more fully. I sometimes hear "I want to take a break from therapy, I need to get on with my life", as if spending one hour a week in my consulting room were preventing them from doing so.

The principle of integration

If the direction of therapy is towards better neural integration, the obstacles to integrated hemispheric working in situations where the client struggles need to be overcome. Hypothesising … when all goes well enough in childhood, the hemispheres develop in an integrated way that carries into adulthood. But when there's unresolved emotional wounding and trauma while the brain is maturing, the hemispheres may not develop in the integrated way nature intended, and a divided psyche results.

People may come to therapy because their hemispheres are in conflict and so they (or their left hemispheres) don't know how to make them co-operate. They need a human relationship, with its potential to evoke what's missing and enable new integration. Their left hemisphere may be unable to let go to their right's inherent capacity for healing, so they need the therapist's (hopefully better) integrated hemispheric functioning to make it possible for them to do so. Cozolino says, "we teach clients a method by which they can learn to attend to and translate right hemisphere processing into left hemisphere language" (2017: 114).

When therapy works, there's a shift in the relationship between the hemispheres. They co-operate in places where before there was conflict. Once this happens, everything starts to feel different.

Encouraging processes arising in the right hemisphere

Therapists must work with the client's left hemisphere, and we might characterise this as working cognitively. One approach is to teach it to listen to the right and allow it to play its role in his psychological life.

They should also know how to work with the right hemisphere. The transformative processes of therapy arise in the right and then engage the left as well. Many therapeutic interventions point towards the right:

- emotional and bodily awareness
- imagery

- exploring attachment patterns, family systems, transference and countertransference
- dreamwork, drawing, sand trays, movement etc.

But dialogue also engages the right when it's to the point and meaningful, and the advantage of such talking is that it happens seamlessly during the therapeutic process. It involves supporting the client to bear painful feelings, tolerating confusion and uncertainty, and encouraging him to experiment and take risks.

The right hemisphere is where unexpected transformative moments arise, so we must trust our instincts. It's not magic, but it can appear magical to the left hemisphere that's taken by surprise at the completely different nature of the world of the right. Left cannot predict what will come from right, so we should always "expect the unexpected".

Working with the psyche

Therapy involves working with the psyche, which points towards the right hemisphere and the subcortical and somatic processes that underpin it. "The right hemisphere is dominant in treatment", says Schore (2009: 128). It's where the client encounters his vulnerability, his forgotten childhood, his imaginal world and the potential for healing.

Perhaps the right hemisphere *is* the inner world – a world of feelings, somatic sensations, forgotten memories, images, dreams and symbols – where one thing naturally leads to another thanks to its interconnected composition. We tend to live in the more conscious processes of the left, and clients may need help to venture into the very different world of the right.

The right hemisphere is where the client begins to integrate the raw emotional forces within him, where his capacity for intimacy grows, and where he opens up to the transpersonal dimension that transforms his perspective. It's where he encounters his shadow, experiences depression and breakdown, but also where he senses his way forward. If client and therapist can withstand the turmoil and keep the therapeutic dialogue going, then better left-right integration takes care of itself.

In general terms, any movement towards the right hemisphere in therapy is therapeutic, and the more ways we engage with it, the better. There are two riders to this. First, right must also engage with left in the process, for example, in articulating inner experience. Second, this principle is not an absolute. Relying on the same right hemisphere process repeatedly may not help – for example, always inviting an image. The more repetitive an intervention, the more it becomes familiar and therefore lacking the novelty of the right. Beware the trickery of the left! But I would exclude genuinely meaningful dialogue from this observation.

Conclusion

Nature has carved the brain in two. There must be an evolutionary advantage in having two different minds humming alongside each other, able both to compete and to co-operate. But if things go badly during our neural and psychological development, it's along this divide that we might expect to find clues to the problems that ensue.

The left-right axis provides a model of mind and body that can be empirically researched. To understand it requires learning a little science, appreciating the subtleties of nature's arrangement, and taking time for reflective thinking. If you're careful to avoid simplistic dichotomies, your experience of observing others' brains (maybe even your own) can guide you. I find this model more practical than some models of the psyche that decorate the therapy world; the following chapters will put this to the test. And it has the potential to build bridges between the worlds of therapy and of neuroscience.

I've used a model of two minds for many years that's helped me make sense of people's inner experience. I draw it on the flipchart when teaching focusing workshops, so we have a diagram illustrating how, when we turn our attention within, the body speaks back to us. I call these two minds the 'foreground mind' and the 'background bodymind'. Everything I've learnt about the hemispheres fits with this intuitive model and elaborates on it, so I use these terms as well as refer to the hemispheres.

The left-right model of the divided brain, including the right brain-body ensemble, is a primary point of reference for the topics that follow – starting with the rather important one of human relationships.

Notes

1 McGilchrist also describes the right hemisphere's global attention as 'open' attention (2009).
2 I use 'map' here in a figurative sense rather than the neural 'mapping' sense described in Chapter 2.
3 'Animus' and 'anima' are Jung's terms for the contrasexual aspect of the psyche – the masculine for a woman, the feminine for a man.

Chapter 4

Relationships and social engagement

Introduction

We may see ourselves as separate individuals who spend some of our time relating with others. This is the view from the left hemisphere, whilst the view from the right is of the interconnectedness of inner and outer worlds, which include other people. We begin life by attaching to others, and only later do we develop an autonomous self. As we progress through life, our relationships are fundamental to our well-being, and our right hemisphere does much to look after them in the background, without our left noticing.

Images of brains usually show a single brain, which is misleading because brains imply other brains – the context of relationship, family and community which supports them. Keeping brains isolated is a technique used either for spiritual advancement, as in silent retreats, or for punishment, as in solitary confinement, and both are a challenge for the nervous system. So let's look at real brains that relate to other brains: the contributions of each hemisphere to relating, the state of the autonomic nervous system in the pleasurable and painful aspects of relating, the role of the body – and the dynamics of therapeutic relationships.

The 'social brain'

Brains are inherently social, so the idea of the 'social brain' is a construct that points to brain areas and biochemicals involved in relating. Much social brain activity happens implicitly, outside our awareness. Psychotherapy is full of mysterious manifestations of the social brain, including projection, transference, countertransference and projective identification, and we'll see how the nervous system provides a platform for them. But first, we need to get some more neuroscience detail onboard.

Social brain areas

Certain areas are key players in the social brain and feature in discussions of this subject. We need to work bottom-up here, and return to the three levels

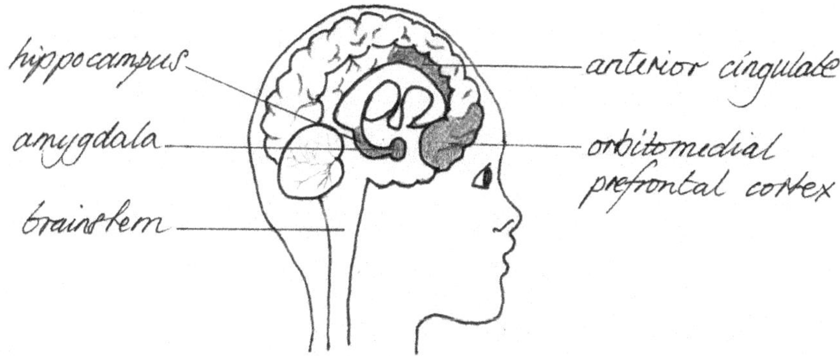

Figure 4.1 Social brain areas: brainstem, amygdala, hippocampus, anterior cingulate, and orbitomedial prefrontal cortex. The insula, not shown, sits next door to the anterior cingulate, hidden behind cortical areas

of the triune brain – reptilian, mammalian and human – adding a fourth level between the limbic system (mammalian) and the neocortex (human), that of the paleocortex ('paleo' meaning old). The paleocortical areas, the insula, cingulate and orbitomedial prefrontal cortex, were the first cortical areas to evolve, and neural development in infancy re-traces the path of evolution. These areas sit above the limbic areas below and contribute to the bodily and emotional aspects of our social life (see Figure 4.1).

The *brainstem* is working at birth. As well as handling aspects of bodily life such as breathing, it's the home of reflexes that kick-start attachment, such as orienting to the sound of mother's voice.

The *amygdala* is a limbic area working at birth, which means it's well-connected within itself and with areas it links to. One such is the hypothalamus which raises heart rate and blood pressure, another is a motor nerve in the face that triggers fearful expressions. The amygdala generates stress, anxiety, fear and fight-flight reactions to certain stimuli. Babies arrive in the world ready to become stressed and anxious if circumstances warrant it. Circumstances for babies mainly concern relationships, and the amygdala fires if mother's behaviour seems threatening. It pairs particular feelings with a fear reaction, and a baby can learn to fear attachment itself. Worse, the amygdala has a tendency to 'generalise': the more it fires in reaction to genuine threats, the more it appraises other stimuli as threatening even when they aren't.

The *hippocampus*, also in the limbic system, is associated with memory. It can dampen the amygdala's reactions because it organises memory by context, a more sophisticated method than the amygdala's simple pairings. If it appraises a stimulus the amygdala considers a threat to be a false alarm, it can trigger a parasympathetic response to slow heart rate and breathing. Unfortunately, it isn't sufficiently developed to do this until we're around 2 years old, hence the potential for infants to experience stress and fear.

Cingulate is Latin for surround, and this area surrounds the thalamus, the limbic area that relays sensory signals. The *anterior cingulate*, the front half that borders onto the frontal lobes, gets talked about more than the *posterior cingulate*. Being paleocortical, it's an evolutionary step beyond the capacities of limbic areas that enables mammals to take care of their young and to play together. An association area for emotional and somatic pathways, it fires in infants when they cry out in distress and in mothers when they hear their cry, when we feel emotion in our body, and when we experience pain or witness others experiencing pain.

Insula is Latin for island, and this is a well-hidden island, usually absent from brain diagrams. Also paleocortical, it handles body signals conveying physiological and emotional sensations on their way to the *somatosensory cortex* in the parietal lobes above. It contributes to our awareness of what's happening in our body, and fires when we see changes in another's facial expression or eye gaze that affect us. Attachment trauma can lead it to associate body awareness with feelings of shame and disgust, leaving us reluctant to sense within.

Prefrontal cortex is the main part of the frontal lobes, and the more social life a mammal has, the larger it is. It's an evolutionary improvement on the cingulate, permitting greater neuroplasticity and therefore more scope for learning and conscious control. The prefrontal cortex is an 'association area' for sensory signals from the posterior lobes, knitting them together into one big picture, which enables it to inhibit brain areas lower down the hierarchy, including the amygdala. We need it to imagine another person's inner world.

Orbitomedial prefrontal cortex is the key area of the prefrontal cortex for the social brain. 'Orbito' means above the eye sockets, 'medial' means in the middle, and it features a lot in neuroscience discussions. Sitting at the apex of social brain networks organising attachment, it's the first frontal lobe area to develop in infancy. The highest level of integration of signals from external senses and internal ones from the body happens here, especially in the right hemisphere (Cozolino 2017). It's needed for considered social responses based on the awareness of both self and other.

Mirror neurons are a type of neuron rather than a brain area because the research that discovered them involved attaching electrodes to particular neurons in monkeys' brains – to avoid having to persuade them into brain scanners (Ramachandran 2011). When a monkey watched another monkey eating a banana, the same neurons fired as when the monkey ate a banana itself.[1] Mirror neurons are found in the frontal and parietal lobes and fire both when we observe another person make a movement, such as a facial expression, and when we make such a movement ourselves. The implication is that when we observe another's movement, our brain prepares us to make the same movement. They enable us to imitate others and anticipate their intentions.

Social brain chemistry

Certain neurochemicals appear frequently in discussions of social experience. This subject gets very complex very quickly, so I'll keep it simple.

Dopamine is associated with feeling motivated and excited. It fuels our social lives and energises us to engage with the world and other people (Panksepp 2012). Infants need dopamine to forge their attachments, and we all need it to seek the rewards of social interaction.

Noradrenaline is associated with feeling energised and in a good mood. It's released when we experience something new, especially in the right hemisphere (McGilchrist 2009). Too little and we may feel bored and lethargic, too much and we may feel anxious and irritable.

Serotonin does different things in different places in the brain.[2] It lowers emotional arousal (Panksepp 2012), thereby helping us control our impulses, remain even-tempered and have social confidence. Too little and we may feel awful, become aggressive and sleep badly.

Endorphins generate feelings of well-being when we enjoy others' company.[3] Also referred to as 'endogenous opioids', Panksepp calls them 'comfort and joy' chemicals (2012). Low levels of endorphins correlate with feeling lonely, distressed and miserable.

Oxytocin facilitates the good feelings that come with emotional bonding with others.[4] It promotes attachment and intimacy. Oxytocin has a big effect on a mother's body, helping her to give birth and to breastfeed and, combined with endorphins, to experience motherhood as rewarding.

Vasopressin facilitates aspects of bonding and attachment, including sexual and paternal behaviour in men.[5]

Social hemispheres

Our patterns of relating, along with the affect and somatic regulation that accompany them, are biased towards the right hemisphere, "the mediator of social behaviour", according to McGilchrist (2009: 58). This is due to its richer connectivity with subcortical areas and the body. It keeps our autonomic state in sync with the needs of relating and communicating, such as more arousal for speaking and less for listening, and provides the implicit foundation for our finding relationships rewarding or frustrating.

So my 'real' emotional self (that I experience inside) lies in my right hemisphere background, while my persona or social self (the person I want to be and want others to see) is a construct in my left hemisphere foreground. When the two are congruent, relationships are rewarding, but when they're not, I may present a 'false self' and feel uncomfortable. Others are affected by my real self, whether they realise it or not, and whether I like it or not.

The relationship patterns of the real self in the right hemisphere form in early childhood in attachment relationships. They guide our habitual behaviours and felt experience for the rest of our lives, or until we reflect on them with our frontal lobes in a close relationship or in therapy.

The right hemisphere maps our inner sense of self that's rooted in the body. Developing more rapidly than the left in the first 18 months, it absorbs our early experience of attachment and family (Schore 2012). It learns how others are and how to respond to them, shaping our appraisal of social safety or threat, and our ability to regulate our emotions with others.[6] These patterns manifest in relationships later in life, especially when we're under stress.

The right hemisphere's bias for regulating body and emotion in the background frees the left to focus attention on others and our interactions with them. But left's ability to inhibit right can lead to its focus on others disconnecting from right's self-awareness and empathy. What we say (left) and how we say it (right) may not be congruent. Our social self can become grandiose and unaware of its failings, whereas our real self is more realistic about its place in the social milieu (McGilchrist 2009).

Social engagement

Social engagement is about what happens when nervous systems come into contact with each other. Do they fight, withdraw, or do they engage in rewarding ways? The *social engagement system* is the contribution of Stephen Porges, an American neuroscientist with a mammalian perspective. His work is important to therapy because it describes the different states of the nervous system in relationships, including the therapeutic one.

This 'system' is a branch of the autonomic nervous system that enables "positive social interactions in safe contexts", states Porges (2011: 270).[7] It links facial expression and voice prosody with heart rate and breathing to allow mammals to engage with each other without lapsing into fight-flight behaviours. Central to it is the *vagus* nerve, one of the bundles of cranial nerves descending from the brainstem into the body and the main nerve bundle of the parasympathetic nervous system (Porges 2017). Vagus refers to wandering in Latin (think vagrant), and the vagus nerve wanders to many places in the body, including heart, lungs, gut, face and throat. It includes sensory nerves that allow the body to signal its state to the brain, and motor nerves that allow the brain to signal the body to change something.

The following is based on Porges's *The Polyvagal Theory* (2011).

Polyvagal theory

The basic model of the autonomic nervous system is of a 'paired antagonism' between sympathetic and parasympathetic branches. But three is more interesting than two, and polyvagal theory describes a more elaborate model with three levels in the neuroanatomy underlying our social reactions (see Table 4.1). Porges first developed the theory while researching heart rate changes, and heart rate is the key here. He thinks "affect and interpersonal social behaviour are more accurately described as biobehavioural than psychological processes" because of the effect of bodily processes on psychological ones (2011: 257).

The prelude to the three levels is that there are two branches of the vagus (hence 'polyvagal') which enact different behaviours, one related to safety and the other to threat:

1 The *dorsal vagus* evolved first in primitive vertebrates, and it can immobilise us so we 'play dead', shut down and dissociate.
2 The *ventral vagus* evolved later in mammals, linking the heart to the face, dampening the sympathetic nervous system and the stress response, and enabling social engagement.[8]

The ventral vagus, unlike the dorsal, is myelinated, so it works more efficiently. It's the foundation of attachment in the nervous system.

Our physiological reactions to social stimuli, which underlie our psychological reactions, are ordered in a three-level hierarchy, which means they kick off in order:

Table 4.1 Polyvagal theory, following Porges (2011). In response to triggers from the environment and from within the brain and body, the autonomic nervous system goes into one of three states: safety, danger or life threat. Social engagement is only possible in a state of safety

safety	*danger*	*life threat*
ventral "smart" vagus		dorsal vagus
optimal balance of sympathetic and parasympathetic	*sympathetic arousal*	*parasympathetic shutdown*
optimal arousal	hyper-arousal	very low arousal
social engagement	*fight, flight, freeze*	*immobilisation*
eye contact	dissociated rage	dissociated collapse
facial expression	panic	
vocalisation	going mute	

- *Safety*: the ventral vagus, cortically controlled, modulates sympathetic arousal. It adjusts heart rate, breathing rate, facial expression, eye contact and gaze, posture, and voice prosody so that social engagement can be rewarding.
- *Danger*: the sympathetic nervous system, subcortically controlled, triggers high arousal and defensive behaviours including fight, flight, freeze and active avoidance. Dissociated rage and panic, and going mute, also belong here.
- *Life threat*: the dorsal vagus, controlled from the brainstem, triggers very low arousal states of immobilisation, parasympathetic shutdown, passive avoidance and dissociated collapse.

In social situations, nature primes us for safety, but if we feel unsafe (whether we're aware of it or not) our sympathetic nervous system propels us into danger. If this doesn't lead us back into safety, we fall back on our evolutionary past and into life threat.

Two more physiological states are needed for a complete picture of human behaviour:

- *Play*: a hybrid state requiring both the sympathetic mobilisation of danger and the social engagement of safety.
- *Immobilisation without fear*: the safe sort of immobilising associated with intimacy and childcare, quite unlike the immobilisation of life threat.

Together, these five states colour our perception of others. If the other person is in the safety zone, social engagement is reciprocal, but if they're aroused in the danger zone, they may respond aggressively or withdraw. Each person's right brain and subcortex dictates what happens since, whatever their respective conscious stances, their autonomic state determines the nature of their interaction.

We take social engagement for granted. It allows us to co-operate in groups and look after children, both of which require subtle regulation of the autonomic nervous system. The social engagement system works implicitly in the background, interacting with the stress response and immune system, and releasing neuropeptides and hormones, including oxytocin. Some people, however, have difficulties sustaining social engagement. Their ability to read social cues and their affect regulation may be compromised, and in children this affects language development. They may have difficulty establishing and maintaining relationships.

The three levels are not mutually exclusive so, for example, we can experience a mix of safety and danger simultaneously. The precise balance may determine the outcome of many interpersonal encounters. Too little safety between colleagues and partners, or amongst group members, and a human version of the fight response may be enacted, whatever each person claims ("I'm not the problem, you are").

On the left-right axis, we may tell ourselves all is well and we feel safe ("I'm fine"), but in reality our right brain-body ensemble may be experiencing danger. We may become highly aroused with anxiety or anger, or find ourselves going strangely mute, in a way that causes problems in our relationships. Genuinely rewarding interactions only happen when there's biological safety amongst the nervous systems present.

Underlying such phenomena is what Porges calls 'neuroception': "the neural evaluation of risk does not require conscious awareness … the term *neuroception* was introduced to emphasise a neural process, distinct from perception, that is capable of distinguishing environmental (and visceral) features that are safe, dangerous, or life-threatening" (2011: 273). So our inner world can go into danger or life threat without our realising, and we may be so accustomed to this that we don't pause to consider the effects.

A further possibility is that, even with our nervous system in relative safety, we habitually enact danger behaviours learnt during past experiences when we *were* in the danger zone. Left hemisphere defences may rule the roost even without emotional threat in the right, having developed to *avoid* triggering danger. This would be a reversal of the above scenario of thinking we're safe when our body says otherwise.

Vagal brake, vagal tone

A secure attachment or a loving relationship helps develop our *vagal brake*, the capacity of our frontal lobes to use the ventral vagus – the brake is on the sympathetic nervous system. This releases oxytocin and vasopressin so we feel safe and can trust others, and inhibits defensive aggression in response to cues that might distress us. The result is the ability to engage and disengage quickly with others, and to remain calm when there's disagreement or conflict (or when you're in a group waiting your turn to speak).

An effective vagal brake means having good *vagal tone*, the nervous system's capacity to regulate the heart and other organs in support of social engagement. Good vagal tone means we can express upset or anger without withdrawing or becoming aggressive. We're safe to express our feelings.

With good enough parenting, children can grow up with good vagal tone. This supports their ego strength and ability to sustain relationships, and contributes to a healthy heart and lungs. The foundation lies in early attachment relationships, but vagal tone can improve later on in supportive relationships.

Good vagal tone correlates with:

- the ability to self-soothe, instead of becoming irritable
- emotional range and control, instead of emotional dysregulation
- social engagement, instead of social withdrawal
- secure instead of insecure attachment
- suppression of *heart rate variability*, the autonomic smoothing out of heart rate ups and downs, instead of a racing heart in social situations.

Social engagement is therefore about the capacity of the vagus to link the nonverbal aspects of communication with the rapid adjustment of heart rate and breathing. It's part of the weaving together of inner and outer that happens in the right brain-body ensemble.

Social reward

'Reward' is a term associated with pleasure and motivation, succinctly summarised as "whatever makes us feel good and want more" – food, sex or the stimulation of social engagement – by Lewis (2012: 135). It refers to the pleasure of anticipation which involves seeking rewards, rather than of their consummation. Reward helps with understanding addiction and compulsion, our motivation to consume things that aren't good for us.

Our expectations of social reward are learnt in attachment relationships. A brainstem area fires with such expectation, leading to the impulse to approach someone with whom we seek social engagement (Cozolino 2010).[9] Social engagement *feels* rewarding. These expectations needn't be conscious; they trigger patterns of thinking and behaving in interpersonal situations, and become self-fulfilling prophecies. If we expect social reward, we're likely to seek it, but if we don't, we may not bother.

Reward system

The notion of a reward system pops up frequently in neuroscience. It's potentially misleading as it concerns the *pursuit* of rewards rather than their enjoyment (Panksepp 2009). It fires when we expect social reward, such as getting approval. The system is active from birth to stimulate attachment and bonding, and our attachment relationships regulate the biochemistry.

Dopamine gets all the attention here. The brainstem triggers its release along 'dopaminergic' pathways to many brain areas leading up to the frontal lobes (Sapolsky 2004). Reciprocal links back down from the frontal lobes modulate further release. Dopamine fuels the effort of seeking rewards, and is thought to facilitate the synaptic change that accompanies our learning how to get them (Goldberg 2009).

Dopamine combines with endorphins to drive social reward (Watt 2003). Endorphins increase the flow of dopamine in the brainstem where it's produced. "In the neural mechanics of feeling good, the excitement orchestrated by dopamine joins the soothing balm of opioids", says Lewis (2012: 135) – opioids meaning endorphins. And with the pleasures of life, it's "dopamine's flame of desire, unleashed by the *ahhhh* of opioids, that causes animals to repeat behaviours that lead to satisfaction" (2012 135). First you feel good thanks to endorphins, then you want more and dopamine helps you get it. Endorphin release triggers further dopamine release, leading to a virtuous cycle of behaving in ways that lead to satisfaction.

A little transient stress helps this process. When cortisol levels rise in moderation, dopamine is released (Sapolsky 2004). The sympathetic activation means more glucose and oxygen going to the brain, leaving you feeling motivated and focused. In a word: stimulation.

A child who grows up experiencing rewarding contact with parents and others has plenty of dopamine flowing in his brain, which encourages a positive approach to life (Gerhardt 2015). The dopamine in his orbitomedial prefrontal cortex helps him to delay gratification and pause to consider his options.

Implicit social memory

Long before we start collecting explicit memories, implicit memory of our embodied experience is being laid down.[10] It includes motor skills such as learning how to walk, and "guides us through well-established routines that are not consciously controlled", states Kandel (2007: 279). For therapists, the interesting part is what we learn about the social and emotional aspects of life. Explicit memories we recall are merely the tip of the iceberg of our memory, most of which is implicit and beneath awareness (Cozolino 2010).

On the top-bottom axis, implicit memory is more subcortical than explicit memory which is more cortical. On the left-right axis, Schore is clear that "the right hemisphere is the locus of implicit memory" (2012: 88), and we could say that the right brain-body ensemble is guided by it. It includes attachment patterns, transference dynamics and family systems. It influences how we relate and how we end up feeling in relationships and groups.

Implicit memory starts in the womb and then encompasses our birth and early experiences with mother, other attachment figures and the world. We learn how we feel when we see our parents' faces, and what happens when we cry or reach out for help. "We learn how to walk and talk, whether the world is safe or dangerous, and how to attach to others.... we do not remember how we learned them", says Cozolino (2010: 78).

Implicit memory responds to cues, such as the tone of a parent's voice or family tension around the dinner table. As it functions independently of the hippocampus that adds context (place, time, narrative) to explicit memories, our reactions are not modulated by the reality of the present situation. Feelings are generated in the background that may conflict with family or social norms in the foreground. A child who suffers early abuse may be aggressive at school; his behaviour may be seen as his intrinsic personality, and he may see himself as essentially 'bad'. But he's aggressive for a reason.

Implicit memory leads to 'acting out'. The emotional and behavioural patterns it embodies can be observed by others, and by ourselves if we're open to others' feedback or become self-aware. 'Enactments' happen in therapy when implicit memory is triggered (Cozolino 2010). The client may experience criticism and abandonment where to the therapist there's none. Implicit memory can be explored in therapy using imagination – the look on a parent's face and how it made us feel, for example; it can be brought into awareness for frontal lobe reflection.

Implicit memory is less bordered than explicit memory. It connects us to genetically inherited memory, to our parents' unconscious, and to the collective unconscious of the world we grow up in.

Nonverbal communication

Nonverbal communication tends to be spontaneous, meaningful and outside awareness. We may underestimate the degree to which ours is apparent to others. It's implicit, expressed bodily, and biased to the right hemisphere (McGilchrist 2009). While we focus attention on what we say with our left hemisphere, our right conveys our emotional state via muscles controlling eyes, face, voice and body. And while we focus attention on what others are saying, we absorb their emotional communication, especially their responses to us (Trevarthen 2009). We're affected by it, even if we're unaware. Our right hemisphere registers the felt meaning behind the words so we can understand how others are really feeling.

Nonverbal communication, including bodily mirroring reactions, allows mother and baby to engage and understand each other (Trevarthen 2009). The infant has a means of expression and of sharing his interest in what's around him.

Eye contact and gaze

How and where the eyes look, the dilation of the pupils, and the rhythm of making eye contact, are all significant. Another person's eye movements and the direction of their gaze fire up the insula, so we have emotional reactions (Cozolino 2006). We depend on the eyes to judge others' trustworthiness, the right hemisphere detecting deceit better than the left partly because it pays more attention to them (McGilchrist 2009).

Facial expression

The face is the main way we communicate our feelings and read others' feelings. Muscles controlling face, eyes, mouth, head and neck are involved (Trevarthen 2009). Changes in facial expression also fire up the insula and trigger emotional reactions, and mirror neurons if our face reflects the same expression. The right orbitomedial prefrontal cortex is the key area for responding to facial expression; small facial changes can be mirrored by the observer's right hemisphere in less than half a second, outside awareness (McGilchrist 2009).

Gestures, postures, movements

'The body doesn't lie'; our body language is usually a good reflection of our real feelings and attitudes. We take in others' body language, gestures, the speed and variations of their movements, including of their hands (Trevarthen 2009). When we get our words wrong, our body may nevertheless give away what we really want to say. The right hemisphere expresses feeling authentically, while the left's speech may or may not be congruent with it.

Prosody

This means the rhythms, pitch, intensity and quality of the voice – intonation (Trevarthen 2009). Prosody conveys the feeling and real meaning behind our words, while our left hemisphere may try to say something completely different. Schore says "the right hemisphere is important in the processing of the 'music' behind our words" (2012: 38). When words and prosody are congruent, we communicate effectively.

Conversational habits

There are many aspects to how we conduct a conversation; they're biased to the right hemisphere and may contrast with what the left wants to say. They manifest in therapy, which is a good place to point them out. They include:

- *Intensity*: speaking more intensely than seems warranted, or with a lack of intensity that suggests emotional deadness.
- *Pace*: speaking so quickly it's hard to follow what the client's saying, or so slowly that he seems half-dead.
- *Taking turns*: who speaks first, who has the last word? When the client speaks, at what point does he pause and allow you to respond? Some people don't pause, as if they don't expect us to respond helpfully.

Others say something and then stop prematurely before we have a sense of how to respond. If someone replies before we've finished speaking, they may be hearing us with just their left hemisphere rather than *really* listening with their right.
- *Coherence*: clients may leave us with the sense of a coherent story, or not. A lack of coherence may reflect fragmentation and dissociation in their right hemisphere.

These habits may lie outside awareness until the therapist brings them to the client's attention, expressing curiosity without judging or interpreting. The therapist can speak from her felt sense of the dialogue, and be mindful of her own conversational habits.

Attachment

Relating starts with attaching to mother, and babies are born primed to attach. They seek interaction with others but turn away if they feel overwhelmed, or freeze if they feel endangered (Gerhardt 2015). They influence mother as much as she influences them, by seeking to engage and by smiling. Mother gets a lot of attention when we discuss attachment, but babies also form attachments to others, including their father – so 'mother' here means the actual mother and others in a mothering role.

Newborns start out with their brainstem reflexes ready to kick-start attachment. They smile, imitate mother's facial expressions, and try to make her feel good. Their embryonic social engagement system means they can experience polyvagal safety, danger or life threat. Subcortical areas get them started, and then the cortex gradually takes over as the brain develops. Brainstem reflexes are replaced by the frontal lobes, especially the right, and voluntary control of social engagement behaviours becomes possible.

Attachment experiences organise the growing pathways between cortical and subcortical areas (Schore 2012). Babies form working models of attachment in implicit memory networks biased to the right brain. Attachment supports healthy neuroplasticity (the number of synapses peaks in infancy) and brain development; poor attachment can hinder them. Enjoyable interaction aids the healthy development of their biochemistry and sympathetic nervous systems, stimulating oxygen consumption, energy metabolism and gene expression.

The right hemisphere develops faster than the left in the first 18 months, weaving attachment together with affect and somatic regulation (Schore 2012). Facial expression facilitates this: "emotionally expressive facial expressions between mother and baby in the child's early maturing right hemisphere means that, long before the infant either comprehends or speaks a single word, it possesses an extensive repertoire of signals to communicate its internal state", McGilchrist says (2009: 108). Disapproving or angry looks trigger unhealthy parasympathetic activation, with lower blood pressure, shallow breathing and shame (Gerhardt 2015).

Enjoyable interactions release endorphins in the brain, and a good attachment relationship is an "endogenous opioid addiction" (Panksepp 2012b). They relieve pain and stress, bringing feelings of well-being and pleasure. "Babies love opioids, and presumably their mothers, because of the feelings of warmth and safety produced by these molecules", says Lewis (2012: 133). Breast milk contains endorphins, and they're released with soothing touch and holding.

Rewarding attachment experiences also boost oxytocin and dopamine, both of which contribute to warm feelings (Cozolino 2010). When babies are stimulated, they produce more dopamine and noradrenaline, which enhances their enjoyment and neural development. Plenty of dopamine primes them for approaching attachment, and everything else, with enthusiasm.

The quality of the attachment relationship affects the orbitomedial prefrontal cortex in particular, and the development of the vagal brake associated with it. One aspect of this is the regulation of heart rate: the more secure the attachment, the more regular it is (Porges 2011). Then the social engagement system can restore safety after moments of danger, and the frontal lobes can replace subcortical areas, especially the amygdala, as arbiters of neural life.

Attachment centres on communication between mother and baby that's essentially right brain to right brain (Schore 2012). Their left hemispheres are activated by enjoyable exchanges (the baby's isn't entirely idle at this point) and do focused attention, but the intuitive responding to each other arises in their right. Mother's right hemisphere appraises her baby's nonverbal communication faster than her left. Mothers tend to cradle their babies on their left side, which makes it easier to take in their emotional communication, since the visual signals go to her right occipital lobe and onwards to her right frontal lobe.

The right brain enables attachment to grow in "episodes of mutual gaze" in which "mother and infant engage in intuitive and nonconscious facial, vocal, and gestural preverbal communications", says Schore (2012: 228). Attunement creates 'affect synchrony' in which their emotional arousal is matched. Periods of social engagement need to be followed by periods of disengagement for rest – there can be too much attachment (Fonagy 2010).

The inevitable misattunements and ruptures need to be followed by repair. Learning that positive feelings can be restored helps the child tolerate negative feelings and develop emotional security (Gerhardt 2015). Patterns of rupture and repair, comforting or its absence, become implicit memory. Self-esteem comes from learning that mother will comfort him when he's distressed.

Attachment patterns reflect neural networks from infancy in which implicit memories of interactions with mother are paired with feelings of safety and warmth, or of danger and fear. But they're not set in stone, since these networks remain plastic into adulthood (Cozolino 2010). A happy consequence is that parents who grew up with insecure attachments can nevertheless provide secure attachments for *their* children – the power of love to heal.

Secure and insecure attachments

Secure attachments form when mother is available and responsive to her baby and can use her right hemisphere to sense what he needs. His brain develops with good vagal tone and good integration across the three axes. His right hemisphere is imprinted with the implicit expectation that interpersonal ruptures will be repaired (Schore 2012). But if mother is engaged sometimes and withdrawn at other times, the attachment may be insecure. Her child may grow up with poor vagal tone, and his brain may develop with poor integration, leaving him with a tendency to either emotional reactivity or deadness (Gerhardt 2015).

In *avoidant* attachments, mother tends to be distant and rejecting, while her baby doesn't seek closeness or appear to be upset. He tends towards parasympathetic dominance, which manifests in avoidance of eye contact and little emotional expression, as he learns to suppress his feelings lest he upset or anger her. He may also appear calm when his heart rate is high (Gerhardt 2015).

With *anxious-ambivalent* attachment, mother may oscillate between overstimulating her baby and neglecting him. He may be hyperactive, tending towards strong sympathetic arousal which manifests as irritability, dependency and acting out. He may cling to her and seek attention (Gerhardt 2015). He becomes over-sensitive to his mother's feelings, and insensitive to his own. As an adult in therapy, he may keep returning to his parents, still looking for safety as an adult despite the accumulated evidence that he won't find it with them (Cozolino 2010).

In *disorganised* attachments, mother may feel devoted to her baby but struggle to be emotionally available and responsive, often because of her own unresolved traumatic childhood (Gerhardt 2015). She may be unpredictable, sometimes dissociating and other times getting too close to him. Often frightened by her, his social engagement system may not develop, leaving him in a helpless but dependent state, prone to fight-flight or freeze reactions in relationships. Such chaotic behaviour is better understood as a sign of hyper-arousal rather than as a coping strategy.

These attachment styles aren't mutually exclusive, of course. They become biological structures that affect how we respond and react in our relationships. The therapeutic relationship is a fresh attachment experience, and the client's original attachment to mother is often central to the work, whether it's addressed explicitly or implicitly through what transpires between therapist and client. There's time and space to repair ruptures and misattunements. Incursions into polyvagal danger and life threat states can be explored if there's enough safety and trust in the relationship.

My own experience of therapy was ultimately of being gazed at, and responded to, calmly, kindly and approvingly, in stark contrast to my mother's tendency to lurch from idealising me to becoming fearful, angry and disapproving. It was only then that I was able to settle happily in a long-term relationship.

What social brains do

There are some common phenomena in the social life of brains (and bodies) that may appear in any relationship, whether the original attachment relationship, the therapeutic relationship or any others. Some of the terms come from the neuroscience and psychology worlds rather than the therapy world.

Resonance

Underneath our focused attention to others is the emotional effect we have on each other. 'Resonance' describes this implicit communication between right brain-body ensembles. It results in people finding themselves in similar emotional places: enjoying a good conversation, getting into arguments, or picking up each other's anxiety. Resonance leads to 'atmospheres', and to the contagious nature of emotion whereby someone inspires us or a group descends into mass hysteria. It happens outside awareness, and can leave us wondering which feeling belongs to whom ("is this my sadness or your sadness?"). It determines whether we experience polyvagal safety or danger. Young children absorb their parent's feelings, whether positive or negative, and adults sometimes need self-awareness to protect themselves from being unduly affected by others' emotions.

Neuroscience ascribes resonance to our capacity for automatic imitation of others via mirror neuron systems. Cozolino describes 'resonance behaviours' such as mutual smiling or yawning as reflexive, implicit and obligatory (2006). Resonance is also called 'contagion'. Watt, for example, refers to "primitive emotional contagion" that's faster than the cognitive aspects of relating (2005). But is there more than imitation going on?

Resonance is fundamental to neural development. The infant brain uses it to link with adult brains: "the intrinsic regulators of human brain growth in a child are specifically adapted to be coupled, by emotional communication, to the regulators of adult brains", says child psychologist Colwyn Trevarthen (1990: 357). The adult's feeling towards the child colours his emotional experience. "Resonance phenomena are now thought to play one of the most important roles in brain organisation", states Schore (2003a: 32). It underlies attunement in attachment relationships; enjoyable resonance states are part of secure attachment. Conversely, anxious parents are liable to have anxious children.

Resonance is a right brain to right brain phenomenon (Schore 2003). Mirror neurons play a role, as does the insula which links sensory perception with emotion and body. At the top of the neural hierarchy, resonance networks in the orbitomedial prefrontal cortex enable empathy and compassion (Siegel 2007). It's based on nonverbal communication, including movements that imply intentions.

Resonance happens whether we're aware of it or not. Therapists are trained to notice resonance effects, which evoke countertransference feelings and 'the feeling in the room'. Our frontal lobes can reflect on what we feel as we listen to a client, whose feeling it is, and whether and when to draw attention to such feelings. As Panksepp says,

> if therapists cannot assume an interpersonal stance in which they resonate with the psychic pain of the client, there can never be that sense of trust that is critically important for the healing touch ... to take hold in the client's mind.
>
> (2009: 14).

Attunement

Attunement enables a mother to intuit what her baby needs, and a couple to dance together. It allows us to 'feel felt' by each other (Siegel 2007). When this happens, we feel understood and the relationship feels alive, and neither partner dominates. Attunement builds on resonance, and if resonance evokes positive feelings, it flows easily. I have good memories of simple attunement exercises in workshops designed to break down the sense of separation from others – they evoked profound experiences of interpersonal unity.

Attunement is more conscious and less reflexive than resonance. It involves the prefrontal cortex with its inhibitory pathways to the amygdala that dampen anxiety. It also includes motor areas and mirror neurons, as it involves movements. It contributes to good neural integration and healthy development in the child (Siegel 2007). The right hemisphere is dominant for the implicit process of attunement; if we deliberately try to attune via our left, our right may undermine us.

Social engagement is facilitated by attunement, and neural integration flows from attuned relationships (Siegel 2007). Without it, we have to manage the effects of misattunement, compromising ourselves in vain attempts to attune, or acting out our frustration. Our left hemisphere then defends against negative feelings in our right, rather than co-operating to pursue the rewards of social engagement.

Attunement happens through nonverbal communication. Facial expression, for example, allows us to attune faster than talking, and is important in infancy before we have language. It's part of a child's early right hemisphere development that enables him to express his emotional state (McGilchrist 2009). It also happens through touch, as mother attunes to her baby's visceral communication. Their attunement builds neural pathways in the child's right brain-body ensemble that last a lifetime. The success of mother-infant attunement in the first year predicts a toddler's degree of self-control when he's 2 years old (Cozolino 2010).

When misattunement happens, the rupture needs repairing for positive feelings to be restored. Some children experience a lot of misattunement and negative feelings, which sets up trouble for the future – or until other relationships and their own efforts enable them to learn the art of attunement (I think I've spent much of my adult life doing this).

Therapy offers the opportunity to experience better attunement. The therapist has to be flexible in attuning to clients who bring patterns of misattuning into the relationship. Some clients expect misattunement and are therefore defensive. They enter polyvagal danger states easily, or avoid going to places where they might. The therapist must adapt; for example, by listening patiently for long periods before giving feedback to the client about his nonverbal communication. Here lies the art of therapy: attunement can't be explicitly taught, but we absorb it in our own therapy and fine-tune it sitting in the therapist's chair.

Theory of mind

Theory of mind isn't about a grand theory of the mind, but the more humdrum matter of reading other people's intentions and motivations. If resonance allows us to be in a similar emotional state as another person, and attunement to enjoy social engagement with them, next up is mapping their mind. This is the realm of projection, and what we assume others are thinking. We get a sense of 'where someone is coming from', and anticipate what they'll say and do, what they know and don't know. Ramachandran thinks we "automatically project intentions, perceptions, and beliefs into the minds of others", and are able to "infer their feelings and intentions and to predict and influence their behaviour" (2011: 138). This starts outside awareness with our brain mapping others' minds based on nonverbal cues.

The term was coined from observing how primates read each other's intentions. Theory of mind can be seen in animals and birds that hide food from each other. Camels, goats, squirrels and pigeons have been spotted displaying it (McGilchrist 2013). It starts early in life: six-week-old babies already have a theory of mind about the implications of people's gestures (Gazzaniga 2016).[11] A baby is figuring mother out from the outset, learning to guess from her facial expression and tone of voice whether or not she'll feed him or comfort him. Secure attachment enables theory of mind to develop and support social engagement, whereas insecure attachment can lead to the child imagining that others will reject him as his parent does, damaging his ability to form relationships.

Theory of mind, with its automatic nature, independence from language and roots in early attachment, is biased to the right hemisphere. Neuroimaging studies show it centred in the right frontal lobe and cingulate (McGilchrist 2009). But it starts down in the brainstem since it manifests in the first weeks of life as a visceral sense of mother's intentions based on her eye gaze, facial expression and tone of voice (Cozolino 2006). Later in development, cortical areas enable a more elaborate capacity for theory of mind to emerge. The involvement of the brainstem and the cingulate implies the body's involvement: theory of mind starts with the right brain-body ensemble and how another person affects us emotionally and somatically. Reasoning in our left hemisphere about what they're thinking is merely the icing on the cake.

Clients sometimes say shocking things that reveal wild inaccuracies in their theory of mind; for example, "you think I was to blame for my father beating me when I was a child". Responding helpfully to such seemingly bizarre statements isn't easy. The therapist has to manage her shock and reflect on the sort of scenario that might give rise to such a self-destructive theory of mind.

Empathy

Resonance, attunement and theory of mind are the ingredients for empathy. Resonance happens naturally, while the capacity for attunement may have been damaged in early childhood, and theory of mind may be prone to inaccuracy – hence the differences in people's capacity for empathy. I once worried that I lacked it, though working as a therapist has convinced me otherwise. It's clearly not something you can make up in your left hemisphere. Empathy implies not only that I'll feel something when I listen to you, but also that I'll respond with sensitivity.

Empathy brings together psychological capacities that enable us to sense not only what another person *is* feeling, but also what they are *on the edge of* feeling – and *may* feel if we respond sensitively. Cozolino says it requires "conceptual understanding, emotional attunement, and the ability to regulate one's own affect" (2010: 118). The latter ability implies the need to experience our own feelings without being overwhelmed by them.

It's a more conscious ability than resonance, attunement and theory of mind, although it may rely on unconscious perceptions. Cozolino (2006) points out that we need an awareness of our own inner world while we imagine that of someone else. He describes empathy as a hypothesis we make about another based on our own visceral, emotional and cognitive perceptions. This accords with Damasio (2010) who thinks that since our brains map our body states, they can simulate equivalent body states in others. This implies that the better integrated our body state is in the workings of our whole brain, the more natural empathy will be.

McGilchrist (2009) places empathy in the right frontal lobe as an association area for signals from other areas that contribute to it. He adds a front-back dimension: the right frontal lobe tempers the immediacy of emotion and body in the right posterior lobes, and allows others to be mapped as separate individuals, like me but not me. So a sense of self and a sense of other are necessary for empathy – which involves the body, as we'll see.

As empathy is centred in the right hemisphere, it functions implicitly and isn't normally the focus of our attention. But in the therapy room, we notice it and make it explicit. I may find myself listening to my client, responding to the content while simultaneously allowing my empathic sense to come into awareness. At some point, something in that empathic sense wants to become foreground, so I change tack and say something about it.

Self and other

The difference between us is obvious to our eyes and ears. But in our felt experience in the background, things may be less obvious. If we talk and I feel sad, is that my sadness or your's? Are you 'making me feel sad'? What are we projecting onto each other, and who decides? Things can get messy.

The left hemisphere distinguishes between self and other easily, as in "I'm right, you're wrong!" For the right hemisphere that weaves together inner and outer worlds, however, it's less straightforward. Our sense of self develops in the context of attachment so, as Cozolino says, "perhaps the separation of self and other is always a dicey distinction" (2010: 315). This is reflected in the fact that the right hemisphere is responsible for both our sense of self and our sense of other that are rooted in attachment patterns and the implicit aspects of relating.

A network linking right frontal and parietal lobes enables the brain to distinguish self from other (McGilchrist 2009). The parietal contribution includes the body, and bodily feedback to our thoughts and feelings allows the brain to distinguish self-mapping from other-mapping. We're talking here of a *sense* of self and a *sense* of other, the sort of wholistic picture favoured by the right hemisphere. The frontal contribution includes the distance needed to distinguish self from other in our awareness so that others stand out as individuals, 'like me' but also different. The insula, where body signals arrive on their way to the somatosensory cortex, contributes to the distinction (Cozolino 2006), as do mirror neurons with intentional movements, mine and your's (Ramachandran 2011). So a lot of neural resources, and the body, go into distinguishing the two senses.

From birth, our senses of self and other are coloured by our experience of polyvagal safety or danger. Implicit memory develops along social engagement lines or along defensive ones. Later in development, the left hemisphere starts thinking about the differences between ourselves and others. Abstract ideas about personality types may be added (Cozolino 2006). But the right brain-body ensemble continues to provide the foundation for relating: either we enjoy fluid social engagement based on hemispheric integration and sensing self and other, or we repeat left hemisphere routines which suppress these senses to defend against the unpredictability of relating that feels alive.

Self and other awareness in therapy requires both hemispheres and the mind-body connection. A client's lack of such awareness implies a lack of awareness of his body. Bringing attention to his body may increase his capacity for self and other awareness, and directing it to what's happening in the therapeutic relationship may improve his mind-body connection.

Boundaries

A sense of self and a sense of other enable us to have boundaries. A person 'with no boundaries' lacks such senses and his right brain mixes himself and others up, perhaps because someone didn't respect *his* boundary in early childhood. When we imagine we're feeling exactly what another feels, the sense of a boundary isn't present: this isn't empathy, it's identification and fusion. To create a boundary, we need to sense where it feels right to have one – a job for the right brain-body ensemble.

Intersubjectivity

Senses of self and other are accompanied by a sense of 'we', the quality of the relationship in the moment ("it feels like we're getting along well"). This is intersubjectivity, a shared field in which we can empathise and communicate while experiencing ourselves as individuals. We each have feelings and thoughts that may sometimes coincide and sometimes differ, and can sense the quality of our interaction underneath our words. Intersubjectivity allows for rewarding social engagement, and is coloured by implicit memory.

Relating starts with shared experience and develops into a sense of our own inner experience and that of others (McGilchrist 2009). The sense of a separate self emerges from relationship, sometimes promoted by misattunements that get repaired. The shared intersubjective field of 'we' is centred in the right hemisphere, and bodily experiencing facilitates intersubjective processes because it enables the brain to distinguish self from other.

Intersubjectivity begins with what Trevarthen calls the "lyrical duet" between mother and baby, as their bodily mirroring helps them adjust to each other's sounds, gestures and behaviours (2009). The first task is the linking of his body and feeling with mother's responses so he can get his needs met and feel better. Intersubjectivity also enables him to learn playful games and, later on, learn about the culture he's been born into, as the intersubjective field becomes cognitive as well as affective. He learns what his parents know.

The intersubjective field is polyvagally coloured. "It is through this language of intersubjectivity that children learn from their mothers about the fundamental safety or dangerousness of the world", says Cozolino (2010: 184). Intersubjectivity flourishes in an atmosphere of safety; danger in the attachment relationship may lead to rigid defensive states lacking intersubjectivity. Our experience of intersubjectivity becomes etched into networks of the right brain-body ensemble. Schore says "the essential biological purpose of intersubjective communications ... is the regulation of right brain-mind-body states" (2012: 40). If we can't regulate each other, intersubjectivity evaporates, and we get locked into defending against polyvagal danger and interpersonal stress.

A relationship that feels alive is one where each person's left hemisphere welcomes the intersubjectivity of the right. It feels rewarding, rather than a dull ritual that protects against danger. You can be yourself, I can be myself, and we can enjoy social engagement – spiced with the risk of occasionally tasting polyvagal danger.

A good therapeutic relationship enables a person's capacity for intersubjectivity to grow, and deep and difficult issues to be addressed. Explicitly or implicitly, both bring their senses of self, other and 'we' into the interaction; perhaps the content doesn't matter so long as there's an intersubjective process. This may lead to 'edgy' moments of polyvagal danger, where the therapist asks the client to check whether, really, he feels uncomfortable or threatened. She must keep the relationship sufficiently grounded in safety for the danger places to be processed ("when you said that, I began to feel anxious"). If things become wholly dangerous, the intersubjective field is lost.

Projection

Projection, an aspect of anticipation, is automatic and reading others' minds is instantaneous and obligatory (Cozolino 2010). We can go with first impressions or patiently allow a deeper sense of other to form.

Inevitably our brain puts what we know about ourselves into this, below the radar, so we think we see in another what's really in ourselves. We understood this as schoolchildren when we retaliated to taunts with 'it takes one to know one'. To know ourselves, we should notice what we think of others.

Projections can become routine ways our left hemispheres relate. But if we listen to the senses of self and other in our right brain, we have a more nuanced picture of others and can withdraw faulty projections. Safety and social engagement are needed, as feeling threatened tends to cement the projection in place. We may *think* we're making good intuitive assessments of others; maybe we are, but it's better when they agree with us. Sometimes we get into strange interpersonal situations where we find it hard to distinguish a projection from an accurate perception of the other that they don't accept. Beware the certainty of the left hemisphere!

In therapy, the therapist thinks it's the client who projects. This isn't unreasonable if she allows her felt sense of him to unfold gradually, session by session. Therapists often think of projection as a defence mechanism, but since it's automatic, this is questionable. However, when it's repetitive and he avoids the intersubjective field where he might see both the therapist and himself differently, it's clearly defensive.

The therapeutic relationship

Therapists usually agree that the therapeutic relationship is the key to therapy. A trusting alliance enables therapy to work irrespective of the 'approach'. Empathy and compassion work their magic in the background, creating a relationship conducive to neuroplasticity and supportive of the client in tolerating the stress required for neural reorganisation (Cozolino 2010). At the same time, the emotional dynamics between client and therapist tend to mirror those in the client's attachment relationships. The therapeutic relationship is an opportunity for his emotional vulnerability to interact with the therapist's emotional availability (Schore 2009).

Explicit content and implicit engagement

Talking therapy focuses on the explicit content the client brings, but in a context of implicit engagement of two social brains. Therapy provides a regular time and space for the client's background relationship patterns to become foreground and be addressed. Attention can be drawn to the intersubjective field of bodily and emotional experiencing. Insecure attachment patterns can be healed in the secure attachment available in therapy, and the client's senses of self and other brought to awareness and reality-checked ("as you talk about this, I feel I'm not being very helpful").

Schore says the therapist's capacity to address implicit communication requires her to be in a state of right brain "receptivity" (2012). Such receptivity means responding reflectively: not arguing back or withdrawing, not rushing to judgements, and not taking remarks personally. Therapists hear things that are uncomfortable, challenging, and that they would rather not hear – *really* listening isn't easy.

Left and right hemispheres

If the aim of therapy is better left-right integration, then therapist and client must engage both hemispheres in the room. Right hemisphere contributions can be examined, and therapists are trained to use *their* right hemispheres to notice felt senses and images ("my sense is this was really painful for you"). Therapy is where what transpires between right brain-body ensembles can be safely explored; "the right hemisphere is dominant in treatment", says Schore (2009: 128). Exactly *what* the therapist says to the client may matter less than her *manner of being* with him, especially when he feels vulnerable.

While the left hemispheres talk to each other, the right hemispheres communicate nonverbally. Although the therapist's life isn't discussed, her feelings and attitude are conveyed to the client. "Implicit right brain to right brain intersubjective transactions lie at the core of the therapeutic relationship", says Schore (2012: 39). The therapist can notice her own nonverbal signals and their effect on the client. She can notice his nonverbal signals while she listens – his body language, facial expression, eye contact, voice prosody, conversational habits, narrative coherence – and their effect on her. She can make her impressions and feelings explicit when it feels right ("I notice you looked away while you told me that").

Polyvagal theory in therapy

The client needs to feel safe enough, and so does the therapist. Effective therapy must be rooted in social engagement, from which a 'blank screen' may detract. The therapist's efforts to attune to him can create a safe atmosphere where the threat of rejection is minimised (Cozolino 2010). It becomes possible to explore danger and sometimes even life threat states together. The more social engagement, the less need for concern over psychopathology and diagnosis.

How the client perceives the therapist depends on his autonomic state in her presence. If he feels threatened, he may go into danger and enact fight-flight or freeze behaviours; if very threatened, he may go into life threat and dissociate. The therapist must tread carefully since what works in safety may not work in danger or life threat. Many people seek therapy because close contact with others triggers danger or life threat. "If the individual is in a state of mobilisation, the same engaging response might be responded to with the asocial features of withdrawal or aggression", states Porges (2011: 278).

The therapist can influence the client's neuroception but not control it. If her social engagement system is easy to access, then "reciprocal prosocial interactions are likely to occur", says (Porges 2011: 278). But tendencies to enter danger and life threat in close relationships will manifest sooner or later in the therapeutic one as unresolved emotional wounds and trauma are worked through. She has to tolerate moments of danger without withdrawing or becoming aggressive. The client's heart rate and breathing patterns may make him feel intensely uncomfortable, and her job is to make these moments bearable.

Transference and countertransference

Transference is what the client's right brain 'transfers' onto the therapist, namely his unconscious expectation of her response to him based on his early attachments. It's a projection, the nature of which depends on what happened in those attachments and the extent to which he's already become aware of it. Countertransference is what the therapist's right brain transfers onto the client, supposedly conscious thanks to her training. It's her sense of self in his presence rather than a projection, thanks to her receptive state. So they're not really two sides of one coin, as these terms imply. My perception of someone is of a different nature if I want something from her and tell her *my* life story than if she wants something from me and tells me *her* life story. If countertransference was merely the therapist's projection onto the client, therapy wouldn't work.

Both transference and countertransference are right hemisphere mappings. The client's early implicit memories and attachment patterns are activated when he engages with the therapist (Cozolino 2010). When a client tells me I haven't understood him and is angry about it, or when he tells me how much better I am than his previous therapist, I smell transference and administer a large pinch of salt. Countertransference, on the other hand, refers to feelings and thoughts evoked in me when I listen to a client. When he leaves me feeling alive and engaged, or half-dead and sleepy, I take note and don't administer salt. My sense of him might be tainted by my past relationships, but the practice of therapy tends to minimise this. Client and therapist use their right hemispheres differently, and for different purposes.

The client's transference mapping may include old attachment dynamics he's unaware of and which haven't been integrated across left-right and front-back axes. In the brain's quest for better integration, they're enacted and the therapist can bring them to the client's awareness. To the therapist, they're distortions of reality. It's possible, of course, for the client to have a 'healthy' transference that sees her as she is – implying a secure early attachment and good self and other awareness.

Transference is important because it demonstrates the client's earliest struggles for love that aren't part of his autobiographical memory (Cozolino 2006). Clients often come to therapy with negative expectations of how the therapist will respond to them, and the therapist's job is to counter these expectations with patience and kindness, drawing attention to them. By listening to her countertransference feelings, she can make good guesses about the nature of her client's attachment to, most often, his mother. Transference and countertransference are royal roads to resolving problems in the right brain-body ensemble.

Projective identification

This happens when the therapist identifies with the client's emotional projection and reacts without troubling her frontal lobes to reflect on its meaning. A moment later, she has a disturbing feeling that says "whoops! I shouldn't have said that". A similar phenomenon happens in close relationships when people fall in love, the happy version, and when couples argue with mutual recriminations ("I didn't start the argument, you did!"), the unhappy version. Intersubjectivity goes out of the window. But projective identification is a technical term best reserved for a therapist's theoretical understanding of challenging emotional interactions in therapy.

It's a resonance-fuelled right brain to right brain nonverbal communication that bypasses both parties' frontal lobes. Both act out in a subcortically-driven manner, their nonverbal communication conveying strong emotion that leaves both in a dysregulated state. Therapists catch themselves speaking in a different tone of voice, shifting posture or making a gesture they don't intend (Schore 2012). Such moments are re-enactments of the client's attachment trauma in which mother reacted to his strong emotion with disorganised hyper-arousal, as if two babies were screaming at each other. They embody both the force of his rage and terror, and the therapist's difficulty in containing the enactment.

The therapist's orbitomedial prefrontal cortex goes 'offline', so she reacts impulsively, becoming fearful without realising it. Schore considers the interaction as essentially subcortical in both parties, enacting a 'deep unconscious' communication rather than a 'preconscious' one closer to awareness (2012). The challenge is to get the cortex back online as soon as possible to recover the situation.

Projective identification is part of how therapy works, with intractable attachment trauma erupting in the room, bringing the possibility of resolution. The client might attack the therapist with "you're not hearing me! I'm not coming again", and the therapist react angrily like a scolding parent with "I *am* hearing you!". The therapist is landed in trouble; she must re-establish safety, reflect on what happened and make something useful of it. If the therapeutic alliance is poor, such moments can be damaging, but with sufficient trust, they can be breakthrough moments.

Conclusion

Relationships are powerful transformers of psyches – since half the brain beavers away in the background with the implicit aspects of relating when we're in company, this is unsurprising. A better polyvagal experience means more rewarding relationships and a happier sense of self.

Enjoyable relationships require the integration of the hemispheres, subcortical areas and the body. The right brain-body ensemble provides the implicit foundation for the left hemisphere's conscious efforts to relate. A solid foundation enables rewarding social engagement, while one weakened by unresolved attachment conflicts may divide the psyche and undermine the left hemisphere's persona.

Therapy involves drawing attention to implicit aspects of relating that affect the client's relationships. Enactments of old attachment wounds and traumas can be responded to with compassion, perhaps by offering comfort in places of deep distress where the client's implicit memory is of being rejected, or by the therapist not taking it personally when he acts out rage his parents were unable to withstand. Unhealthy relationships can be questioned to encourage reality-testing, while healthy ones can be supported. Sometimes I'm grateful to a client's partner who's doing most of the work, while I support the relationship by helping my client remain in it.

We all have a lifelong need to attach to others for companionship, support, physical contact, emotional regulation and a sense of belonging. Relationships are emotional experiences, and we need other people to acknowledge our feelings if we're to accept them. So, in the next chapter, we look at emotions and feelings.

Notes

1 People get excited about mirror neurons. Ramachandran calls them "the closest thing to telepathy nature was able to endow us with", and thinks they facilitated the rapid growth of culture and language when we emerged from caves (2011: 22). Some claim they demonstrate that brains can do empathy (we knew that anyway!). The capacity of infants to imitate faces and tongues early in life may begin in brainstem areas because of the relative immaturity of the frontal lobes and their mirror neurons at that stage (Trevarthen 2009).

2 Serotonin does different things in different areas of the brain because of the large number of different types of serotonin receptors.

3 Pert says endorphins were discovered by researchers at Aberdeen University who called them enkephalins, but when the Americans found out they rediscovered them and called them endorphins in an act of transatlantic one-upmanship (1997).

4 Oxytocin is sometimes labelled a neuropeptide. Panksepp says the idea that it's the hormone of love "has a few ounces of truth as well as, all too often, pounds of exaggeration" (2012: 249). He thinks oxytocin's effect is more about confidence than love.
5 Vasopressin is another hormone/neuropeptide.
6 The child's right hemisphere is biased for receiving mother's communicative signals, while his left is biased for giving, or being proactive, in communicating with mother (Trevarthen 2009).
7 'System' is used to refer to large scale networks in the nervous system, with particular neural pathways and neurochemistry, that it helps to think of as such in understanding the brain.
8 The ventral vagus is also known as the 'smart' vagus – it enables the smarter aspects of mammalian relating.
9 The brainstem area where dopamine release starts is the *ventral tegmentum*, which projects to the *nucleus accumbens* and from there to many places in the brain fuelled by dopamine (Sapolsky 2004).
10 Implicit memory is also called *non-declarative* or *procedural* memory.
11 Gazzaniga observes that "the field of developmental psychology keeps driving back the age at which babies reveal their cards" (2016: 337–338). It's as if the earliest signs of everything we take to be human can be traced back to the first weeks of life. And further down the evolutionary ladder too: for example, deception was a purely human trait until someone noticed that a species of crow was messing around with its food to stop other crows from stealing it (never underestimate a bird).

Chapter 5

Emotions, feelings and the felt sense

Introduction

Most things in life evoke feelings, which are bound up with emotion. Damasio summarises the history of this subject:

> Romantics placed emotion in the body and reason in the brain. Twentieth-century science left out the body, moved emotion back into the brain, but relegated it to the lower neural strata associated with ancestors whom no one worshipped. In the end, not only was emotion not rational, even studying it was probably not rational.
>
> (1999: 39)

But in the 1990s some neuroscientists risked their professional necks by venturing into emotion, including Damasio, LeDoux and Panksepp (whose work is the backbone of this chapter). Neuroscience became relevant for therapists, and interesting for everyone.

Feelings are linked with specific systems in the brain, just as vision and speech are (Damasio 1996). The key is finding the neural networks underlying emotional experience, and means correcting the normal bias of looking top-down from the cortex by looking bottom-up from the subcortex. Science has finally crossed paths with therapy by recognising that emotion is "part of the glue that holds the whole system together", says neuropsychologist Doug Watt (cited in McGilchrist 2009: 88).

The left hemisphere view puts emotion secondary to cognition, but the right hemisphere view reverses this, as will become clear. Emotion is "essential for any attentional function, volition, or consciousness", Watt states (2003: 110). It facilitates co-ordinated learning across different brain systems and "by coordinating parallel plasticity throughout the brain, emotional states promote the development and unification of the self", says LeDoux (2003: 322).

Feelings tell us what something *means*. They leave their mark in the nervous system so that we have "a record of the benefits and risks of behaviours", says Trevarthen (2009: 55). It follows that feelings colour our behaviour in relationships. They link families and communities together, enabling both co-operation and conflict. They sustain our spirits and protect us against stress. They influence what we remember from the past, and what we imagine will happen in the future. Emotions allow children to play, learn and start acting in a world that's meaningful. Because they're "the primary *mediators of social life*", they have healing power (2009: 55). Understanding their neurobiology sheds light on therapy.

Feelings are "first and foremost about the body", says Damasio, offering us "a glimpse of what goes on in our flesh" (1996: 159). The body connection means that they come first in our development and thereafter are fundamental to our psychological life (McGilchrist 2009). If this isn't obvious, it's because the left hemisphere can be oblivious to the background emotional life of the body. Therapists ask their clients "and how does that make you feel?" to bring the background into the foreground.

Neuroscience now sees the significance of emotion to our mental lives. "Feelings have a say on how the rest of the brain and cognition go about their business", continues Damasio, and "their influence is immense" (1996: 160). Body mapping in the brain links with cognitive activity so we know what's good and what's bad for us, what brings pleasure and what brings pain. Feelings are therefore an essential aspect of reasoning and decision making.

Emotional terminology

We may use 'emotion' and 'feeling' interchangeably, but Damasio distinguishes them (1999): emotion is what happens in body and brain when we're emotional, while feeling is the neural mapping of emotion that influences the brain, even when the emotion has dissipated. Emotions are public and involve movement, whereas feelings are private and inward – and sometimes conceptual ("when I feel sad, I prefer to be alone"). Emotions allow direct communication, feelings allow us to understand each other. It's possible to be unaware of both; children need help to name their feelings lest they grow up to be adults who are unaware of them.

The term *felt sense*, originally coined by Gendlin (1996), refers to background feelings that are hard to articulate ("I'm feeling something about this . . ."). Less intense than emotion and less conceptual than feelings, a felt sense is *of* a whole situation ("this whole thing makes me feel uneasy"). We experience it as a subtle intuition, or as a physical sensation such as tightness in the chest. It's the right hemisphere's take on a situation when we're neither overwhelmed nor dissociated. Listening to it brings meaning ("oh, *now* I see what this sadness is about") as the left hemisphere finds words to match the sense in the right.

Damasio's 'feeling of what happens' is a similar notion, which he distinguishes from emotions and feelings:

> I separate three stages of processing along a continuum: *a state of emotion*, which can be triggered and executed nonconsciously; *a state of feeling*, which can be represented nonconsciously; and *a state of feeling made conscious*, i.e. known to the organism having both emotion and feeling.
>
> (1999: 37)

Bringing feelings into awareness requires sensing what happens when we feel them.

Affect denotes everything emotional, including mood, our general state of being (relaxed, tired etc.), and emotional arousal. Panksepp adds 'homeostatic affects', such as hunger and urges to go to the loo, and 'sensory affects', such as pleasure and pain (2012). For our purposes, affect is generally interchangeable with emotion.

Damasio proposes two more terms in unravelling the neurobiology of feelings (1996):

- *'As if' feelings*: neural mappings of past emotional states that provide a reference point for feelings without having to re-enact them in the body. We can reflect on what it's like to *feel* sad without necessarily *being* sad.
- *Somatic markers*: fleeting sensations we may or may not notice, 'gut feelings' perhaps, associated with past experiences of similar situations. They help the brain decide how pleasant or unpleasant an option might be; in making decisions, it follows implicit memories of how something felt in the past.

Feeling our feelings

How do we know what we're feeling? Damasio's view is that feelings needn't be in awareness, since we often notice a feeling that's already present (1999). The neural mapping of changes in body and brain that constitute a feeling happens anyway, but knowing we have that feeling, 'feeling' it, requires another level of mapping of our feeling self affected by that feeling (1999). So we know a feeling via having another feeling – a felt sense. Turning our attention inwards and listening to the body helps us know what we're feeling.

Suppressed feelings and dissociated emotions

Feelings may or may not be in awareness, but the question is whether they *can* be in awareness. I think neuroscience points to two sorts of problematic feelings and emotions:

- Feelings we *suppress, avoid or deny*. The left hemisphere's defensiveness leaves them unattended in the background in the right hemisphere.
- Emotions that are *dissociated*. They remain in a fragmented state in the right brain, prone to erupting.

The former aren't 'unconscious' because they can enter awareness when the safety of the therapeutic relationship melts defensiveness. And the latter aren't 'repressed' in a dark place, having been experienced and then banished: they belong to overwhelming, traumatic experiences in the past, and they erupt as seemingly unwarranted reactions to triggers. Schore thinks that "unconscious affects can best be understood not as repressed but as dissociated affects" (2009).

The primacy of affect

Which comes first, affect or cognition? We may believe cognition comes first, especially given our ability to suppress emotion, but from a neuroscience perspective "the affect comes first, the thinking later", as McGilchrist puts it, and "emotion ... is closer to the core of our being than cognition" (2009: 184–185). Hence the 'primacy of affect' (Zajonc 1984). First we have an emotional stance, then cognitions flow from that stance. When I sit down to resume writing this book, I'm already feeling enthusiastic or anxious about it, before I think what to write next.

Despite the prevalence of 'cognitive neuroscience', neuroscientists agree on this. "Emotions colour our cognitive states almost moment to moment", says Gazzaniga (2016: 79). For LeDoux, emotional arousal dominates and controls thinking and, although thinking can obviously trigger feelings, "we are not very effective at wilfully turning off emotions" (1999: 303). Furthermore, "feelings are just as cognitive as any other perceptual image", says Damasio (1996: 159), implying that emotion precedes cognition which includes the feelings that emotion gives rise to. We need to listen to the felt sense to get underneath the purely cognitive level that includes talking about feelings.

Feelings and emotions in therapy

People come to therapy because they experience unwanted feelings that won't go away, feelings they struggle to express, or feelings that overwhelm them. The direction of therapy is to accept feelings rather than fight them, the left hemisphere ceasing its battle against feelings stirred up in the right. Helping people accept their feelings has many aspects: making it safe to experience uncomfortable feelings, responding compassionately to painful feelings, and naming feelings and understanding where they come from.

Since affect is primary, we needn't go looking for it. Whether the client expresses feelings explicitly or not, they're implicitly present. The therapist must both respond to feelings that are expressed *and* draw attention towards feelings implicit in what's being discussed. The notion of 'repressed' and 'unconscious' feelings can encourage 'digging'. The digger is the left hemisphere, and the right resists being dug – what works in therapy is for feelings and emotion to unfold naturally from the right as trust and safety grow.

I was once very confused about feelings. When I did experiential 'self-transformation' workshops in the 1980s, my emotions erupted, but afterwards I was still unsure what I was feeling. It was only when I learnt focusing and started listening to my felt sense that I 'found' my feelings and everything shifted. Working with feelings is about many things, but experiencing them and allowing a natural 'bodymind' process to unfold, left hemisphere letting go to right, is the key.

The emotional brain and body

We experience emotions in the body, but neuroscience tells us they arise in the brain. "A few ounces of brain tissue constitute the bedrock of our emotional lives", Panksepp says, by which he means the subcortical areas where emotions are generated (2012: 1). Emotions then play out in the body, which feeds back to other areas of the brain, changing its cognitive landscape. All levels of the brain have a role in our emotional lives. Let's unravel this.

The most complete account is Damasio's (2010). Emotions begin when subcortical areas are triggered by particular external or internal stimuli – such as the amygdala in the case of fear. We may be alone and remembering something, or we may be talking to someone; the context needs to fit the particular emotion, and the signals generated by the stimuli sufficiently intense. It's "as if certain stimuli have the right key to open a certain lock" (2010: 112).

The idea of an emotional centre in the brain (such as the amygdala or limbic system) is misleading because, from a neural perspective, different emotions concern different aspects of living. Rage and grief, for example, involve different movements. While different emotions involve different brain areas, a key area for generating them is the *periaqueductal gray* (PAG) at the top of the brainstem. According to Damasio, "laughter and crying, expressions of disgust or fear, as well as the responses of freezing or running in situations of fear are all triggered from the PAG" (2010: 80). The triggering generates widespread changes:

- biochemicals are released in the body by endocrine glands (such as cortisol for extra energy when we're scared), and in the brain from subcortical nuclei

- inner changes including raised heart rate and faster breathing
- movements including facial expression and body posture, e.g. fearful ones when we're scared
- altered cognitive activity, including attention and working memory, as the process spreads in the brain, e.g. when sadness takes over, we think sad thoughts.

In under half a second, "the emotional cascade manages to transform the state of several viscera, the internal milieu, the striated musculature of face and posture, the very pace of our mind, and themes of our thoughts", says Damasio (2010: 114). Much energy is consumed, so being emotional is tiring.

The brain then generates feelings of the emotion in different areas from the triggering ones. The feelings are inner 'perceptions' that comprise both the changed body state and changed mental landscape. Body state is mapped in a sequence of areas from upper brainstem to somatosensory cortex, which link back to the triggering areas, creating loops that amount to a "near fusion of body and brain", says Damasio (2010: 119).[1] The insula links body signals and feelings with other aspects of cognition; it's the primary cortical area for inner body state, just as the visual cortex is for our eyes.

After visual stimuli reach the brain, it takes half a second before we report feelings about them (Damasio 2010). That's quick, but emotional states can then continue long after the initial trigger ends. The human brain is more subject to emotional turmoil than the animal brain, thanks to our capacity to think about emotive things. Explicit memory enables us to look backwards in our lives, and imagination enables us to look forwards. Our cognitive enhancements bequeathed by evolution bring a greater vulnerability to emotional problems.

The role of the body

The brain tells the body to enact an emotion, and they then engage in a dance (Damasio 2010). Thoughts can trigger emotional states in the body, and "the body can change the brain's landscape and thus the substrate for thoughts" (2010: 96). The intensity and duration of an emotional state is influenced by the body's feedback to the brain (LeDoux 2003). For example, anxiety may start with an anxious thought, enlist the heart into an anxious state, and then continue as signals from the heart prompt further anxious thoughts.

Bodily feedback is intrinsic to sustained emotion, and is a main ingredient in the ensuing feelings. What unfolds in the body is new, not stereotyped, so bodily feedback keeps our feelings fresh and alive. Our felt experience depends on the body and, if we listen to our felt sense, our feelings change rather than stay the same – our frontal lobes come into the loop, and our left hemisphere engages with our right. Emotion is a double act of body and brain, each with their role but working as an ensemble.

The neurochemistry of emotion

Specific emotions don't reduce to specific biochemicals. Knowing what chemicals are involved in emotions doesn't itself explain how we feel. What generated those chemicals in the first place? "Knowing that a substance is working on certain systems, in certain circuits and receptors, and in certain neurons, does not explain why you feel happy or sad", warns Damasio (1996: 160). In the therapy room, we can only guess what biochemicals are coursing through our client's veins.

Emotion unfolds bottom-up

Subcortical areas that generate emotion can overwhelm the cortex, and the challenge for the cortex is to form a working alliance with them. Babies can generate strong emotions, and neural development enables them to integrate these emotions into their emerging self. If the parent's cortex doesn't help them do so, their cortex may spend years in therapy achieving it. A good top-bottom balance involves the frontal lobes being able to inhibit the generating areas, and allowing us to reflect on our emotional experience.

Panksepp's view is that the "ancient neural territories below the neocortex constitute our ancestral mind – the affective mind ... that we share with many other animals" (2012: x). This is the source of our most powerful feelings – rage and grief, panic and terror. The source of more nuanced feelings like shame and guilt is more cortical, and the fine-tuning of emotion requires the cortex.

In therapy, catharsis works bottom-up and changes the cortex, hence its catalytic power, especially for previously unexpressed emotion.

Three levels of emotional control in the brain

A useful model of the role of different levels of the brain in emotion comes from Panksepp (2012). He describes three such levels, working bottom-up (see Table 5.1):

- *Primary-process* affects are our instinctual emotional reactions that guide our behaviour from infancy onwards. Based in the brainstem, especially the PAG, they comprise the "emotional systems" (described below) that include rage, grief and terror. They can be intense and overwhelming, and touching into this level in therapy means emotionally charged moments.

Table 5.1 Three levels of emotional control in the brain, following Panksepp (2012). We can only be conscious of the tertiary level

	brain area	*psychological function*	*examples*
tertiary process	cortex	emotional reactions and habits mixed with cognition	awareness of feelings, attitudes towards feelings
secondary process	limbic areas	ingrained habits based in implicit memory	attachment dynamics, social emotions, e.g. pride, shame, guilt
primary process	brainstem, especially the PAG	core emotional systems	primary emotions, e.g. rage, grief, fear, joy

- *Secondary-process* emotions are ingrained habits rooted in implicit memory in subcortical limbic areas.[2] They develop as primary affects mixed with sensory perceptions: for example, implicit memory of attachment relationships can make people fearful of intimacy. They're unconscious processes; as Panksepp says "we cannot readily will ourselves out of underlying emotional turmoil that has been created through the consolidation of maladaptive affective patterns at primary and secondary levels" (2012: 448). Social emotions like pride and shame arise from this level.
- *Tertiary-process* functions take place when our emotional reactions and ingrained habits mix with cognition in the cortex. They include becoming aware of feelings, thinking and talking about them, and exercising free will around them. Our attitudes towards different feelings, absorbed from parents and culture, belong here.

As Panksepp points out, "in maturity . . . higher brain functions seem to be in complete control – which, as every psychotherapist knows, is rarely the case" (2012: 15). But therapists can only work directly at the tertiary level, with the client's awareness of his feelings. We must allow primary and secondary levels to reveal themselves, which they do, especially when the dialogue feels meaningful. Emotions that erupt can be welcomed in safety, and emotional habits brought into awareness.

Emotional hemispheres

Pop psychology holds that the right hemisphere is the emotional one, but the reality is more nuanced. This hemisphere belongs to the right brain-body ensemble that weaves together the inner bodily world with the outer world of people and situations into a feeling-toned background picture. The left hemisphere can stand aside and focus attention on something foreground, including or excluding the felt experience of the right.

The subcortical generation of emotion may not be lateralised, according to Panksepp (2012a). But once generated, the bodily feedback that influences our emotional state means that "the right hemisphere is more in touch with true inner feelings" (2005: 334). The left hemisphere can *pretend* to feel something, but to know what we're *really* feeling, we need the right's felt sense.

The right hemisphere is central to spontaneous emotional expression via the face, voice and body language (McGilchrist 2009). It mediates smiling, laughing and crying; the left side of the face, which it controls, is more emotionally expressive than the right. Sadness is biased to this hemisphere, anger to the left, which may explain why sadness leads into our inner world while anger does the opposite. The right hemisphere is also best at perceiving emotion, and colouring what we see and hear with emotional tones. If the left ignores it, our experience lacks emotional richness – a common complaint amongst people presenting for therapy ("I don't feel anything much").

But the left hemisphere contributes important aspects of our emotional lives beyond anger. We need it to articulate our feelings and understand them. It enables emotions, such as cheerfulness, that oil our social experience (McGilchrist 2009). It thinks it knows what we're communicating emotionally although, without listening to the right, it lacks congruence. To remain emotionally neutral, we need this hemisphere, and the distance provided by our frontal lobes.

The idea that the right hemisphere does 'negative' emotions and the left 'positive' ones doesn't persuade McGilchrist, though he acknowledges that left may tend towards optimism and right towards pessimism (2009). The right's involvement with sadness might be construed as negative, but both hemispheres contribute to our feeling positive. Overall, the right has a more inclusive range of feelings, the left a more partial one. Mixed feelings can be problematic: left prefers one feeling at a time, but must work with right to untangle confused feelings.

We feel our feelings with our right hemisphere, and articulate them with our left. A balanced emotional life requires both, and we need left to let go to right to mourn our losses. Left can suppress feelings that arise in right, avoid them, even deny them – but only at a price, because resonance means that other people sense them and wonder what's going on. Feelings in right are at the edge of awareness rather than 'unconscious', although dissociated emotions erupt in the right.

The right hemisphere gives us the felt sense of a situation. Gendlin called the process of noticing a felt sense in the background, bringing it foreground and allowing words to come to describe it, 'focusing' (1981).

What at first seems fuzzy comes into focus when we turn attention towards the body.

Two hemispheres in therapy

The left hemisphere approaches therapy from a foreground cognitive stance, while the right experiences it from a background affective one. Cognitively, client and therapist have a therapeutic goal, while emotionally they enter unknown territory and must 'trust the process'. In my biodynamic training, we were taught to 'expect the unexpected'.

The foreground mind may have intentions for action as the client wills changes to his behaviour, while the background bodymind simply enacts its current state through transference, projective identification and by acting out. We need both minds for psychological transformation. Acting out is emotionally driven behaviour that happens when clients lack a sense of where they're 'coming from' inside, their frontal lobes lacking awareness and unable to inhibit their subcortical reactions.

With his left hemisphere, the client can report what he feels, but with his right he can really feel it. Incomplete emotional cycles from the past, 'old' emotions, may erupt unexpectedly from the right brain as nature tries to complete the cycle. When they do, the therapist can respond in a way the client doesn't expect – with compassion rather than disapproval, for example.

Emotional systems

Emotion isn't one thing that comes in different flavours; there's no single emotional system (LeDoux 1999). Instead, there's a number of them, each of which has evolved with its own purpose. My main source here is Panksepp, whose account has become part of the emerging consensus amongst neuroscience-oriented therapists. Unless otherwise indicated, what follows comes from *The Archaeology of Mind* (2012).

Panksepp's work was based on his research into other mammals. He believes that "we can finally understand the rudiments of our nature by understanding the emotional neurology of our fellow creatures" (2006: 25). Human emotion is hard to study in brain scanners where people lie still in a small space, and brain imaging works better with the cortex than the subcortex. His classification of emotions is a bottom-up perspective based on neural networks and biochemistries, which makes it quite different from a top-down psychological one. They start with subcortical 'action tendencies' and only later give us the cortical feelings we reflect on.

Emotions have "a mind of their own – an ancient form of phenomenal consciousness that preceded language and sophisticated human thoughts by hundreds of millions of years", says Panksepp (2009: 2). They manifest via genes as our evolutionary inheritance, become linked to the cognitive mind through experience, and have the power to ride roughshod over cognitive awareness. But the human cortex takes emotion to places not available to other mammals. We can enjoy fear (think fairground rides), we can turn loneliness into creative activity and we can experiment with sexual orientation. We can hide our real feelings, and we "can be warm or acerbic, supportive or sarcastic at will" (2005: 301).

Seven core emotional systems

Panksepp outlines seven primary-process systems.[3] They're distinct in terms of neural pathways and the emotional behaviours and visceral responses they generate, though they sometimes overlap. There are three "primordial" systems, found in reptiles as well as mammals – SEEKING, RAGE and FEAR – and four "social" systems found only in mammals – LUST, CARE, PANIC/GRIEF and PLAY (the capital letters distinguish these terms from common usage of the words). They're subject to neuroplasticity, so they can become sensitised and triggered more easily, or become weaker through lack of use. But they can't be got rid of; the client who wants me to remove his anger needs to develop top-down inhibition from his frontal lobes so he can control it.

These systems are based in deep subcortical places including the PAG, and they energise and colour what the cortex does. Each of them generates core emotional states and typical behaviours. They lie at the heart of much therapeutic work, sometimes evoked in the room and sometimes emerging in the client's life. Here's a summary (see Figure 5.1).

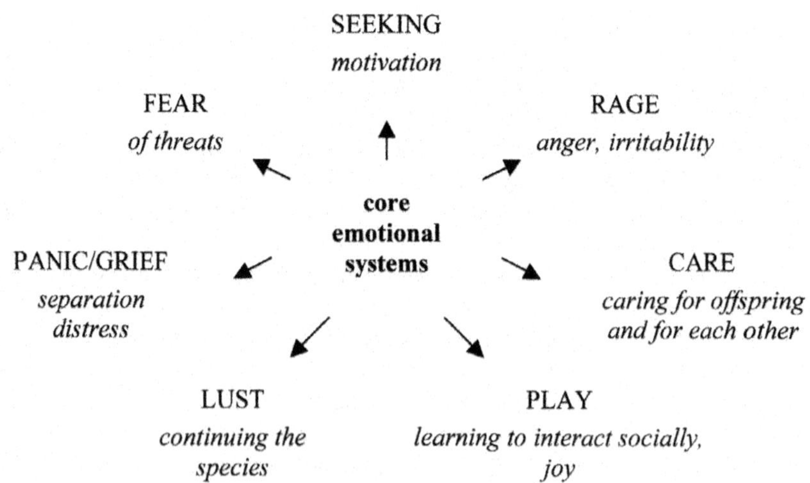

Figure 5.1 The seven emotional systems proposed by Panksepp (2012)

SEEKING

Emotions are about action, and this system motivates us to get what we need and want. It's "a general-purpose system for obtaining all kinds of resources that exist in the world, from nuts to knowledge" (2012: 103). It's fundamental to living, and combines with each of the other emotional systems so they can fulfil their goals. The sense of purpose it provides feels good.

When animals sniff and forage, they're SEEKING. Humans hunt, explore, seek mates, go shopping and surf the internet. SEEKING energises our intellectual and creative activity so we keep going and overcome obstacles. We use this system to express ourselves, to fuel our self-esteem. It can take us away from social contact as we pursue something (e.g. getting a book written), and can fuel obsessive and addictive behaviours – it needs training lest it become "just a super-efficient get-up-and-go-get-it system" (2012: 103).

Based in the brainstem, it stretches via dopamine pathways to the hypothalamus, from where it energises the body, and to the frontal lobes, from where it energises our mind to fulfil our needs. Because it's powered by dopamine, it feels good to be SEEKING. Many feelings arise from it including hopefulness, anticipation, excitement and, when combined with fear, thrill. It turns mundane activities into exciting ones.

We use SEEKING to search for meaning in life, so therapy depends on it. Clients seek help, and we ask them what they want from therapy. Their motivation may diminish as they encounter personal blocks, so reviewing how they feel about their progress is an opportunity to renew their SEEKING motivation. Therapists seek meaning in experiences that may seem meaningless to the client,

RAGE

RAGE is the source of our anger when we don't get what we seek or lose what we already have. Mildly activated, this system makes us irritated and annoyed, while strong activation can lead to aggression. Frustration, animosity and hostility stem from it. RAGE is central to the fight part of fight-flight and, when combined with SEEKING, we may fight to get what we want.

The three levels of emotional control play their roles:

- *primary*: raw RAGE is triggered subcortically
- *secondary*: habitual patterns of perceiving people as obstructing us result in our making them the object of our anger
- *tertiary*: our frontal lobes may elaborate angry feelings into resentments which feed continued subcortical RAGE arousal.

RAGE pathways start in the amygdala, where sensory and cognitive links that provoke our anger arrive, and proceed to the hypothalamus and the

PAG where aggressive behaviour is generated.[4] The cortex can both promote and restrain RAGE: "cortical processes, especially in the frontal lobes, can provide inhibition, direction, and other forms of cognitive regulation over this impulsive urge, yielding internalised irritability, hatreds, and resentments" (2009: 11). Biochemically, RAGE is fuelled by noradrenaline and acetylcholine, and diminished by serotonin and endorphins. A clenched jaw indicates RAGE arousal.

When we feel put down, ignored or abused, RAGE is triggered, especially in childhood. The resulting anger may be directed against those responsible or turned inward against ourselves – possibly because RAGE and FEAR pathways overlap in the amygdala. The effective expression of anger can feel good, but just feeling angry and irritable feels bad. To recover from excessive RAGE, we must grow the capacity for warm relationships that supply endorphins.

RAGE sometimes erupts in the therapy room. If the therapist can contain its force, the client can learn, implicitly and explicitly, that anger can be expressed safely. An angry transference needs to be *responded* to, rather than *reacted* to through the therapist's projective identification.

FEAR

When we seek what we want, we sometimes run into danger: this system helps us deal with the threat by freezing or fleeing. We're born with the capacity for free-floating fear, so baby may experience fear without any external stimulus. During development, the amygdala links FEAR with particular stimuli (e.g. scary sounds, scary faces) that trigger it. The system can become over-sensitised if we're frightened too often for too long: "experience can create fearful memories that henceforth can be triggered by previously neutral events" (2012: 176).

The amygdala is part of the FEAR network, forming two-way loops with both the hypothalamus, generating sympathetic arousal, and the PAG. The PAG evolved before the amygdala, and fear can emanate from here too. The amygdala's involvement can make matters worse because of its tendency to generalise and thereby add more stimuli to the list of FEAR triggers.

Mild FEAR arousal results in chronic anxiety and proneness to freezing, powered by modest levels of dopamine. High arousal means terror and flight, a high dopamine state in which muscles tense and heart rate rises as the body prepares to run. Generalised anxiety, paranoia and startle are all aspects of FEAR. We can be afraid without realising it, but in becoming aware we join the human race – we're all afraid of something.

In therapy, FEAR may be expressed directly, or the therapist may sense it in her countertransference. It needs to be named and managed to avoid re-traumatising the client.

LUST

Unsurprisingly, this system organises sexual behaviour. The primary level of sex and gender begins in the womb (and probably that of sexual orientation too although the underlying biology remains unclear). Experience and culture add secondary and tertiary level layers of complexity. Unlike animals, humans can exercise choice around whatever LUST has decreed for them.

Male and female LUST networks are centred in different parts of the hypothalamus, and their differences are sufficient to ensure that men and women don't always understand each other.[5] In puberty, hormonally-driven changes take place to sexual brains and bodies laid down in the womb. Sexual awakening for girls involves oestrogen and progesterone, and for boys, testosterone. Female sexuality has more complex underpinnings than male sexuality.

Because of the way sexual brains and sexual bodies are organised in the womb, "male-type desires can flower in female brains and female-type desires can thrive in male brains" (2009: 12). This leads to transgender phenomena later on, and may influence sexual orientation.

For both sexes, LUST recruits SEEKING to the cause of finding a sexual partner and fulfilling desires. Sexual preferences, rooted in LUST, are partly innate and partly learnt; neuroplasticity means that their development after puberty is influenced by the culture we inhabit. Other feelings affect LUST: fear and anger reduce sexual arousal, mild pain can increase it.

LUST manifests in therapy as erotic transference and countertransference. If it can be experienced without being enacted, the client's confidence in their sexuality and the capacity of their frontal lobes to channel it creatively may grow. Outside the room, a healthy experience of LUST supports well-being and intimate relationships.

CARE

This system enables parents to care for their children, and anyone to help another person. It's part of the delicious cocktail of love and passion, and of many good things in human relationships including altruism, compassion and empathy. At the primary level lies the instinct to care for others, especially children, and especially strong in women. The secondary level includes habitual patterns of caring we learn from parents, and the tertiary level includes what we believe about caring, its 'socially constructed' aspects.

CARE is based in the anterior cingulate, higher up in brain evolution than other systems, which implies its nuanced nature. It also suggests that it develops after birth as the anterior cingulate develops, but nevertheless early enough to explain why children can care for a parent from an early age. CARE pathways lead down to many subcortical areas to combine with other systems needed for parenting; for example, to dopamine-producing brainstem areas to combine with SEEKING to "add urgency to the maternal intent" (2009: 13).

Oxytocin is the key biochemical, and female brains produce more than male brains. In pregnancy, it's released before birth along with other hormones to prepare women for the physiological and emotional changes required to become maternal. "Oxytocin . . . promotes female confidence in the face of the difficult task of raising children" (2012: 259). After birth, a mother's affectionate contact with her child both generates oxytocin and is enabled by it. Fathers have less oxytocin and may require tertiary level understanding to be motivated carers. CARE generates good feelings in everyone, partly because it generates endorphins as well as oxytocin.

CARE can be part of the therapeutic relationship. Despite not having children myself, I often experience caring parental feelings in the room, paternal ones and sometimes maternal ones. This suggests something was missing for the client in childhood.

PANIC/GRIEF

This system concerns separation distress. Young animals and children panic and cry in distress when separated from mother to call her back. If she doesn't return, panic turns to grief, hence PANIC/GRIEF.[6] Later in life, it underlies mourning, sadness, crying and separation anxiety.

Following birth, this system is 'objectless' and will link to anyone who's caring even if they're also abusive since someone is better than no one – which may explain a lot of adult relationship problems. It helps babies get fed and looked after, and to become securely attached to parents. When children are separated from parents and become lost, PANIC/GRIEF is triggered.

This system lies in the subcortical PAG which generates the emotional pain of separation. As the brain develops, it can also be triggered by the amygdala and anterior cingulate; brain imaging shows these areas firing up in adult brains experiencing sadness. The anterior cingulate becomes involved in separation distress during the first year. If we're unable to mourn our losses and cry, the routes to PANIC/GRIEF may be inhibited at the secondary and tertiary levels – we can't just decide to cry.

Biochemically, the distress of PANIC/GRIEF involves stress hormones that lead to adrenaline and cortisol being released in the body, for separation is stressful.[7] When separation distress subsides and we're cared for again, endorphins and oxytocin replace the stress chemistry.

PANIC/GRIEF links with feelings of rejection. It contributes to both depression and some forms of chronic anxiety including panic attacks (other forms relate to FEAR). Both FEAR and PANIC can underlie anxiety, but they're separate systems, so anxiety about separation and anxiety about danger are different states.

In therapy, PANIC/GRIEF manifests as deep sobbing, periods of mourning, and panic attacks. Distinguishing FEAR and PANIC is a useful application of Panksepp's work. Sometimes both are present, as when a client's apparently irrational fears irritate their partner who then threatens to leave; this is the only situation I've encountered when I've felt that more than two sessions a week might be helpful.

Crying depends on letting go to PANIC/GRIEF. If we don't let go to it, the blocked emotion can be held in the body as chronic muscle tension and tissue 'armour' (Stauffer 2010). But the heart of the problem may lie in the brain and the secondary-process level expectation of an unsympathetic response. If I imagine my mother seeing me cry, I see her look of alarm, not the softness of sympathy – I cry easily watching movies or listening to music, but less so in company.

PLAY

Play is essential for healthy social brains. "Playfulness ... brings young animals to the perimeter of their social knowledge, to psychic places where they must learn about what they can or cannot do to each other" (2009: 16). All young mammals have the urge to play so they can use their minds and bodies to develop social skills and prepare for life's challenges. PLAY allows humans to be woven into a social system and underlies sports, dance, music and theatre – everything that brings joy, laughter and creativity. It turns routine work into enjoyable play.

The neural substrates for PLAY lie in the thalamus and in dopamine networks, which implies the interplay of mind and body. In childhood, much play is rough-and-tumble, which integrates movement with social behaviour. The subcortex and body are sufficient for primary level rough-and-tumble play, but the cortex becomes involved at secondary and tertiary levels as children start inventing games and acting roles. In adulthood, play allows us to rest our busy left hemispheres and let go to our bodies and sense of fun.

Panksepp thinks children deprived of opportunities for play are more likely to become "reclusive and a potential menace to society as an adult" (2012: 386). The roots of many social problems, including sadistic and cruel behaviour, may lie in unhappy homes with parents unable to enjoy rough-and-tumble play with their children, and in the lack of safe places for children to play together in adventurous ways.

Invoking PLAY invigorates both child and adult therapy. It can make the therapeutic relationship feel safe, so it becomes a context for exploration. A therapy room that's sometimes filled with spontaneous laughter is a healing room.

The systems interact

The systems often work together. Most of them can invoke SEEKING to achieve their aims: for example, LUST and SEEKING to find a mate, or RAGE and SEEKING to campaign for a cause. Or they can be in conflict. In FEAR, we flee from someone threatening, whereas in PANIC/GRIEF we seek an attachment figure. If the latter person is also the former, the nervous system is flummoxed and affect regulation goes haywire; this dynamic underlies much early childhood trauma from abusive parents. The PANIC/GRIEF need to let go and cry may conflict with the RAGE need to protest and seek redress. Such an emotional conflict can last a lifetime if we don't get to the bottom of what first triggered RAGE.

And the systems affect each other. For example, CARE inhibits PANIC/GRIEF, and PANIC/GRIEF reduces PLAY – unsurprisingly.

Social emotions

What about other emotions such as shame and guilt? Panksepp sees these as secondary-process emotions that are 'socially constructed' and 'cognitively elaborated' (2012). Unlike some of the primary emotions, they only emerge after birth as primary emotions interact with developing secondary-process habits in attachment relationships. They link with the emotional systems, especially the separation distress of PANIC/GRIEF.

We can experience the primary emotions when alone but social emotions are, as Trevarthen says, "*basic* self-and-other human feelings" that arise in company (2009: 56). They are part of the context in which we experience primary emotions, and they affect what we do with them. We may suppress RAGE, for example, because we feel guilty about expressing anger.

In therapy, social emotions can block the expression of primary ones. When the client overcomes his shame or embarrassment, he may find his mojo (SEEKING), express bottled-up anger (RAGE), let go to tears (PANIC/GRIEF), or make space for creativity (PLAY) – then transformation occurs. The power of social emotions lies in keeping primary emotions hidden.

Shame

Shame is a feeling of being bad that grows around emotions and behaviours when we perceive others as judging us in disapproving ways. The opposite feeling is pride – others' approval feels good. Watt thinks shame is rooted in separation distress and reflects "a sense of oneself as exposed and defective in the eyes of significant others" (2003: 86).

Experiencing some shame is essential, of course, lest we become monsters without a conscience. But children who are shamed excessively by parents trying to control their behaviour may later feel criticised and rejected in their adult relationships, which can lead to anxiety and depression. It's a "powerful, preverbal, and physiologically based organising principle", says Cozolino (2010: 193), a state we enter rather than a feeling that flows through us. It affects our social standing until we face whatever it obscures inside.

While "you can take action to alleviate guilt ... shame offers no redemption", Cozolino points out (2006: 234), hence we learn to conform to avoid further shame. But we must overcome our shame if we're to discover our real feelings underneath. Group therapy works because others overcome their shame in our presence.

Shame envelops us with a shift from the mild sympathetic arousal of social engagement to a very low arousal parasympathetic state (Schore 2012). There may be a degree of immobilising with fear, implying dorsal vagal activation (Porges 2012). We look down, hanging our heads in submission. Blood pressure drops, breathing becomes shallow. People who make little eye contact may be experiencing shame. Dorsal vagal activation means a life threat state – we 'want to die' when we feel shamed.

The parasympathetic low arousal of shame implies a right brain dominant state. The implicit self collapses, undermining the left hemisphere's capacity for enjoyable social engagement and conversation. Left may defend against the risk of right collapsing into shame – which means avoiding feelings that might trigger such a collapse. This can reach the point where, as Gabor Maté says, "our abiding fear of shame impairs our ability to see reality" (2011: 12).

Shame begins with misattunement in attachment relationships; Cozolino says it's "the emotional reaction to the loss of attunement with the caretaker" (2006: 234). This begs the question of when we first experience it. At 6 months says Trevarthen (2009), around 12 months according to Cozolino (2010), and in the second year when we start crawling and hearing parental 'no's' thinks Schore (2012). But misattunement between mother and baby leading to parasympathetic low arousal can happen before six months old, so shame may be part of early attachment dynamics – which might explain some of the persistent shutdown states some clients display in therapy.

Shame is hard to feel physiologically, since the body shuts down. But it's easy to recognise in feelings of inadequacy and at a cognitive level in superego attacks ("I'm not good enough", "I don't belong in this group"). If rejection by others was life-threatening in our evolutionary history, is it any wonder that shame can be so pervasive and worth avoiding?

Shame in therapy

It's easy to miss the low arousal of shame in therapy. Schore thinks therapists have over-emphasised the importance of anxiety and rage, and under-emphasised that of shame (2009). It's present in clients who go quiet when what's being discussed touches into unresolved early trauma.

If not swiftly resolved, misattunements in the therapeutic relationship trigger shame, rupturing the implicit right brain to right brain communication (Schore 2012). They manifest as the client avoiding eye contact, and the therapist sensing his withdrawal as something painful is touched on and his implicit self collapses. For the therapist, this can be "the most difficult countertransference ... to consciously recognise and tolerate", and "mutual projective identifications that set off reciprocal shaming" may ensue (2012: 98). The therapist may be unaware of her own shame, let alone the client's, rendering therapy ineffective because the underlying trauma is ignored.

Shame is hard to work with since the neural networks generating it are by definition cut off from the client's capacity to relate. It descends like a wet blanket, dampening the interaction. But the therapist can learn to recognise shame and talk to the client's left hemisphere about it. She can express curiosity about whatever lies underneath, making it safe for the client to go there, and support the client's primary emotions – the more they come into play, the less he's beset by shame.

Guilt

While shame involves the judgement of others, we can feel guilty without anyone knowing about our wrongdoing. We feel bad about what we've done rather than about who we are. Compared to shame, guilt is "a more complex, language-based, and less visceral reaction that exists in a broader psychosocial context", says Cozolino (2010: 194). It emerges later in development than shame, when the child learns about right and wrong.

Feeling guilty can be central to some people's experience. The person who feels guilty may resolve one situation and instantly find another to feel guilty about. Might guilt be a pervasive feeling of being in the wrong (right hemisphere) and a cognition of needing to apologise to others and attack oneself (left hemisphere), an unholy hemispheric constellation that maintains a familiar social stance learnt in childhood from parental punishments?

Arousal

As well as different emotions, we experience different levels of emotional intensity. Too little emotion and our brain doesn't notice what's happening, too much and it becomes unproductive (LeDoux 1999). In the body, too much arousal makes us tense and our breathing shallow, while too little drains our zest for life. Furthermore, LeDoux points out that "arousal locks you into whatever emotional state you are in when arousal occurs" (1999: 290), so we can get stuck. Emotion works best with just the right amount.

The right hemisphere mediates emotional arousal. It's "generally more important than the left in activating arousal systems" and "superior in processing emotional arousal", says Schore (2012: 88), as it's more closely linked with the body and affected by bodily feedback than the left. The right frontal and temporal lobes exert inhibitory control over emotional arousal (McGilchrist 2009). However the left hemisphere plays a role in dampening arousal (Watt 2003), and while the right triggers sympathetic arousal, the left triggers parasympathetic relaxation (Craig 2015).

Regulating emotional arousal is learnt in attachment relationships. Parents look after their child's arousal levels through their capacity to regulate their own arousal, and if they lack such capacity, the result may be affect dysregulation in the child (Schore 2012). Arousal may be very high or very low, but either can be painful and potentially traumatic.

The window of tolerance

Optimal arousal means we're within our 'window of tolerance' – affective tolerance (Siegel 1999). Within the window, there's a felt sense of what's happening, we're able to maintain social engagement and think, and our emotional reactions are tolerable – for us and hopefully for others. Outside the window lie the extremes of hyper-arousal and very low (hypo-)arousal, which may relate to trauma and dissociation. Moving in or out of the window happens autonomically, and only the resulting feelings and states of mind come into awareness (see Figure 5.2).

Windows of tolerance are personal. We inherit them from our parents in our temperament, and by how they respond to our emotional expression in childhood (Siegel 1999). Secure attachment supports a wide window which helps us tolerate strong emotions, while a narrow window means they can disrupt our thinking and behaviour. How wide our window is may vary with the emotion evoked, anger or sadness for example, and whether we're with people with whom we feel safe. Another factor is our physiological state – if we're hungry, tired or in pain, our window may narrow.

Being outside our window can mean one of two things: either we go into high sympathetic arousal with accelerating heart rate and breathing, or into low parasympathetic arousal where they slow, our mind shuts down and we feel numb (Siegel 1999). In either direction, our capacity for self-reflection and responding flexibly with our frontal lobes to what's happening evaporates.

Within the window, both hemispheres can contribute, the left dominating when there's a need for verbal and explicit cognitive activity (Schore 2012).

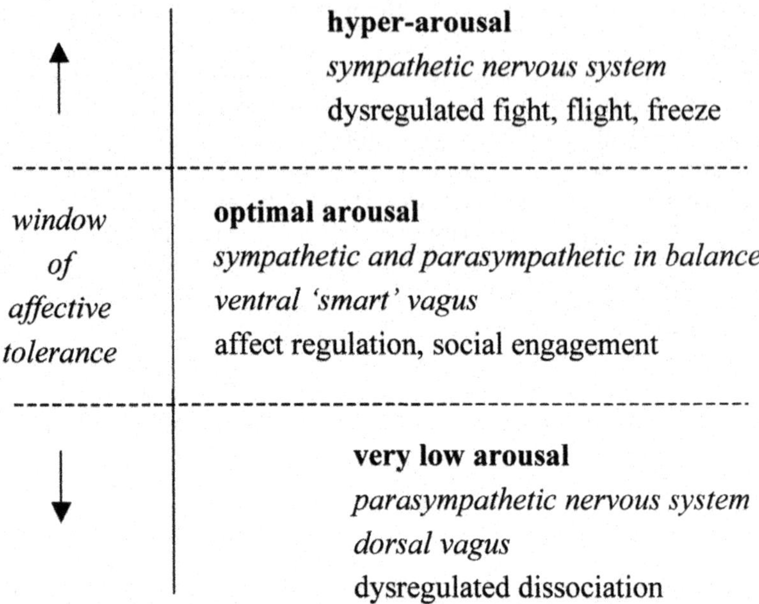

Figure 5.2 The window of tolerance, following Siegel (1999) and Ogden (2009), which aligns with polyvagal theory. The diagram fails to show the direct link from hyper-arousal into very low arousal

It can do this because the right can manage the moderate level of arousal without intruding. With both frontal lobes available, we can control our behaviour and choose our actions.

Hyper-arousal

When our emotions fly out of control, we're hyper-aroused. Overwhelmed with rage or anxiety, we over-react. The niceties of social engagement give way to polyvagal danger – sympathetic fight-flight states in which we behave impulsively and defensively, and are hyper-vigilant for threats. Hyper-arousal includes freezing, where we immobilise, experience agitation and go mute. In adults, it points to childhood abuse.

Hyper-arousal sends the right brain into overdrive and derails the left hemisphere's ability to talk about what's happening (Cozolino 2010). The right brain is dominant (it has its downsides) and intrusive images, unwelcome feelings, racing thoughts, and possibly flashbacks and nightmares, torment us (Ogden, Minton & Pain 2006). The sympathetic arousal involves accelerating heart rate and unpleasant physical sensations (Schore 2012). Hyper-arousal doesn't feel good.

Very low arousal

In parasympathetic very low arousal, heart rate and breathing slow right down, we experience shame and hopelessness, and we may dissociate (Schore 2012). We can lack the energy to *dis*engage from whoever we're with. Autonomically, we're in the life threat zone governed by the dorsal vagus. The right brain takes over in survival mode and the implicit self implodes, leaving the left hemisphere struggling to work out what to do next. The lack of emotion and sensation in this state is itself torment (Ogden et al. 2006). We feel numb and empty, and behave passively, as if paralysed, unable to make sense of the situation. We can't defend ourselves, so we submit. The roots of such states may lie in childhood neglect and giving up on being helped by parents.

It's possible to shift rapidly from hyper-arousal to very low arousal, from fighting to submitting, so the window of tolerance diagram fails here: there's a direct route from the top to the bottom.

Cycles of arousal

Safe emotional arousal runs in cycles in which a charge builds in the sympathetic nervous system, is expressed, and then we wind down and recover with the parasympathetic (see Figure 5.3). In early childhood, children need parents to soothe their high arousal and help them through the cycle (Gerhardt 2015). Without this, they don't learn to self-soothe and, if left in high arousal, may give up and flip into very low arousal.

The cycle of arousal is about our capacity for self-regulation and for 'completing' experiences. Humans are adept at interrupting these cycles. We may suppress the charge as it builds, so we appear calm despite underlying agitation. We may stop ourselves midway, leaving some of the charge in the body. We may not allow ourselves to recover. When a cycle isn't completed, something of it remains in both body and brain. Our breathing may be shallow, our muscles tense, and our endocrine and immune systems may be disrupted (Gerhardt 2015). Emotional healing is about finally completing the cycle. We can't just decide to 'move on' – we need to complete the cycle, a joint project with our right brain-body ensemble. Doing so generates feelings of aliveness and fulfilment.

An example of an incomplete cycle: a child wanders away from his parent, becomes lost and frightened, and when reunited with the parent is scolded. The child's PANIC/GRIEF arousal remains underneath his shame, and he's left in an emotionally confused state, less able to trust others to care for him.

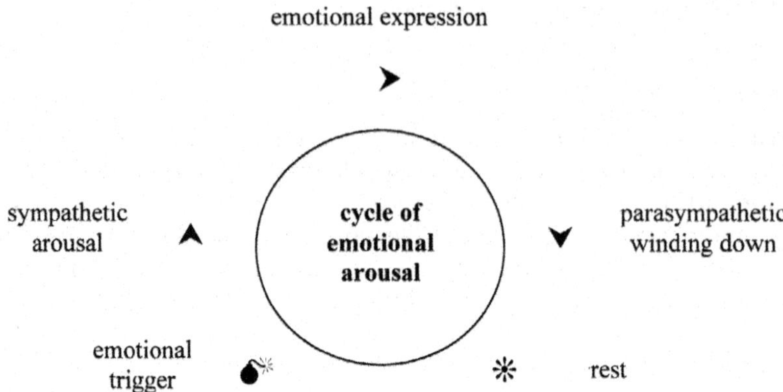

Figure 5.3 The cycle of emotional arousal, adapted from Stauffer (2010). The cycle starts with an emotional trigger, whether external or internal, and we may block it midway so it doesn't complete

Arousal in therapy

Psychological transformation happens within the window of tolerance. However, the client needs sometimes to go outside it in order to experience unresolved emotional cycles and allow them to complete. A good session can go through a full emotional cycle that leaves both client and therapist satisfied that something worthwhile has happened (Stauffer 2010).

The therapist can respond to signs of increasing arousal, such as changes in facial expression and skin colour, eyes moistening, or the body tensing up. The client's arousal goes outside his window of tolerance when early relational trauma is triggered in the therapeutic relationship. When this happens, the therapist needs to keep her countertransference arousal within *her* window (Schore 2012). She acts as a buffer for the client's excess arousal, allowing herself to be affected but not overwhelmed.

The client can learn to recognise the signs of these arousal states (Ogden et al. 2006). Bringing awareness into the body and making eye contact with the therapist can bring the arousal level back within the window. Very low arousal happens when the client becomes distant and possibly dissociates; he needs to make contact with the therapist again. The better he understands this process, the easier it is to work with when it happens. Bringing the client back into his window of tolerance widens it. Outside the window, interpretations are useless – the arousal must be attended to first.

Moderate levels of arousal allow us to work with the left hemisphere, so cognitive and insight-driven approaches can be effective (Schore 2012). Moderate arousal allows the client to feel in control and use his frontal lobes. The evidence is that "moderate levels of arousal optimise the production of neurotransmitters and neural growth hormones that enhance ... cortical reorganisation", says Cozolino (2010: 342).

Therapy can help people tolerate intense emotions, explore mixed feelings and allow them to unravel, and enjoy positive feelings. A wider range of emotions can come within the window of tolerance. For example, the client who cries easily may discover that it's safe to express anger – maybe he'll be less overwhelmed by tears thereafter.

Affect regulation

This is a technical term for managing our emotions and staying within our window of tolerance in polyvagal safety. It involves tolerating strong emotions and ambivalent feelings, and shifting easily from feeling one emotion to feeling another. It happens in relationships when I'm angry and you remain calm, or vice versa. When we can regulate each other and ourselves, we enjoy social engagement and cope with life's ups and downs. Affect regulation is autonomic, but it doesn't happen autonomously: it's best done in relationships, lest we use food, alcohol, computers and televisions, for example, which are less effective.

Affect regulation begins in attachment relationships if the child is comforted when he feels hungry or scared, for example, and if his happy feelings are encouraged in playful exchanges (Schore 2012). It accompanies attunement, giving the child a feeling of safety and confidence to explore the world. The way the right brain-body ensemble develops reflects early emotional experiences and responses between child and parent, and these unconscious patterns guide us in social situations thereafter. Affect regulation and attachment patterns intertwine in the right brain.

After birth, we only have our amygdala for affect regulation, so we can easily become stressed and fearful. Later, our anterior cingulate develops so we can attune to our parents. We can then learn to use our frontal lobes to regulate our feelings, and develop top-down networks between the orbitomedial prefrontal cortex and subcortex for affect regulation from around 12 months (Cozolino 2010). When tired or scared, for example, we may cry and howl; parents can help us back into a regulated state, and the implicit memory of many such cycles of affect regulation then becomes a foundation for life and relationships. We learn the art of "positive state transitions ... 'good inner objects' that bias us toward restoring regulation when we are challenged", says Cozolino (2006: 87).

Good affect regulation means we use our feelings as signals to respond to others and sustain relationships (Gerhardt 2015). Paying attention to feelings means we can adjust to each other. But implicit patterns of poor affect regulation are common. For some people, happy feelings signal the need to spoil them (my mother excelled at this, unable to feel happy for more than one day before finding something to get extremely upset about), while angry feelings can signal the need to withdraw rather than resolve a disagreement.

Affect dysregulation

This means being unable to regulate the intensity of an aroused emotional state (Schore 2012). Both hyper- and very low arousal states are potentially traumatic. Severe affect dysregulation lies at the core of dissociation, and psychiatric and personality disorders. Such disorders may reflect breakdowns in attachment relationships in infancy, as the child's right brain absorbs his parent's dysregulated emotional arousal. Later, he resorts to extreme attempts at affect regulation: substance abuse, self-harm, suicide attempts.

If the child isn't helped to regulate his emotional states, the brain falls back on automatic survival reactions (Cozolino 2010), discussed in Chapter 7. The prolonged stress of dysregulated affect damages pathways between cortex and subcortex that look after emotion (Cozolino 2006). The plasticity of the growing brain is inhibited; levels of endorphins and dopamine fall, while those of noradrenaline and cortisol rise.

The most severe dysregulation is experienced by people who lacked a secure and consistent attachment relationship in early childhood (van der Kolk 2011). They have a history of chronic misattunement with others. Quite apart from lacking positive emotions, they suffer from negative emotional states they can't manage. A vicious circle develops: their lack of self-regulation leads to being rejected, and the pain of rejection fuels further unmanageable emotion.

Affect regulation in therapy

Both client and therapist can allow emotion to be expressed in the room in a way that feels safe, so that arousal cycles are completed. Clinical enactments can be withstood, whether high arousal explosions or low arousal implosions of the implicit self. "Psychotherapy is not the 'talking cure' but the affect communicating and regulating cure", suggests Schore (2009: 128). When the client feels overwhelmed, the therapist can support him so the emotion becomes more manageable ("it's OK to feel like this").

If the client can let go to painful and traumatic emotional turmoil, his implicit self can remain intact so he stays in touch with himself and the therapist, allowing for a continuity of inner experience (Schore 2009). Affect dysregulation becomes affect *regulation*. The possibility of reflecting on the experience opens up, and the emotion is integrated across his neural axes.

Awareness of bodily experiencing of emotion facilitates affect regulation. Why? Because it engages the frontal lobes, both of them, and their engagement with the rest of the brain.

Feelings in the therapy room

If affect is primary, then feelings are at the heart of therapy. Schore's belief is that "the more therapists facilitate the affective experience/expression of patients in psychotherapy, the more patients exhibit positive changes" (2009: 113). That's my experience too, but there are many aspects to such facilitation. When I began my healing journey, I thought catharsis was needed for psychological transformation, but soon realised it's more complex than this.

The therapist's task is to evoke feelings, contain emotion, bring background feelings into the foreground, and turn emotion into feelings that can be reflected upon. She needs to do more than just ask "how does that make you feel?". In our quest for neural and psychological integration, we might approach the task with the three axes of neural architecture in mind:

- *top-bottom*: integrating raw emotion with acceptance and understanding
- *front-back*: reflecting on habitual emotional reactions and their cognitive aspects
- *left-right*: allowing the felt sense of feelings and emotions to unfold.

Let's explore this by looking at what we actually do in therapy.

Evoking and experiencing emotion

Brain and psyche don't become better integrated simply by talking about feelings. Rather, therapy itself must be an emotional experience. Client and therapist need to engage with primary and secondary processes, despite these levels being unconscious – we can't turn raw emotion on and off, or enact habitual patterns, at will. But in therapy, as in life, they're often evoked. For example, the therapist may show compassion the client doesn't expect, or challenge him in a way no one has ever done.

There are many ways to evoke emotion. Pointing attention into the body, exploring imagery, gestalt third chair work, and steering the dialogue towards whatever feels meaningful – all tend to engage the right hemisphere and feelings. Instead of looking for emotion, we can tease out the emotional nub of what's being discussed, since emotion is implicit in everything important. Emotion is then *experienced*, bottom-up, in the room; or it's experienced outside the room and discussed inside it. Experience generally precedes understanding, though sometimes understanding primary emotions can make it safer to feel them.

Therapy gets edgy sometimes. The client may erupt in rage at the therapist who must withstand the onslaught, or he may be overwhelmed with grief that triggers her own painful feelings. If she can work experientially, the opportunity arises for a natural integration of primary emotion with higher levels of neural control. When emotion arises, and the session becomes experiential, I change gear. Holding and support are needed, followed by bodily and felt sense awareness, and the expression of new feelings arising from the emotion. Bottom-up catharsis can be balanced with top-down reflection. LeDoux puts it succinctly: "psychotherapy is interpreted as a process through which our neocortex learns to exercise control over evolutionarily old emotional systems" (1999: 21).

Containing emotion

To encourage the integration of the different emotional process levels, the therapist must first contain the client's emotional outbursts, not taking them personally, maintaining intersubjectivity so she can respond creatively. His emotion may take him into hyper-arousal or very low arousal.

When old emotion first emerges, it can be messy, erupting from the primary level without the frontal lobes knowing what's happening. Rage may be excessive and seemingly unreasonable, but the key is that it's OK to be angry. Grief may struggle against suppression, but what matters is that the client can choose whether to let go to tears or hold them back.

If the therapist can hold onto both sides of her brain during emotional storms, she can support the client through the experience and gradually give what erupts back to him. He discovers that his emotion is both tolerable and understandable, and can then contain it himself, holding onto both sides of *his* brain. He's no longer alone with his feelings, which now make sense to him.

Feeling feelings

Feelings can be explored by feeling them in the here-and-now. What we *think* we feel lies in the left hemisphere, what we *really* feel lies in the right – they may or may not be the same. Client and therapist can enter right's world of felt experiencing – not an *experience* so much as a *flow of experiencing* – and explore the felt sense: where feelings arise in the body, how they change the body, and how the client feels about them, welcoming or resisting them.

Exploring the felt sense means the hemispheres working together, and client and therapist working in partnership. The client feels in control, approaching painful feelings and dissociated emotions in safety, sensing how far to go. Sitting with a felt sense is itself an integrated experience, and whatever arises comes in an integrated way (Gendlin 1964).

Conclusion

To heal wounded and traumatised aspects of the psyche, emotions and feelings must be at the heart of therapy. Some very different emotional experiences were part of my healing journey: explosive catharses in workshops, finding my way through my feelings in focusing practice, the compassion of individual therapy, and emotional honesty in group therapy. From finding the whole feelings business confusing and scary, I'm now comfortable feeling uncomfortable in working with it. I trust my feelings and my felt sense.

Affect is primary, so why don't we have 'affective therapy' to complement 'cognitive therapy'? This raises questions about therapy trainings: do students learn to work with strong emotions, and are they taught to work experientially? Confidence, skill and understanding are needed. Therapists have to go through the emotional wringer themselves, otherwise they work with one arm tied behind their backs.

Feeling and thinking needn't be in conflict with each other, but they often are. Discussing the bigger evolutionary picture, LeDoux wonders whether "the struggle between thought and emotion may ultimately be resolved ... by a more harmonious integration of reason and passion in the brain" (1999: 21). Such integration is the therapeutic enterprise.

Both experiencing and suppressing our feelings can lead to problems in the form of stress and anxiety. In the next chapter we'll explore what happens in these debilitating conditions, and in the state that sometimes follows them – depression.

Notes

1 Somatosensory cortex is in the parietal lobe, and the upper brainstem areas that map body state are the *nucleus tractus solitarius* and *parabrachial nucleus.*
2 Secondary-process level emotional habits are called 'conditioned learning' by behavioural psychologists, e.g. a rat learning to fear the sound of a bell on a cat's collar.
3 LeDoux doesn't agree with all of Panksepp's conclusions, but his disagreement is more about the nature of conscious feelings than his account of the emotional systems (2015). I think Panksepp offers the more complete description of our emotional lives.
4 The overlap of RAGE and FEAR in the amygdala: corticomedial areas elaborate the former whereas basolateral areas, that lie alongside, mediate the latter (Panksepp 2009).
5 The male system is centred in the anterior hypothalamus, the female in the ventromedial hypothalamus – one reason why male and female sexuality differ. Another reason is that men produce more testosterone in the adrenal glands

than women do, and have more testosterone receptors in the hypothalamus; testosterone works with vasopressin, of which men have more than women, to energise male sexual assertiveness. The brains of each sex contain "residual sexual circuits typical of the opposite sex", says Panksepp (2012: 258) – anima and animus? These enable men to benefit from oxytocin that helps them be gentle and support their offspring, and women to benefit from vasopressin that helps them protect their child, aggressively if necessary.

6 In Panksepp's earlier work he referred to this system simply as PANIC (2005), but later he called it PANIC/GRIEF.

7 The stress hormone here is corticotropin releasing hormone (CRH), the first hormone in the HPA axis sequence (Chapter 6).

Chapter 6

Stress, anxiety and depression

Introduction

Armed with an overview of the nervous system, the hemispheres, and how relationships and emotions fit in, let's now delve into the afflictions people bring to therapy, starting with the unholy trinity of stress, anxiety and depression. Most if not all of us experience these in at least mild form sometimes, but to what degree – and do we recover? All mental health problems include one or more of them, and if we experience them excessively in childhood they can lead to lifelong problems.

They overlap and interlink. Stress makes anxiety more likely, anxiety implies stress, stress is depressing, and anxiety and depression can afflict us in tandem. The stress response is over-active whether we're super-stressed, very anxious or severely depressed. And the stress response is an aspect of affect regulation and attachment, so relationships are involved.

Stress

A little stress makes life stimulating and enjoyable, but too much causes trouble – we lose our normal homeostatic balance. The issue is whether we recognise when we're stressed and get help to recover, so that healthy homeostasis is restored. If we don't and it isn't, then stress becomes problematic.

So stress here really means excessive stress, the beginning of much that afflicts mind and body. It contributes to "the expression and severity of most, if not all, psychiatric and medical disorders", says Cozolino (2010: 349). People are said to suffer 'stress-related' illnesses, which may be a euphemism for depression or what was once called a nervous breakdown. As Damasio says, "stress over time destroys life, mentally and physically" (2010: 114).

What is stress?

Normal stress involves brain and body mobilising inner resources for action, such as getting up in the morning. An excellent account of the subject comes from Robert Sapolsky, a Stanford neurobiologist with an affinity for African wildlife. His definitive guide to stress is *Why Zebras Don't Get Ulcers* (2004). The reason is that their stress response switches off when it's not needed, whereas humans can get stressed without any external stimuli and our stress response may not switch off to restore healthy homeostasis. Like zebras, we need a burst of energy to deal with the (metaphorical) lions we encounter and, thanks to our highly evolved brains, these lions include emotional and psychological stress that may linger. We worry, we try to do too many things at once, we get into inner conflicts we can't resolve.

Stress is more than just tension. It's a cascade of physiological events involving the brain, certain organs, hormones and the immune system. We can be stressed without being aware of it; we don't necessarily *feel* stress. Which is part of the problem.

Stressors

Stressors are things we get stressed about: anything that disrupts our homeostatic balance, or things we anticipate will do so (Sapolsky 2004). They may be external or internal stimuli that threaten our well-being; they may be physiological such as being injured, or psychological and emotional – *dis*tress. "The core of psychological stress is loss of control and predictability", says Sapolsky (2017: 127).

Stress can be caused by an event that presents a threat, such as losing your job, but Maté thinks that more harmful in the long run are stress-inducing situations that occur regularly in relationships (2011). Suppressing feelings, being unable to say 'no', and having poor psychological boundaries leave us with unmet needs that make us stressed, whether we're aware of it or not. Social support helps reduce stress, but "whatever undermines autonomy will be experienced as a source of stress", he says (2011: 197). It's possible to be in a secure relationship in which we lack autonomy.

The stress response

This is essentially a physiological and biochemical fight-flight response to emotional stimuli, an "ancient physiology, found in mammals, birds, fish, and reptiles", according to Sapolsky (2017: 126). It kicks off in the brain and involves the sympathetic nervous system preparing body and muscles for a burst of energy. A healthy stress response enables us to remain cool in a crisis, stressed enough to deal with it but not so stressed that recovery is compromised.

The stress response evolved for short-term emergencies but in humans can be triggered merely by thinking about potential disasters (Sapolsky 2004). If activated too often, it can do more damage than the stressor itself ever could. Designed for brief periods of stress, it can fire up for weeks or even years at a time (Cozolino 2010). Where there's affect dysregulation, there's also stress.

The physiological details vary depending on the particular stressor and the psychological context. Getting stuck in a traffic jam, being overloaded with work, or repeatedly suppressing anger if we can't say 'no', are very different situations, but the broad outline of the stress response holds true for them all (Sapolsky 2017a).

Stress thresholds

Each of us has our individual threshold for perceiving something as stressful and triggering the stress response. This threshold is partly innate and partly learnt from experience. The perceiving may be unconscious.

People with a low threshold who react more to stress and recover more slowly are 'high reactors' (Sapolsky 2004). Such a person may get stressed easily, be emotionally insecure, unable to self-soothe, and be prone to overeating and getting depressed (Gerhardt 2015). 'Low reactors' are people who appear to have a high threshold because their stress response is blunted, but who are prone to sudden outbursts of stress-fuelled anger and aggression. We can be a mix of the two.

Triggering the stress response

This happens via neural and biochemical routes (Sapolsky 2017). The neural route involves the amygdala and brainstem inhibiting the parasympathetic nervous system and activating the sympathetic by signalling the body to release adrenaline and noradrenaline into the bloodstream, especially the former from the adrenal glands. Within seconds, the heart beats faster with sympathetic arousal.

This fast neural route is backed up a slower biochemical one, the 'HPA axis', HPA standing for hypothalamus-pituitary-adrenal. The amygdala starts the sequence by signalling the hypothalamus to release hormones that head for the nearby pituitary gland (Sapolsky 2004). The pituitary releases another hormone which tells the adrenal gland to release cortisol into the bloodstream within minutes.[1] Cortisol gets most of the attention in stress discussions, probably due to the damage excessive amounts cause.

Stress in the body

The stress response mobilises energy for muscles. "Glucose ... proteins and fats come pouring out of your fat cells, liver, and muscles", enthuses Sapolsky (2004: 11). Heart rate, blood pressure and breathing rise to get glucose and oxygen to muscles quickly. Adrenaline from adrenal glands and noradrenaline from elsewhere in the body get visceral organs into gear. Cortisol follows on, reinforcing the adrenaline-initiated activity over minutes and hours, keeping the heart pumping. It also biases brainstem neurons to trigger further sympathetic arousal.

Other bodily processes slow down. Digestion is inhibited, tissue growth and repair are curtailed, sexual drive drops, pain perception becomes blunted. Complicated things happen to the immune system: moderate and transient stress enhances immunity, severe and prolonged stress impairs it (Sapolsky 2004).

Cortisol gets a bad press, but it helps the body recover when the stress response stops (Sapolsky 2004). When the brain decides the stressor is over, it stops triggering the HPA axis, and the parasympathetic nervous system then slows the heart and calms the body, restoring homeostasis. But if it continues generating a stress response, this may not happen and the body may not recover. Repetitive stressful thoughts and continued sympathetic arousal can combine to make us stressed most of the time. Although there may be tension in the body, we can be stressed without *feeling* tense (Maté 2011).

Prolonged cortisol release causes problems. Ongoing stress "changes the weather in the gut" by slowing digestion and reducing blood supply, explains Giulia Enders in her wonderfully informative *Gut* (2015: 125). Gut health suffers as the gut lining weakens and becomes more sensitive to further stress. We become prone to diarrhoea, loss of appetite and general fatigue. Signalling to the brain causes a sense of malaise. These negative effects of stress may continue long after the stressor itself ends.

Stress doesn't lead directly to illness, but it does increase the *risk* of certain illnesses (Sapolsky 2004). Common stress-related conditions include high blood pressure, heart disease and intestinal ulcers. Emotional stress contributes to illness, thinks Maté, because it affects our major organs and immune defences (2011). Although emotional expression resolves stress, incomplete emotional cycles can disorganise our physiological defences, which then undermine health instead of protect it. The cycle re-starts repeatedly, rather than ending with parasympathetic recovery and restored homeostasis.

Low cortisol

Most damage from cortisol concerns high levels, but low baseline levels also cause problems. Very low cortisol has been found in PTSD patients (van der Kolk 2014). It seems that while trauma involves high cortisol, correlating with agitation and anxiety, the adaptation to chronic stress from unresolved trauma can mean unusually low cortisol, correlating with feeling numb. Avoiding painful feelings stemming from early neglect, abuse and unresponsive parenting may reflect low cortisol (Gerhardt 2015). Boys prone to impulsive aggression often have low baseline levels, but when they feel threatened there's a sudden spike.

Stress in the brain

A little stress sharpens the senses and improves cognition, but too much for too long causes damage (Sapolsky 2017, 2004). There's a nasty feedback loop: the amygdala triggers the stress response, and the resulting cortisol flowing into the brain amplifies the glutamate-releasing excitement of amygdala neurons, so they process emotional and sensory signals more quickly but less accurately. The amygdala has lots of cortisol receptors and is particularly sensitive to the stuff. Over time, new dendrites and synapses grow there. Stress encourages it to learn new fear associations, and weakens the ability of the prefrontal cortex to extinguish them. Hence, chronic stress makes us more fearful.

While cortisol facilitates amygdala function, it impairs hippocampus function, so explicit memory suffers and we remember less (LeDoux 2003). The hippocampus regulates the stress response and slows cortisol release via its links with the amygdala and hypothalamus, but excess cortisol compromises its ability to do so. Chronically high levels correlate with reduced hippocampus volume: dendrites shrink, neurons die, and there's less neurogenesis.

Sustained stress and high cortisol can also damage the frontal lobes (Sapolsky 2017). Dendrites retract and synapses are lost as less excitatory glutamate is released to energise them. Attention and decision making are then impaired. Sapolsky warns that "we're more fearful, our thinking is muddled, and we assess risks poorly and act impulsively out of habit" (2017: 131). Stress erodes intelligence and good sense.

Stressed hemispheres

The stress response is a right brain specialism, part of the implicit background of affect regulation. The right hemisphere regulates emotional stress via subcortical links with the sympathetic nervous system and the HPA axis (Schore 2009).

Clinical experience suggests that when we're stressed but coping, we're less in touch with our body and inner world, implying a left hemisphere biased state.[2] But with too much stress, the balance flips to the right and into high arousal. Our focused attention and mental abilities suffer; this is one of the right brain's unwelcome states. Severe stress disrupts the integrative working of the hemispheres (Cozolino 2017), and chronic emotional stress induces hyper-vigilance (Maté 2011), implying right hemisphere dominance. Gerhardt reports rat research showing stress activating the left frontal lobe, but when prolonged or uncontrollable, the right becomes dominant (2015); high cortisol levels correlate with an over-active right hemisphere and an under-active left.

Stress in childhood

What stresses a young child? Abuse and neglect, obviously, but also parental unresponsiveness and hostility (Gerhardt 2015). Young children need to feel cared for and have some control in the matter. If they don't, they become distressed. The more stressed parents are by work, life and parenting itself, the less sensitive they may be towards their children's needs.

Stress can begin in the womb. Mother's stress is thought to affect the foetus via cortisol in the amniotic fluid, and can lead to low birth weight and epigenetic changes (Gerhardt 2015). The placenta protects him from her cortisol only up to a point: high levels enter the amniotic fluid. The baby's HPA axis is moulded by mother's emotional state. If she's chronically stressed, her baby may be born with a highly reactive stress response and low serotonin levels, crying more readily. Prenatal stress can affect lateralisation, resulting in anxiety in childhood and poor functioning in adulthood (Cozolino 2017). Maternal stress has been linked to children being irritable, hyperactive, and having learning disabilities. These research findings beg questions about the prenatal origins of mental health problems.

Birth may be stressful, but baby and mother can recover afterwards if she's supported in her demanding new role and can regulate her own stress. Breastfeeding can calm both of their stress responses (Gerhardt 2015). The way a baby is cared for affects the way his stress response develops: if mother is responsive when he's distressed, his cortisol level doesn't rise unduly, but if she isn't, it can go very high. A mature cycle of cortisol release – high in the morning and low in the evening – only appears around age 4. How our stress response develops at the beginning of life determines our stress threshold, how our brain and body react to stress, and whether we can turn to others for support when we're stressed. The stress we grow up with becomes our expectation of what a normal level of stress is, even if it's unhealthy, so early stress can handicap our capacity to recognise stress later in life.

Prolonged early stress is linked to children having smaller than average hippocampi, reflected in memory deficits (Cozolino 2010). Without enough holding and touch, insufficient cortisol receptors may develop in the hippocampus, weakening its capacity to inhibit the amygdala so that the child grows up with poor affect regulation and less emotional resilience (Gerhardt 2015). Prolonged high cortisol can mean a more reactive amygdala, fewer pathways from the orbitomedial prefrontal cortex and anterior cingulate to modulate the stress response, and low serotonin, reflected in impulsivity and aggression. The frontal lobes are affected, impairing attention and impulse control, and creating a vulnerability to depression later in life.

Early attachment stress

Whilst attachment relationships should help us recover from stress, they can also be sources of stress. Early attachment stress may lead to chronic stress in close relationships later in life (Maté 2011). Fight or flight are natural reactions to stress, but since babies can do neither a 'learned helplessness' in relationships may develop. We can grow up believing it's normal to meet others' needs while ignoring our own, unable to say 'no' and lacking autonomy. Whether we shut down emotionally and avoid intimacy, or become emotionally dependent and vulnerable to separation and loss, the outcome is chronic stress.

Stress at the beginning of life can occur in families where the child is loved but his stress and anxiety aren't eased (Maté 2011). His stress can be hidden in states of very low arousal. I suspect this happened to me: my mother intended to be loving, but her frequent anxiety, anger and hostility, followed by invasive attempts to express love, certainly didn't feel like love – I learnt to 'space out'.

Stress in therapy

Stress plays a role in most mental health issues, yet it "often flies under our diagnostic radar", thinks Cozolino (2010: 350). Current stress in the client's life can block reflection, and the therapist's first task may be to bring this into awareness ("do you think you're stressed?"). The therapist can help him identify what's stressing him, encouraging his frontal lobes to play their role in inhibiting the amygdala from firing up his stress response unnecessarily.

However, *some* stress in the therapy room is needed to trigger fresh plasticity and psychological transformation, as chronic relational stress the client has suffered all his life without realising gets addressed. The avoidance of relational stress may be an issue; the client tries 'not to go there' lest he become aroused and stressed in the room. He may be in a low cortisol, shutdown place in which he avoids core issues from old trauma. But his actual experience in attachment relationships, and in the therapeutic relationship, can be explored. The therapist has to balance stress-inducing challenge with stress-relieving support – the art of therapy. If relational stress can be safely navigated in the room, the client may become able to tolerate necessary stress in his close relationships.

Anxiety

While stress generally concerns what *is* happening, anxiety revolves around the expectation of what we fear *may* happen. They overlap: stress can make us anxious, and anxiety can be stressful. The distinction lies in their biochemistry: noradrenaline is key to anxiety, energising us, up to a point, while cortisol is key to stress, exhausting us if prolonged.

When we face a threatening situation and are uncertain what's going to happen or how best to respond, we become anxious (LeDoux 2003). So some anxiety is unavoidable, and many people prosper despite it, such as great actors who always feel stage fright. Social engagement is still possible. Too little anxiety may make us reckless and insensitive, while a modest amount keeps us alert. But too much becomes a problem: it obscures our felt sense, blocks our inner life and restricts what we do by plunging us into polyvagal danger states. Anxiety that stops us doing what we feel like doing needs to transform into a manageable companion. It can be eased if we feel it and allow others to know we feel it. Whatever lies underneath, unexpressed feelings and thoughts and so forth, can become foreground – then anxiety ceases to be an insurmountable obstacle.

What is anxiety?

We experience anxiety as tension and agitation in the body, and a mental state of expecting bad things to happen that's hard to shake. It may, in effect, be the continuation of scary experiences from long ago.

Sapolsky describes anxiety as "a sense of disquiet, of dis-ease, of the sands constantly shifting menacingly beneath your feet", requiring constant vigilance (2004: 319). Our nervous system constantly mobilises resources to cope with a perceived or anticipated threat, while our mind exaggerates the likelihood of things going badly. For LeDoux, it's an emotionally-fuelled state of cognitive arousal and worrying thoughts in which the brain is uncertain how to respond to a threat (2003). The amygdala is central to generating this state, which takes over our mind. "One's general level of anxiety is a fairly stable personality trait", he says (2015: 2) – and we might wonder whether it's innate or the outcome of early experience. Anxious parents create anxious children.

While fear concerns a real threat, anxiety involves our imagination running away with us (Sapolsky 2004). Different neural networks fire when we face a real threat than when we imagine something that may or may not happen (LeDoux 2015). We don't feel fear without also becoming anxious, but we can be anxious without fearing anything in particular. Nevertheless, when we're anxious, fear is triggered more easily than when we're not.

Anxiety suggests old trauma, which may be why some people experience it more than others. Sapolsky explains: what makes us anxious is associated with a trauma or with something similar to an experience associated with a trauma (2004). Anxiety reflects implicit learning from autonomic reactions to trauma, including early attachment trauma. Implicit memory can be triggered unconsciously; for example, hostile early parenting can make us anxious that other people we meet will become hostile, without our making any conscious connection to our past.

Finally, Panksepp's distinction between PANIC and FEAR systems (Chapter 5) allows us to distinguish different kinds of anxiety:

- PANIC-anxiety concerns separation distress and the fear of rejection. It underlies grief and crying, which may be why shedding tears can reduce anxiety.
- FEAR-anxiety concerns a threat to our physical or psychological integrity. Modest arousal triggers freeze reactions, while high arousal triggers fight-flight ones.

The former may have its roots in childhood neglect, the latter to childhood abuse.

Anxiety in the brain

Anxiety involves emotional arousal in brain and body, and cognitive changes. While particular regions play key roles, LeDoux says "anxiety itself is best thought of as a property of the overall circuitry rather than of specific brain regions" (2003: 290). Noradrenaline is released in the amygdala, hippocampus, prefrontal cortex and elsewhere, generating arousal which is energising up to a point, helping us cope and even thrive in social situations and in life generally. Severe anxiety is reflected in excess noradrenaline (Sapolsky 2017a).

Fast and slow fear pathways

The power of fear and anxiety in the brain owes much to there being two pathways for anxiety-provoking sensory signals. One is fast: sensory area to thalamus to amygdala, bypassing the cortex, as if signalling 'go directly to fear, do not pass the frontal lobes'. LeDoux calls it "a quick and dirty processing system" (1999: 163), and it has survival advantages, reacting to stimuli so fleeting the cortex never registers them, only the fearful state they trigger. Worse, the amygdala is unconcerned about accuracy, which is the job of the cortex. Worse still, the pathway develops early in life in the context of attachment.

The slow pathway takes twice as long, giving the brain time to consider whether there really is a threat: sensory area to hippocampus to frontal lobes, enabling context and awareness to check the signals for accuracy. Sometimes we're able to stop unnecessary fear reactions quickly, and we calm down again. But the two pathways may become disconnected during prolonged early childhood stress so that the slow one fails to inhibit the fast one (Cozolino 2010).

Amygdala

Anxiety and fear centre around the amygdala (LeDoux is so enamoured of this brain area, he has a band called 'The Amygdaloids'). It pairs a sensory stimulus (e.g. from eyes or ears) with a fear reaction, triggering arousal in body and brain via the brainstem and HPA axis. The fine detail of where outgoing pathways go to reflects different manifestations of fear and anxiety, such as raised blood pressure, freezing and startle (Cozolino 2010). With its penchant for inaccuracy and generalising, over time a growing range of stimuli may fire up the amygdala – hence 'free-floating anxiety'.

Amygdala and prefrontal cortex are reciprocally related, and the key to anxiety is which one predominates (LeDoux 2003). If the prefrontal cortex does, it inhibits the amygdala and we overcome our anxiety; if the amygdala does, we become anxious and fearful, straying into the polyvagal danger zone.

The amygdala is particularly sensitive to unsettling social circumstances (Sapolsky 2017). Much relational and social experience may be laden with anxiety, even if we hide it. Such anxiety can persist, and the cortisol unleashed by the stress involved may encourage dendrite growth in the amygdala that underlies the generalising effect of learning more fear associations. Furthermore, persistent stress weakens the ability of the prefrontal cortex to unlearn fear reactions.[3]

The amygdala is also involved in generating aggression. Fear may not make us aggressive, and not all aggression is rooted in fear, but it does make people who are prone to aggression more aggressive.[4] Sapolsky gets wistful: "in a world in which no amygdaloid neuron need be afraid and instead can sit under its vine and fig tree, the world is likely to be a more peaceful place" (2017: 44).

Anti-anxiety medications work by boosting GABA inhibition in the amygdala in particular. Some do this quickly (e.g. benzodiazepines), others slowly (e.g. certain antidepressants). Alcohol, the oldest anxiety-reducing drug, also boosts GABA inhibition quickly, hence its popularity.

Bed nucleus of the stria terminalis

This elaborately-named area (BNST for short) is an amygdala extension that's also associated with anxiety (Sapolsky 2017). Its different incoming pathways mean that, instead of reacting to present threats from sensory areas, it fires with anticipated ones from the prefrontal cortex (Cozolino 2017). The BNST may trigger less intense arousal over longer periods of time than the amygdala. Maybe we can blame it for worry and mild anxiety, the amygdala for fear and severe anxiety.

Hippocampus

Whilst it contributes to the slow pathway that modulates fear, the hippocampus also provides contextual signals from past experiences that reinforce the amygdala's fear associations (Sapolsky 2017). Stress can strengthen this unholy bond between amygdala and hippocampus, resulting in long-term memory of a fearful nature. But as the hippocampus only contributes from age 2 onwards, it may not feature in social anxiety rooted in early attachment – which might explain why social anxiety can be harder to overcome in therapy than explicit fears and phobias.

Frontal lobes

We need our frontal lobes to calm the amygdala's fearful reactions (LeDoux 2003). But if we're prone to anxiety in ostensibly safe situations, the amygdala may influence the frontal lobes to fret about threats, whether real or not. Bodily feedback and noradrenaline can reinforce its hold on them, so that our thoughts and behaviour are biased towards reacting to threats. When the amygdala holds sway, we need someone else's frontal lobes to quell our fear.

"Learning not to fear ... appears to be a major contribution of the orbitomedial prefrontal cortex", says Cozolino (2010: 254). The larger and better developed it is, the more it's able to inhibit fear reactions.

Anxious hemispheres

The left-right axis sheds light on two kinds of anxiety (Schore 2009):

- *Anxious arousal* is an affective state biased to the right hemisphere which looks out for danger and tries to align somatic state with apparent threats. It triggers strong sympathetic arousal.
- *Anxious apprehension* is a more cognitive state biased to the left hemisphere, manifesting as worry and endlessly turning things over in our minds. Although the body is tense, the arousal level is lower.

This distinction may correlate with that between mild and severe anxiety. Anxious apprehension reflects a fear of uncertainty and a need to be in control (McGilchrist 2009), not uncommon human tendencies. The mildly anxious left hemisphere avoids facing uncomfortable feelings in the right, and may function quite well on its own. But with severe anxiety, right hemisphere arousal dominates, disrupting the left's focused attention. It's evident to others.

Anxiety in the body

Anxiety starts in the brain and then affects the body. FEAR-anxiety generates sympathetic arousal for escape: adrenaline, raised heart rate and blood pressure, fast and shallow breathing, sweating, tense or upset stomach, muscle tension, body shakes and trembling hands (Panksepp 2012). PANIC-anxiety is more parasympathetic and about needing emotional support: wanting to cry, tight chest, lump in throat, feeling weak.

The body signals its anxious state back to the brain, which biases it to continue triggering more anxiety. We can become so accustomed to shallow breathing and muscle tension that we don't notice them.

Some anti-anxiety medications change the body to reduce anxiety: beta-blockers by slowing the heart, and probiotics by improving gut bacteria.

Anxiety in childhood

Both FEAR and PANIC systems develop in infancy and may become over-active with insecure attachment (Panksepp 2012). FEAR is triggered by abuse and punishment, and a parent can become a threat. An over-active FEAR system may mean chronic anxiety in adulthood, manifesting as social anxiety and a tendency to freeze. PANIC is triggered by neglect and separation distress. Being left alone for too long can lead to frequent crying, difficulty self-soothing, and a tendency to panic attacks we don't grow out of. Children need their parents' frontal lobes to calm their anxiety for their own frontal lobes to learn to do this when they're older.

Prolonged anxiety in childhood can mean poor consolidation of long-term memory, which manifests as a lack of recall of childhood as an adult (Cozolino 2006). If memories weren't consolidated, they aren't there to be remembered in therapy.

Anxiety disorders

These are manifestations of severe anxiety that mess up our lives. They come in a number of flavours, including worry, panic, dread, fear and terror, all sharing high sympathetic arousal and excess adrenaline and noradrenaline flowing through body and brain (Sapolsky 2004). We desperately try to cope but in vain, so we feel out of control.

The polyvagal perspective on anxiety disorders is that "the protective anti-stress and self-soothing features of the … social engagement system are lost", says Porges (2011: 273). There is poor regulation of heart rate and less facial expressiveness, which compromises our social experience. A lack of emotional support from others is implied, probably learnt in childhood; the underlying issue lies in the person's relationships, or lack of them.

Both FEAR and PANIC may be involved, either separately or in combination. Safe situations are responded to as if they were dangerous, because the emotional and social foundation of the nervous system is biased to danger and a fear of not being in control.

I'll discuss three anxiety disorders here, and PTSD and OCD in later chapters. There's also 'generalised anxiety disorder' which is what it says it is, implying free-floating anxiety; its roots lie in the FEAR system (Panksepp 2009).

Panic attacks

These are horribly uncomfortable experiences that can happen without an obvious trigger. "The anxiety boils over with a paralysing, hyperventilating sense of crisis that causes massive activation of the sympathetic nervous system", is Sapolsky's description (2004: 319). The chest tightens, the heart races, the stomach churns, we feel hot and sweaty and wonder if we're going to die.

Repeated panic attacks may lead to chronic anxiety and avoidance behaviours to prevent further attacks (LeDoux 2003). We can become over-sensitive to uncomfortable bodily sensations. If the body becomes a battleground for survival, we may avoid bodily feelings in general because some are uncomfortable, risking a life of rigidity punctuated by periodic outbursts of chaos in the form of further panic attacks (Siegel 2007).

Panic attacks are linked to PANIC, the anticipatory anxiety about further panic attacks to FEAR (Panksepp 2009). The role of PANIC points to separation anxiety in a way that isn't apparent to us, and early separation anxiety may leave us prone to panic attacks later in life. When our pot boils over again, surviving the emotional storm becomes the priority.

Phobias

These are innate fears associated with specific dangers such as heights or spiders. The central part of the amygdala is involved, whereas other amygdala areas are associated with learnt fears (Sapolsky 2017). Phobias are less related to our level of stress than other forms of fear, and less likely to subside with a general lowering of anxiety, so they can reappear out of the blue when we thought we'd conquered them. The FEAR system underlies phobias (Panksepp 2009).

Social anxiety

This is the fear that others will shame us. Polyvagal safety slides into danger, and we become socially inhibited. In the absence of social engagement, affective and somatic regulation are compromised. We misread social cues, by imagining hostility where there's none, for example (Porges 2017). If other people are a threat, the right brain implicit self lacks the external support it needs.

This common form of anxiety disrupts our ability to have relationships (Cozolino 2006). We anticipate hostile reactions from others, orienting attention towards anything that *might* be hostile. We avoid eye contact and thereby miss signs of friendliness. We feel we're on trial ("am I good enough?"), and any negative interaction affects us deeply. Sympathetic arousal pitches us into a right brain biased negative state, disrupting the left hemisphere's ability to speak. So we have nothing to say or, in our disconnected state, we say the 'wrong' thing.

The neurochemistry of social anxiety has some particular features (Cozolino 2006):

- low GABA, which translates as a lack of normal inhibition, so we're prone to acting oddly in company and feeling uncomfortable
- low serotonin, implying agitation
- low dopamine, implying a lack of motivation to seek social reward.

This fits with the neurochemical asymmetry of the hemispheres: more dopamine in the left, more noradrenaline in the right.

Poor treatment in early attachment relationships is implicated. Cozolino suggests that "when parents dominate children through physical or psychological punishment, some young brains may be shaped to experience persistently lower social rank" (2006: 247). 'Persistently lower social rank' gets called a sense of inadequacy.

Anxiety in therapy

Let's explore some ideas for working with anxiety in the light of the science. Two rules of thumb: anxiety is about something, and other feelings lie underneath it.

The felt sense of anxiety

Merely talking *about* anxiety may not help much, but pausing to explore the felt sense of it can ("take a moment to notice how this anxiety feels in your body"). The client's left hemisphere may not know what the anxiety is about, but sitting with the felt sense of it may bring something new. Even when painful feelings or realisations come, there can be relief for, as Gendlin says, "the more directly he attends to . . . the felt meaning, the less his discomfort and anxiety" (1964: 116). It feels better to be connected to feeling and body than disconnected – the hemispheres work together, and life moves forward.

Awareness of breathing

The anxious body keeps the brain in a state of anxiety, but we can change the body to change the brain. One way is by encouraging awareness of breathing. Noticing how far down in the chest the breath goes tends to slow it and deepen it. According to Porges, "a breathing strategy of short exhalations supports anxiety", while lengthening the time spent breathing out can "trigger the physiological state that supports social communication and calmness" (2017: 191–192).

Left-right balance

Anxiety obscures the client's inner world. His left hemisphere avoids it and keeps talking ("Peter, I need you to get rid of my anxiety"). He may complain that he feels cut off inside and his life seems meaningless, yet he won't stop talking long enough for something to unfold from the right. However, he may have good reason to be anxious about 'going inside' since old traumas may lurk there.

If the therapist can tolerate her own anxiety, the client's anxiety will tend to ease over time – a resonance effect. *Her* felt sense of the anxiety may enable her to point to what lies underneath ("I wonder if you feel sad about what happened"). It becomes easier for him to let go to his right hemisphere and body than to continue avoiding anxiety and managing the consequences.

Polyvagal safety and danger

The anxious client may start therapy too immersed in danger and the threat the therapist represents to be able to let go, but safety can grow as trust in the therapeutic relationship builds. When fears can be named, the client can experience the therapist's understanding; he has support in facing what makes him anxious and is no longer alone with his feelings. If he then feels on the edge of danger as the process deepens, a door to his inner world may nevertheless open.

FEAR or PANIC or both?

Both sorts of anxiety leave the client with "the internal feeling of tension and persistent negative affect", and it helps to distinguish them, says Panksepp (2009: 15). FEAR concerns threats the client faces, such as losing his job; reality-testing and preparing for what might happen engages the frontal lobes, so they regulate subcortical fear reactions better. PANIC may point towards attachment relationships, including the therapeutic relationship. The client's fears about the therapist's judgement ("you must think I'm a bad person"), or even rejection ("I'm worried you'll say I can't come any more"), can be addressed.

If the client is in the grip of both FEAR and PANIC, there may be a case for upping the frequency of sessions to contain his anxiety. For example, he may fear his partner ending their relationship because of his uncontrollable anxiety. His nervous system can be calmed in the session, but the effect may not last a whole week until the next session.

Neural integration calms anxiety

Anxiety stems from bottom-up emotional arousal, so top-down inhibition of subcortical areas, especially the amygdala, is needed. This means working with the integrative potential of the frontal lobes by encouraging the client to notice what happens inside when he feels anxiety and to reflect on its meaning. Cozolino recommends shifting the client's experience of anxiety "from an unconscious trigger for avoidance to a conscious cue for curiosity and exploration" (2010: 21). Better neural integration through reduced anxiety translates into better psychological integration of affect and cognition, and of mind and body – and a more productive working partnership of therapist and client.

Depression

Most people experience stress and anxiety, but maybe not depression. Whilst *feeling* depressed is a common experience, *being* depressed is quite different – a deep and persistent low mood as opposed to a transient one. The former can be valuable because it opens a door to the inner world, whereas the latter is a serious illness warranting a visit to the doctor. I experienced it once; it was as if my brain stopped working and I was incapable of functioning normally. The awfulness of it is hard to imagine without having experienced it.

Depression is linked to stress, too much thereof for too long. "Stress is depressing", says LeDoux, and depressed people are awash with cortisol in body and brain (2003: 277). It's also linked to anxiety, so much of it that it stops us sleeping properly. We may be predisposed to depression, but something has to happen to become ill with it. Sapolsky describes it as "a genetic/neurochemical disorder requiring a strong environmental trigger whose characteristic manifestation is an inability to appreciate sunsets" (2004: 272).

Here I'll discuss severe depression.[5] Other manifestations, such as unipolar depression, post-natal depression and seasonal affective disorder, share some of the themes.

What happens in depression

The "defining feature of a major depression is loss of pleasure", says Sapolsky of the sunset non-appreciation aspect (2004: 272). We're engulfed in a right hemisphere dominant state in which positive feelings are nowhere to be found, and even feelings like sadness may be so dampened that we feel little except completely awful – an affectively blunted state (Damasio 2010). With the balance tilted to the right hemisphere, we withdraw from the world, the left's capacity to engage with it greatly diminished.

Some depressed people, however, experience overwhelming grief and despair. They may find it hard to stop crying, and feel guilty about their state. The contrast with the affectively blunted state may reflect different manifestations of depression or differences in people's emotional make-up. Another facet can be sudden outbursts of uncontrolled anger.

The stress response and the sympathetic nervous system are so overactive that we're exhausted (Sapolsky 2004). Despite the high arousal, we scarcely have the energy to get out of bed. Our appetite goes, we eat less and lose weight. Everything requires so much effort and concentration that we may move and speak slowly.[6] This is why severely depressed people, despite feeling suicidal, rarely attempt suicide – or at least not until they begin to recover and have the energy to do so.

High levels of cortisol entering the brain leave us fighting inner battles ("can I do this or not?"). In the frontal lobes, cortisol impairs short-term memory and plays havoc with executive functions such as decision making (LeDoux 2003). At night, we battle with insomnia. We struggle to fall asleep, wake early, and may not return to sleep.

Depression in the brain

Not everything about the right hemisphere is wonderful. More activity there than in the left, particularly in the prefrontal cortex, is a marker for depression and the anxious arousal that accompanies it (McGilchrist 2009). Its naturally pessimistic stance runs riot. Is the right brain struggling in vain for affect and somatic regulation to recover from this unbalanced state? The brain is awash with cortisol from the bloodstream, and it has to adapt to the persistent nature of this hormonal state. The effects are widespread because, as LeDoux explains, "change the synapses in one area, and like dominoes in a line, synapses in others will be altered as well" (2003: 307).

The usual neural suspects are implicated in depression. The amygdala is hyperactive, keeping the stress response firing and cortisol flowing (Sapolsky 2004). The cortisol impairs the ability of the hippocampus both to store and retrieve explicit memories. The resting level of activity in the anterior cingulate tends to be high, reflecting fear and foreboding.

Cortisol also attacks the frontal lobes, with dendrites retracting, synapses disappearing and less glutamate being released; meaning poor attention, short-term memory and decision making (Sapolsky 2017, 2004). There can be a loss of volume from a reduction in glia cells with chronic depression. Depressed people may then find it harder to judge situations and control their reactions to others (Gerhardt 2015).

Neurochemistry

Depression isn't caused by a chemical imbalance in the brain, but it certainly involves one – correlation, not causation. The excess of cortisol biases the brain to keep signalling the adrenal glands to secrete the stuff. It's failure to stop the stress response is reflected in "the person fighting an enormous, aggressive mental battle", says Sapolsky (2004: 276). The battle is to self-regulate, and the brain is losing. The more cortisol is secreted, the less effective it is at stopping the secretion.[7] If we're merely anxious, it copes well enough with noradrenaline, but when it gives up, cortisol takes over and depression results.

Noradrenaline, serotonin and dopamine go haywire. Sapolsky thinks this is because cortisol disrupts them (2004). It's about more than their abnormal levels; for example, "stress alters all sorts of aspects of the synthesis, release, efficacy, and breakdown of serotonin" (2004: 295). A shortage of noradrenaline may explain the slow bodily movement, changes in serotonin, the endless gloomy thoughts and angry outbursts, and dopamine dysfunction the not seeking reward and pleasure.

Watt highlights other aspects of biochemistry (2003). Endorphin levels crash, as do those of oxytocin and prolactin, which may link with the social withdrawal. He thinks these changes to peptides and cortisol trigger the shifts in noradrenaline, serotonin and dopamine (monoamines) in an attempt to compensate. The result is the "complex dysregulation of multiple monoaminergic systems" (2003: 90). Chemical chaos, in other words, and feeling awful.

Depression in the body

Depression is a physical as well as a psychological illness. While the adrenal glands churn out adrenaline and cortisol, the body is exhausted yet remains aroused.

Polyvagal theory links compromised social behaviour in depression with less facial expression and difficulties regulating heart rate (Porges 2011). Porges hypothesises "a down regulation of the social engagement system and atypical coordination between sympathetic and dorsal vagal pathways" (2017: 11). Behaviour oscillates between high levels of sympathetic motor activity and dorsal vagal lethargy, reflecting the aroused yet exhausted state. Social engagement declines, interacting with others feels uncomfortable, and the odd behaviour that ensues reflects polyvagal danger or even life threat.

Porges thinks there may be a mobilised form of depression characterised by anxiety linked with a depressed social engagement system, and an immobilised form characterised by grief with dorsal vagal shutdown (2017a). This distinction could point to the burn-out of an over-loaded life on one hand, and the melancholia of loss on the other – a relationship may be such a large part of our life that losing it means our body shuts down to adapt and recover.

Something else that may be happening in the body is an over-active immune system and inflammation – discussed below.

Depression in childhood

A mother's depression can create stress in her child who may show signs of depression himself: high cortisol, raised heart rate, lower vagal tone (less safety, more danger), high noradrenaline (implying anxiety) and greater right frontal lobe activation (Cozolino 2010). He may make less eye contact and engage less with others – a lack of attachment with mother means less attachment with anyone else.

Depressed mothers find it harder to attune with their babies, and are more prone to be angry at them. They may stimulate them in insensitive or coercive ways, and not play enough with them (Trevarthen 2009). Such early stress can mean problems with neurochemistry and frontal lobe development that presage a vulnerability to depression later in life.

A depressed mother's bias towards right frontal lobe activity may be reflected in her baby's brain (Gerhardt 2015). Such babies are less affectionate and less likely to engage in play with her. Perhaps the mother's under-active left frontal lobe is simply not stimulating her baby's left frontal lobe. An unhealthy tilt towards the right frontal lobe in babies of depressed mothers is described by Schore as "the intergenerational transmission of depression" (2012: 359).

All of this points to the need for therapy to support mothers and babies at the beginning of life. Why leave mothers to this demanding job and then deal with the mental health consequences later in life if the attachment experience can be helped at the outset?

Theories about depression

There are many theories about what causes depression, which suggests it's a broad spectrum illness encompassing reactions to many things in life. Here are the main ideas.

Too much stress for too long

The involvement of cortisol points to the fact that stress is depressing (LeDoux 2003). The relentlessness of human stress, whether from work demands, relationship problems or socioeconomic circumstances, can disrupt homeostasis and neurochemistry over time. And the more stressed we are, the less able we are to make the decisions that would help us recover.

Sapolsky also thinks stress plays a critical role (2004). People experiencing a lot of stressors are more likely to become depressed, people experiencing depression are likely to have had recent and significant stress, and people prone to depression are likely to lack social support and therefore be stressed. Stress can be a 'predisposing factor': when another stressor arrives to tip us over the edge, we get depressed. Being 'vulnerable to depression' means not recovering well from stressful events.

Whether stress is a cause or a predisposing factor, it's the "unifying theme that pulls together" the "disparate threads of biology and psychology" around depression, thinks Sapolsky (2004: 305).

An adaptive reaction to intolerable grief

Neuroscience supports the idea that loss of love underlies depression. Separation distress is the main cause of depression according to Panksepp: "it is the pain of social loss, whether the loss of Mommy when one is young or social status when one is older, that opens the gateway to depression" (2009: 15). This is compatible with the stress theory since loss of social support is stressful. Conversely, social dominance protects against depression, because of the endorphins that accompany power.

Depression may be an adaptive reaction from our evolutionary past, thinks Watt (2003). Separation distress can be intolerably painful for a helpless young animal at risk of dying if not reunited with its parent, so depression takes over to quell the grief. It's evolved into a shutdown state when intense emotional arousal doesn't resolve our need to be cared for again, protecting us despite the misery it brings.

In similar vein, Mark Solms, a Capetown 'neuropsychoanalyst', follows the analytic view that depression is "a pathological form of *mourning*" (2015: 101), and hypothesises that "the core brain basis of depression revolves around the process by which separation distress is normally shut down" (2015: 107). The despair of failing to reunite with the attachment figure resembles severe depression: endorphin levels crash and dopamine-driven SEEKING behaviours stop.

These ideas beg some questions. If depression is about loss of attachment, why does the severely depressed person not respond to love and affection until he gets better again? Also, the protective shutdown state sounds like dissociative collapse (Chapter 7), and surely severe depression differs from dissociation? My own experience was nothing like feeling depressed after ending relationships or being dissociated.

Trauma in childhood

Childhood adversity greatly increases the risk of adult depression because of its effects on the development of subcortical networks that include the amygdala, and on cortisol levels that deplete dopamine (Sapolsky 2017). It can lower the threshold for otherwise manageable stressors to trigger depressive episodes. Early trauma can lead to an unhealthy bias towards right hemisphere activation (probably attempting to self-regulate) and therefore impaired development of frontal lobe networks (Cozolino 2010).

Early trauma can create a sense of helplessness in a child unable to attract emotional support which continues into adulthood. Sapolsky describes depression as "a pathological sense of loss of control" (2017: 197). We become prone to giving up, and stressful events beyond our control may then awaken an existing vulnerability, leading to depression.

Genetics

Genes can increase the risk of depression, but only in stressful environments (Sapolsky 2004). They're about tendencies and vulnerabilities, and only rarely about inevitability. One gene in particular causes serotonin to be removed from synapses, but it only increases the risk of depression when coupled with trauma in childhood (Sapolsky 2017).[8]

Inflammation

A recent theory is that depression can arise from inflammation (an immune reaction) in the body. Depression is "robustly associated with increased levels of inflammatory proteins in the blood", and there's "strong evidence that inflammation can precede or anticipate depression", says psychiatrist Edward Bullmore in his book *The Inflamed Mind* (2018: 144). These inflammatory proteins are called *cytokines.* It used to be thought that the blood-brain barrier protected the brain from whatever was circulating in the blood, but it's now known that cytokines circulating in it can affect the brain: "inflammation can cause changes in the brain that in turn cause depressive changes in our states of mind" (2018: 144).

Others have focused on the power of an inflamed gut to inflict its feelings on the brain. Enders, for example, thinks an unhappy gut can mean an unhappy mind: "we should not always blame depression on the brain or on our life circumstances" (2015: 130). Is it a coincidence that antidepressants target serotonin and 95% of serotonin is found in the intestinal walls? Inflammatory chemicals can make intestinal walls so permeable that they leak out into the blood supply to affect the brain. "Depression is an inflammatory disease", thinks neurologist David Perlmutter (2015: 75).

So it appears that depression can have physiological as well as psychological causes. My own experience, including brief depressive episodes following flu, have persuaded me that losing my appetite and not enjoying my food are closely related to mood changes and cognitive depletion at these times. Even if the trigger for depression is psychological, the gut may play a reinforcing role.

Sleep disturbance

Insomnia is usually considered a symptom of depression, although my own experience suggested it caused it. First, I was stressed (by work, family and personal upheavals); then I became anxious about everything I had to do and started waking early; and then my brain became exhausted and largely ground to a halt.

Conclusion

Depression is a complex as well as a miserable phenomenon. A way around the psychological versus physiological causes debate is to follow Watt's suggestion to see it as a "final common pathway" for brain and body to deal with a number of "critical variables" in life, rather than as a "single neurobiological derailment" with defined causes (2003: 91). Its complexity arises from, as Sapolsky says, "the interaction between the ambiguous experiences that life throws at us and the biology of our vulnerabilities and resiliencies that determines which of us fall prey to this awful disease" (2004: 308).

Antidepressants and other treatments

There's no medication that blocks the effects of cortisol in the brain, so antidepressants instead target a consequence of excess cortisol – monoamine disruption, or messed up serotonin, noradrenaline and dopamine. Both tricyclics (e.g. amitriptyline) and SSRIs (the modern favourite) do this. Cortisol levels presumably get repaired along the way.

SSRI stands for 'selective serotonin reuptake inhibitor'. These drugs inhibit the 'reuptake' of serotonin floating in synapses, prolonging its beneficial effects – more bangs for your neuromodulating buck. The greater availability of serotonin enhances gene activation and protein synthesis, persuading the brain to become more plastic so it can overcome its dilapidated state (LeDoux 2003). Some of the newer antidepressants also work on noradrenaline or dopamine. They *all* work by changing the levels of one or more of these neuromodulators (Sapolsky 2004). No one knows who will respond best to which antidepressant, and St John's Wort may be equally effective. SSRIs do not work for everyone, and when they do their effects may be partial or temporary (Solms 2015).

Antidepressants are absorbed into the gut lining (intestinal walls) where most serotonin is found. Apart from possible side effects such as nausea, whether they affect the brain because of their effect on the gut is unclear; they may reduce inflammation in the gut and have a knock-on effect on the brain (Perlmutter 2015).

Other treatments

ECT treatment is still used in psychiatric hospitals and sometimes seems to have positive results, but no one knows exactly how it works (Sapolsky 2004). A newer hi-tech treatment is transcranial magnetic stimulation (TMS): by increasing or decreasing excitability in targeted areas of the cortex, it can restore left-right balance in the frontal lobes to ease depression (Cozolino 2017).

Diet and exercise both help to recover from depression, which implies that there are ways to treat the body that serve to treat the brain as well.

Depression in therapy

A mild depression may be an opportunity for the client to venture into his inner world, as if his right hemisphere is insisting that his left pass the baton for a while. This is often about the need to mourn recent or past losses, or losses of longed-for life experiences that won't happen. The left-right balance may have shifted somewhat to the right, but his brain is functioning 'normally'. The more he understands the psychological value of feeling depressed sometimes, the better.

A severe depression is another matter. It's an illness that needs treatment, in which neither cognitive nor affective interventions are likely to work as the brain is too exhausted to respond to them. Neuroscience warns us not to over-psychologise: we must address the illness. We can tell the difference between mild and severe by enquiring into the state of the client's autonomic nervous system as reflected in his sleep. Having only a few hours' sleep each night, waking in the middle of the night and not returning to sleep, is debilitating. Add to this feeling dreadful, not enjoying socialising, the mind struggling to keep up, and it can be obvious to both client and therapist that he's ill.

A severe depression leaves the client incapacitated, without the resources to explore his inner world. If he's not taking medication, the therapist can talk to him about doing so – his feelings about it, and his understanding of how antidepressants work. It's not her job to give medical advice, but she probably has more time than his doctor to discuss the matter with him. Antidepressants are quite effective for many people, helping them to sleep again so they can benefit from therapy. The therapist can also address ways the client can help himself with exercise, diet, sleep habits and making efforts to socialise.

Can a depressive brain be transformed?

Depression is more likely to occur in adults who suffered childhood trauma, so the question arises whether a brain prone to depression can become less vulnerable. Panksepp hedges his bets: "the massive plasticity of the brain suggests that this achievement is likely, albeit not to the extent as occurs during early development" (2009: 22). We can be optimistic about the possibility of lasting changes, but also realistic – we should avoid creating unrealistic expectations. Many factors go into whatever the outcome may be: the severity of early trauma, the client's willingness to engage in depth therapy, and the success of the therapeutic relationship in addressing both the roots of the depressive tendency and ideas for countering it in the future.

Conclusion

A summary of this chapter might go as follows ... Some stress and anxiety is part of life, keeping us on our toes and guarding against complacency. When some becomes a lot, the left hemisphere may ignore the right as it focuses attention on whatever is provoking stress and anxiety. But when a lot becomes too much, the brain flips into a right hemisphere dominant state, struggling for affective and somatic regulation. If it can't calm the autonomic nervous system, depression may take hold.

Therapists work to help clients lower their stress and anxiety levels, and emerge from depression. Paradoxically, they also have to make therapy sufficiently stressful that real transformation can happen, and evoke enough anxiety for clients to discover what lies underneath. Sometimes they have to help them weather depressive episodes and explore new inner depths.

The therapist must manage her own stress and anxiety in the room, and be open to her own depressive tendencies. She can help the client be aware of his stress and anxiety, how they feel in his body and their effects on his mind. They sometimes need to be an element of the therapeutic relationship so he can reflect on their source and allow fresh responses to unfold.

Finally, stress and fear can be so severe that the nervous system is overwhelmed and we're pitched into trauma – which we'll examine next.

Notes

1 The hypothalamus releases corticotropin releasing hormone (CRH), and within 15 seconds CRH triggers the pituitary to release corticotropin, another hormone also known as ACTH, which enters the bloodstream. Finally, when ACTH reaches the adrenal gland, cortisol is released within minutes into the bloodstream. (Sapolsky 2004). Most writers talk about cortisol, but Sapolsky refers to 'glucocorticoids', the family to which cortisol belongs. Sticking with cortisol seems an acceptable simplification for our purposes.

2 It seems we can be in a left hemisphere biased state overall while the right hemisphere is triggering a moderate stress response.
3 'Fear extinction' happens when the prefrontal cortex is able to inhibit the basolateral amygdala, where stress raises levels of brain-derived neurotrophic factor (BDNF), encouraging dendritic growth to power the amygdala (Sapolsky 2017).
4 Violent psychopaths don't exhibit fear (Sapolsky 2017).
5 Severe depression used to be called 'clinical' depression, and its official DSM term is now 'major depressive disorder'.
6 The technical term for this slow movement and speech is 'psychomotor retardation' (Sapolsky 2004).
7 The reason why the brain doesn't self-regulate to stop cortisol release is that sustained stress reduces the number of cortisol receptors in the brain, making it less sensitive to the amount of cortisol swilling around (Sapolsky 2004).
8 The gene in question is 5HTT (Sapolsky 2017).

Chapter 7

Trauma and dissociation

Introduction

The world is full of trauma, and now we understand more about helping people recover from it. Unresolved trauma underlies much of what goes wrong in our lives, and maybe what goes wrong for humanity as a whole. As Levine says, "trauma defeats life" (2010: 31).

Trauma is a big issue for therapy. If stress, anxiety and depression are the main afflictions clients bring to therapy, trauma and dissociation are the psychological minefields therapists must help them navigate. Trauma experts tell us we must approach trauma differently from everything else clients bring to therapy. Neuroscience supports this advice, because trauma and dissociation imply a serious breakdown in neural integration. The normal top-bottom functioning of the right brain-body ensemble fragments in trauma, and this means front-back and left-right integration also suffer. Polyvagal safety and the felt sense give way to danger and life threat.

The areas of therapy where neuroscience has arguably had the most effect on good practice are trauma and dissociation. This has much to do with the contributions of some American trauma therapists, including Bessel van der Kolk, Pat Ogden, Peter Levine and Babette Rothschild, who bring neuroscience into their training courses on trauma.

Trauma can happen anytime in life, including when we're most dependent on others as babies and infants. A number of terms are now used to distinguish trauma at different life stages; here I separate trauma in adulthood from trauma in childhood much of which is 'early attachment trauma'. They present different challenges in the therapy room. Cozolino says trauma lies on a spectrum of severity and, in general, "the earlier, more severe, and more prolonged the trauma, the more negative and far reaching its effects" (2017: 323). And trauma may or may not involve dissociation, but dissociation always involves trauma. The better we understand them, the better equipped we are to work with them.

If I reflect on personal traumas, certain memories come to mind: a car accident where I escaped unhurt, thinking (briefly) I was going to die during an earthquake in California, my father dying when I was 21.

I don't think any of these scary and distressing events amounted to trauma. Yet I often used to dissociate in social situations: intense discomfort, not being fully present, wanting to get away and be alone. Where was the trauma? I think it lay in my relationship with my mother, and it probably started when I was very young.

There is undoubtedly more trauma amongst people generally than is recognised, and certainly amongst people who come to therapy. Is trauma the exception or the rule in what clients present with? It's obvious that someone who's been tortured or raped is traumatised. What's harder to appreciate is that someone who grew up in an apparently 'normal' family and shows signs of anxiety or depression is also struggling with the after-effects of trauma.

What is trauma?

Trauma is often linked with overwhelming emotion. But is being overwhelmed with grief or anger, for example, traumatic? The storm may subside soon enough and our equilibrium return. Trauma, surely, is about being overwhelmed by *fear*. It's also associated with threats to our well-being, but do they necessarily traumatise us? We may be fully aware of what happens during the experience, and our fear may ease when the threat passes. We may describe intense experiences as 'traumatic', but not be left with the after-effects of trauma.

The state of the nervous system sheds light on what trauma really is. While stress includes the movement of fight or flight, trauma involves becoming immobile in a state of paralysis or helplessness, or both. Levine explains:

> trauma occurs when we are intensely frightened and are either physically restrained or perceive that we are trapped. We freeze in paralysis and/or collapse in overwhelming helplessness.
>
> (2010: 48)

One of my earliest memories is of standing at the top of the stairs after going to bed and trying to call out to my parents. Nothing came out of my mouth, I was rooted to the spot. It may have been a dream, but whether I was dreaming or awake, it suggests trauma: fear, immobility, paralysis. "Fear crosses the line into trauma", says Cozolino, resulting in "fragmentation of sensory, emotional, and cognitive processing" (2017: 323). The right brain-body ensemble comes apart.

In a traumatic experience, normal top-down cortical integration gives way to bottom-up subcortical reactions. An apparent threat to our safety elicits "subcortical mammalian defences" that "*disable* cortical activity", according to Ogden (2009: 207). Our evolutionary history takes over with reactions that are reflexive, not voluntary. The right brain that normally keeps inner and outer worlds aligned in safety goes into survival mode, and we may dissociate.

Another factor in trauma is whether we seek support to restore our sense of safety. An experience may be traumatic, but if we have help to recover afterwards we don't remain traumatised. Inner and outer worlds come back together in the right brain. "Traumatised human beings recover in the context of relationships", says van der Kolk, and "survivors require the presence of familiar people, faces, and voices" (2014: 210). It's other people that restore our sense of safety, so if the trauma occurs in a relationship, recovery is less likely. This is why early attachment trauma can be so damaging: if the people we instinctively turn to for safety are the same people who trigger the subcortical reactions, we may disconnect from our feelings and dissociate. The right brain-body ensemble fragments, and afterwards the left hemisphere defends against this damaged state re-occurring.

So trauma involves fear, life threat, immobility and a lack of support. Whether we should extend the meaning to include habitual fight-flight-freeze reactions is debatable.

Survival reactions

When we're frightened, subcortical reactions are triggered. Ogden organises these into a scheme tied into polyvagal theory (2009). If social engagement is impossible, the ventral vagus gives way to sympathetic arousal and a danger state; if neither fight nor flight are possible, the dorsal vagus generates a life threat state and immobilisation. Different people may react differently to apparently similar frightening events, depending on their (unconscious) perception and previous trauma history (Porges 2017), but these mammalian reactions nevertheless shed light on much human behaviour.

1. Relationship-seeking actions: social engagement

The best reaction is to seek safety in social engagement with someone we trust. Young children cry and call out for their parents. If this strategy (involving PANIC) works in early attachment relationships, we're better able to use it later in life. Faced with a threatening person, for example, we may be able to 'talk them down' from their fight state into social engagement, using our cortex to get us out of trouble.

2. Mobilising reactions: danger

When social engagement isn't possible, sympathetic arousal and fight-flight kick in. If escape is possible, flight (involving FEAR) enables us to run *from* danger or *to* safety. Flight impulses are reflected in leg movements or when our bodies twist, turn or back away. But if we're trapped, or if aggression seems worthwhile, fight (involving RAGE) may predominate. Fight impulses manifest as tense arms and shoulders, making fists, eyes narrowing, jaw clenching, struggling or kicking. Procedural memory may be available. For example, escaping a situation by driving a car: we remember how to drive even though we're scared and unable to think straight.

3. *Immobilising reactions: life threat*

If fight or flight aren't possible, such as when we're very young and unable to resist or run away, immobilising is the only option left. This can manifest in three ways:

- *Alert immobility*: freezing.[1] There's both sympathetic and parasympathetic arousal, so we remain still except for eye movements, with shallow breathing. Heart rate rises, muscles are tense, we're hyper-vigilant, yet we feel paralysed.
- *Floppy immobility*: a last resort of helplessness and submission.[2] The parasympathetic and dorsal vagus take over so we don't move, muscles go limp, heart rate and blood pressure drop, and we may faint. We don't engage, collapsing instead into shutdown with very low arousal. We detach emotionally and dissociate as endorphins are released, so we may not feel pain if we're injured. Afterwards, we may not remember what happened.
- *Submissive behaviour*: passive avoidance after previous trauma, an attempt to protect ourselves by avoiding further aggressive reactions from others. We avoid eye contact and act in subservient and compliant ways.

Porges's view is that "some reactions to traumatic events are highly mobilised, defensive, highly anxious reactive behaviours, while other reactions are manifested totally in immobilisation" (2017: 165). Both mobilising and immobilising reactions are subcortically controlled, with growing degrees of cortical disabling as they become more extreme. They probably underlie most deficits in neural integration during child development. Our brains evolved with cortical capacities above subcortical ones, so when the latter disable the former, the human brain pays a heavy price.

Not recovering from mobilising fight-flight reactions and continuing to feel unsafe may mean we react this way to future threats, even minor ones. But not recovering from the immobilising reactions leave us at risk of the more serious after-effects of dissociation and right brain 'dis-integration' discussed below.

The key point is that these reactions are evoked not only during a traumatic experience but for as long as the trauma remains unresolved. These "instinctive defensive and protective reactions ... persist decades after the original threatening events are over" (Ogden, Minton & Pain 2006: 85).

We may re-enact them for the rest of our lives, and they lie at the heart of many difficulties clients bring to therapy.

Trauma in the brain

The more frightened and helpless we become, the further down the hierarchy of survival reactions we go. The locus of control descends along the top-bottom axis, from the frontal lobes where we can maintain social engagement despite feeling afraid, to the brainstem where the reactions are triggered by specific areas of the PAG. Each reaction has an "exquisite" mechanism for generating "its particular motor routine and physiological accompaniment", says Damasio (2010: 113).

During a traumatic experience, the power of subcortical reactions can mean that awareness disconnects from feeling and body, as integration turns into fragmentation. Awareness narrows down to the threat and any avenues of escape. Afterwards, our brains function in separate compartments due to the breakdown of sensory integration during trauma in the thalamus, which normally combines sensory signals into a coherent experience (van der Kolk 2014). Sights, sounds and smells remain as dissociated fragments in the brain. This is how trauma is remembered implicitly, with powerful emotions but no narrative.

Trauma makes it more likely that "the balance and coordination between left and right will be disrupted", says Cozolino (2017: 364). The right hemisphere may react to reminders of the experience; flashbacks arise there and intrude into the left which is unable to make sense of them. Until we're supported to face what happened and form a narrative, right may struggle with affective and somatic regulation. Left has less capacity to organise the experience into a sequence that makes sense, says van der Kolk: "without sequencing we can't identify cause and effect, grasp the long-term effects of our actions, or create coherent plans for the future" (2014: 45). Left may also have less capacity to articulate feelings and to realise when the past is being re-enacted.

When our nervous system reacts with life threat and immobilisation, there's 'biobehavioural shutdown' (Porges 2017). Less oxygenated blood goes to the brain, causing a worsening of cognitive functions and sometimes fainting. Our ability to evaluate situations and make decisions wanes. After the trauma, we may feel uncomfortable in public places or if others get physically close, and we may develop intestinal problems. These are all characteristic of a massive reaction of the dorsal vagus; neural regulation changes so we don't regain our former homeostasis.

The high stress levels in trauma disrupt neurochemistry in ways that may become chronic (Cozolino 2017):

- *high noradrenaline* accompanies fight-flight reactions: if it remains high, we're prone to anxiety, irritability and being easily startled

- *high dopamine*, correlating with hyper-vigilance, paranoia, and perceptual distortions
- *low serotonin*, correlating with high arousal, irritability, violence and depression
- *high cortisol* disrupts the hippocampus and therefore memory, as well as the immune system
- *high levels of endorphins* cease their feel-good effects and undermine cognition, memory and reality-testing, and may mean emotional blunting and dissociation.

These changes in neurochemistry and neural networks bias the brain towards "sustained arousal, hyper-vigilance, and chronic anxiety", says Cozolino (2017: 320). An aspect of this is the inhibition of the *default mode network*, which means that even the resting brain is in a more stressed state.[3] If chronically inhibited, empathy, introspection and a coherent sense of self are impaired: "chronic inhibition of this important network can drastically change the experience of being human" (2017: 320), especially when it happens early in life.

The right brain-body ensemble is prone to going into hyper-aroused fight-flight states, and/or very low arousal states of collapse. It reacts and overwhelms, or it fragments and dissociates. Left-right constellations (e.g. "let's not go there, I don't want to feel uncomfortable") form to protect against all this. The survival personality can't see the point of risking repeat performances, though they inevitably happen sooner or later.

Trauma in the body

With fight-flight, the body mobilises a lot of energy in sympathetic arousal. We "duck, dodge, twist, stiffen and retract", says Levine (2010: 23), but if the threat remains, we become 'scared stiff' and freeze, or we collapse in defeat. It doesn't help that our fearful expression causes others to react to us with their own discomfort, fear or even paralysis, as if trauma were catching.

If we immobilise, the result is either panic and agitation as cortisol pours into the bloodstream, or collapse (van der Kolk 2014). This may carry on, such that many people "have no idea why they respond to some minor irritation as if they were about to be annihilated" (2014: 66). Without recovery, we may oscillate between hyper-arousal, with disruptive emotional reactions, and very low arousal, feeling empty and dead inside (Ogden et al. 2006). If we develop submissive behaviours, we may duck our head, avoid eye contact and have a bowed back when facing a perpetrator, as if making ourselves look smaller and less noticeable.

Trauma tends to evoke shame, especially if we have an immobilising reaction. "There is an *intrinsic* association of shame and trauma", says Levine (2010: 60). Shoulders drop, heart rate slows, eye gaze is averted, we feel nauseous.

Unresolved trauma

Without recovery, the same subcortical reactions are prone to firing off in response to perceived threats. We can't think our way out of them, so we feel inadequate and blame ourselves. The reactions that helped us survive the trauma become liabilities (Ogden et al. 2006). It makes no difference to realise we're over-reacting. We become hyper-aroused, feeling overwhelmed and lashing out angrily with minimal provocation, or go into low arousal, feeling little and collapsing in the face of minor threats. Submissive behaviour can become ingrained, and may have the perverse effect of encouraging others, via right brain resonance, to abuse us again.

We may "remain stuck in a kind of limbo", not fully re-engaging in life, says Levine (2010: 24). Paralysis can become a 'default response' to emotion; for example, when sexual excitement turns to fear and revulsion. The paralysis manifests as feeling numb and being shut down, or as depression. We may function relatively normally in a 'functional freeze', but lack any zest for life, surviving it rather than enjoying it.

Unresolved trauma "disrupts integrated neural processing so that conscious awareness is split from emotional and physiological experiences", says Cozolino (2017: 340). The changes in neurochemistry mentioned above, and the poor integration of the hemispheres, may affect our relationships and our connection with our body. The brain may go round in circles with repetitive mental activity: repetitive play in children, repetitive dreams and thoughts for both children and adults (Wilkinson 2006).

Post-traumatic stress disorder

Post-traumatic stress following a trauma eventually becomes PTSD if we don't recover. Dissociating after a traumatic experience is predictive of developing PTSD later on (Cozolino 2017). Sometimes non-recovery from trauma in adulthood points to having suffered trauma in childhood that has left us vulnerable to being re-traumatised. PTSD is sometimes subdivided into 'simple PTSD', referring to a single trauma in adulthood, and 'complex PTSD' both for multiple traumas in adulthood and trauma in childhood.

The following can happen in the brain with PTSD:

- the amygdala over-reacts to slightly fearful stimuli, is slow to calm down afterwards, and becomes larger (Sapolsky 2017)
- relationships are endangered by the social engagement system having a low threshold for further fight-flight or life threat reactions (Porges 2017)
- over-activity in networks mapping bodily states, implying the frontal lobes not playing a role (Cozolino 2017)

- affect regulation is undermined by increased metabolism in the right prefrontal cortex and in limbic areas (Cozolino 2017).[4]

The right hemisphere may intrude on the left with flashbacks, negative emotional reactions and somatic sensations.

Trauma in childhood

Trauma is often discussed in terms of gazelles being chased by lions across the African savannah, or of single events such as car accidents. But most trauma in the therapy room happened in childhood, much of it repeatedly in attachment relationships in the early years. This broadens the scope of trauma to include, as Cozolino says, "the everyday interactions during childhood that we depend on for our survival" (2017: 322), and we must consider its effects on the *developing* brain. These are likely to be more damaging than when the brain is mature: the immense plasticity of the developing brain means that it adapts to trauma, but at a cost.[5] If the child's attachment experience is traumatic, the stage is set for trouble in the right brain-body ensemble and the implicit self that may last a lifetime. Depending on the severity of such trauma, it can result in a spectrum of conditions from 'normal' neurosis to psychosis.

Attachment trauma

Parents can frighten their children, and the relationship that should provide safety may be experienced as threatening. Repeated misattunements or being left to cry for long periods can be traumatising. The parents' own unhealed attachment trauma may be evoked by their child's distress, so that they react angrily, over-react by screaming at him, or become unresponsive, freezing or even dissociating (Schore 2012). Such responses can be traumatic if the child isn't helped to feel safe again.

The dorsal vagus is active at birth, and the younger and more insecurely attached the child is, the more likely he will respond to stress with paralysis (Levine 2010). Parents can love their children but nevertheless instil fear in them, leading to what Gerhardt calls a "poisonous concoction of love combined with harm" (2015: 171). My mother loved me, but her love was regularly trumped by her fear and hostility when I wasn't the child she wanted me to be; I grew up feeling wanted but not loved.

The infant's receptive right brain matches the rhythms of his parent's hyper-arousal and low arousal, which Schore terms "the intergenerational transmission of attachment trauma" (2012: 81). He may experience long periods of intense negative feelings. These rhythms and feelings create patterns of implicit memory in his right brain that are re-enacted with other people later in life. They become his working model of relationship, neural mappings of his self interacting with another and of "how it *feels* to be with another person" (Gerhardt 2015: 173). He may expect, unconsciously, psychological mistreatment in later relationships.

When trauma starts in early attachment, we believe we're bad people – why else would we feel so bad? We have no capacity to perceive the failings of those who are supposed to care for us. This cognitive conclusion, and the shame it engenders, is the only way to make sense of our affective experience. But the reality is that we've been maltreated in ways that can be hidden from the world beyond the family, and from our own understanding of ourselves.

If attachment is traumatic, we lack a foundation of safety in our right brain and go through life more vulnerable to being victimised and suffering further trauma and the accompanying shame (Levine 2010). Our capacity to recover from frightening experiences is diminished. New trauma can get heaped onto old.

Neglect and abuse

A child may be abused physically or sexually, or emotionally when the parent dumps their own uncontrolled emotion onto him. Abuse often triggers hyper-arousal, while neglect can mean low arousal. But repeated abuse generally results in immobilising and dissociation (Ogden et al. 2006). Children normally submit to abuse rather than fight back (however, I've seen people who did fight or escape, at least sometimes).

"Severe neglect may be the most damaging of all forms of early stress", thinks Cozolino (2017: 306). This is because social brains need stimulation to grow, and there's evidence of 'neural atrophy' in severely neglected children, probably correlating with sensory, cognitive and relationship problems. Smaller corpus callosums have been found in people abused or neglected in childhood. Early stress affects sensory networks in the brain, with evidence that auditory pathways in the left hemisphere can be disrupted and grey matter in the occipital lobes (vision) reduced. The hippocampi of people who suffered childhood trauma have been found to be smaller than average due to the damaging effects of cortisol.

These developmental deficits pave the way for poor left-right integration and problems with affect regulation and self-esteem for life (Cozolino 2017). The tendency to fragmentation in the right brain makes it harder to understand our feelings as we grow up. We lack a secure foundation of mind-body integration, and are vulnerable to further traumatic experiences later in life.

Traumatic memory

Narrative memory forms *after* an experience, but with trauma this may not happen. The experience may have been so painful that we avoid stirring up further emotion, and there may be gaps in what we recall. In childhood, this can be exacerbated by not having a safe attachment figure to turn to for help. But we usually have at least *some* explicit memory of a traumatic experience, even from childhood – although not from very early childhood when the hippocampus is insufficiently developed. When the hippocampus *is* able to form explicit memories, the stress of trauma can release so much cortisol that its capacity is impaired (LeDoux 2003). One way or another, we don't tell our story.

Whilst narrative memory integrates across the neural axes, traumatic memory mainly consists of fragments in the right brain-body ensemble. Therefore, as van der Kolk says, the implicit memory of trauma "is encoded in visceral experiences such as heartbreaking and gut-wrenching emotions, in autoimmune disorders, and in skeletal-muscular problems" (2011: XIV).

When people *do* recall traumatic fragments, there's generally a shift to right hemisphere activity, implying that the content is more emotional than verbal (Ogden et al. 2006). Is this why when people first speak about a traumatic experience, listening to them, and resonating with their raw emotion, can be so moving?

Flashbacks

Flashbacks are a re-experiencing of a dissociated traumatic fragment, and imply dissociation during or soon after a trauma (Rothschild 2000). They can manifest as nightmares. They're usually visual or auditory, but over-emotional reactions, and somatic symptoms such as unexplained pain, might be considered flashbacks as well. They can also be behavioural, as when young children act out, unable to verbalise traumatic experiences. Flashbacks are triggered by the amygdala in reaction to external or internal sensory cues.

Brain imaging of PTSD patients experiencing flashbacks shows right brain firing (van der Kolk 2014). There's no context to accompany the vivid sensory fragments, implying fragmented subcortical memory not integrated via the hippocampus with the cortex (Cozolino 2017). So it seems that they're happening in the present. Flashbacks correlate with less blood flow to Broca's area in the left hemisphere, which may account for the experience of 'speechless terror'.

Dissociation is often accompanied by a deadening of feeling and bodily awareness, yet flashbacks involve hyper-arousal and heightened feeling (Ogden et al. 2006). This suggests an uncomfortable shifting between low arousal states in which we feel sufficiently in control, and hyper-arousal ones when we don't because of having involuntary flashbacks. They're sensory experiences that we spontaneously *re-experience*, whereas explicit memories are narratives that include sensory elements of the experience and that we *recall*.

Enactments

Fragments of traumatic experience that aren't integrated afterwards live on in the nervous system as 'dissociated' emotions, sensations and implicit memories. Enactments are a revival of the trauma, previously frozen, and are specifically related to dissociation (Schore 2012). Those of a hyper-aroused nature from fight-flight reactions tend to erupt: we act something out in ways that seem unconnected to the reality of the current situation and that we don't understand ("where did *that* come from?"). Those of a very low arousal nature from life threat reactions pitch us into dissociation. These two possibilities can overlap since an enactment may trigger dissociation.

Enactments happen both in the therapy room and outside it – in fact, the world is probably full of people acting out old traumatic fragments, as if this were perfectly normal. They tend to explode suddenly, and normally involve fight and RAGE, or flight and FEAR – strong or overwhelming dissociated affects (Schore 2012). There's a disconnect between cortical and subcortical networks in the right brain, so cortical areas fail to regulate the subcortical explosion. Dissociated grief can also explode, but this is more relational and invites healing – fight-flight is relational but in a potentially destructive way. Self-harm and suicide attempts may be considered as enactments.

Jung's account of this phenomenon is an interesting perspective on what happens with fragments of dissociated experience from a pre-neuroscientific age:

> a traumatic complex brings about dissociation of the psyche. The complex is not under the control of the will . . . Its autonomy consists in its power to manifest itself independently of the will and even in direct opposition to conscious tendencies: it forces itself tyrannically upon the conscious mind. The explosion of affect is a complete invasion of the individual, it pounces upon him like an enemy or a wild animal . . . the typical traumatic affect is represented in dreams as a wild and dangerous animal – a striking illustration of its autonomous nature when split off from consciousness.
>
> (cited in Kalsched 1996: 13)

Dissociation

Dissociation is a horrible state of mind in which we're cut off from ourselves and from others, from the world and from life. Our mind goes blank, the felt sense evaporates, we're all at sea, and shame is the only feeling left. It's where a lack of integration of experiencing in the nervous system gets serious: "the fragmentation of what should be experienced as a whole – the mental separation of components of experience that would ordinarily be processed together", in McGilchrist's words (2009: 235–236). The right brain is unable to weave inner and outer worlds together, leaving the left hemisphere to stumble on alone.

We may dissociate *during* a traumatic experience, which may or may not lead to unresolved trauma and dissociation later on (Levine 2010). It's possible to regain a sense of safety and recover, creating a narrative from the parts of the experience we recall. But if we dissociate *after* a traumatic experience, longer-term problems with dissociation are likely to occur (Rothschild 2000).

Normal experiences such as day-dreaming, where our attention wanders but returns to the here-and-now when needed, are sometimes called 'dissociation'. Perhaps this is the left hemisphere taking a break from focused attention, letting the right drift freely. Traumatic dissociation is something quite different. There's "a sense of being cut off . . . from one's feelings, and from embodied existence, a loss of depth emotion and capacity for empathy, a fragmentation of the sense of self", says McGilchrist (2009: 406). Our mind doesn't just disconnect from body and feeling, it largely stops working.

The flow of experiencing that normally comes as a whole fragments in dissociation, implying a breakdown of integration in the right hemisphere (McGilchrist 2009). Inner and outer worlds are no longer in sync with each other. The result is "a lack of continuity between thoughts, memories, surroundings, and actions" that then creates problems in relationships and in normal functioning, according to Porges (2017: 11). Hence, we can have traumatic memory fragments that we can't piece together to create a narrative of what happened. Complete amnesia is the most extreme form of this.

Dissociation is an adaptive reaction to life threat situations; we're immobile, but with some oxygen intake and blood flow (Porges 2017). Cognitive processing grinds towards a halt as the nervous system backtracks through evolution and survival reactions take over. We feel disoriented, as affective and cognitive neural networks cease linking together (Cozolino 2010). We suffer an inner death, as if nature were protecting us from the agony of approaching actual death.

Dissociation is not a psychological defence

Dissociation is often described as a defence. Gerhardt, for example, writes that it's "one of the most primitive defences against mental pain" (2015: 188), and Jungian analyst Donald Kalsched even calls it "a trick the psyche plays on itself" (1996: 13). But it's quite unlike the left hemisphere defences of suppression, avoidance and denial, over which we have a degree of control. Dissociation happens beyond our control in the right brain after trauma has overwhelmed our defences; we can't decide to stop dissociating. It may be nature's way of protecting us against something acutely unbearable, but it's not a psychological defence. The neurobiological explanation fits the experience of dissociation better than the psychological ones.

However, we do defend against dissociation. If we have unresolved trauma, we may avoid experiences and talking about subjects that might lead to dissociating again, for good reason. And we can always resort to denial of what's happening or has happened, however ridiculous this might look to others. The defence enables us to keep going, at a cost, which is preferable to dissociating and being mired in shame.

Dissociation replaces repression

The term 'repression' gets used in everyday speech to mean suppressing feelings that arise in the right hemisphere, enter awareness and unsettle the left. So we 'repress' our feelings. But the term can encourage the idea that we must have consigned unbearable feelings to a dark forgotten place and should go hunting around inside to find them. This isn't what happens in practice.

Fragments of traumatic experience that aren't pieced together afterwards may remain in a dissociated state in the right brain. When triggered, they return as disturbing enactments, or as unexplained emotions and sensations. They were probably never in our awareness at the time of the trauma, so imagining we 'repressed' them is misleading and reflects a left hemisphere conscious bias. Sometimes in therapy they re-emerge, but this tends to be an unfolding process rather than a discovery.

Schore thinks that "unconscious affects can best be understood not as repressed but as dissociated affects" (2009: 115). Whilst suppression involves the left hemisphere inhibiting feelings arising in the right brain, dissociation reflects a 'dis-integration' within the right brain in which trauma fragments don't come together in conscious experiencing. Cozolino takes a similar line: "simultaneous top-down and left-right inhibition is likely responsible for what Freud called repression" (2010: 158).

Structural dissociation

This concept is used by Ogden to describe divisions in the personality resulting from dissociation (Ogden et al. 2006). She builds on the work of other therapists going back to Charles Myers, the British psychiatrist who coined the term 'shell shock' after World War One while treating traumatised soldiers. The key divide is between the 'emotional person' in the right brain who periodically re-enacts the trauma, and the 'apparently normal person' in the left hemisphere who tries to carry on with daily life (an example of psychological terms that make perfect sense!). The emotional person is driven by their trauma fragments, while the apparently normal person tries to live his life avoiding anything that might re-trigger the trauma, often unsuccessfully.

"The structural dissociation between different parts of the personality represents a profound integrative failure", write Ogden et al. (2006: 137). Not only is there a divide between the apparently normal and the emotional parts, but there can be a number of emotional parts, each driven by a different survival reaction. So a 'fight' part might make the person tense and abrasive when it erupts, while a 'freeze' part might make him immobile and acutely anxious. The division really lies between each of these 'encapsulated action tendencies', so that the person is unable to move easily between social engagement and moments of anxiety or anger. The impulse to fight or flee or freeze isn't integrated into the rest of the personality and isn't available for frontal lobe reflection, because this requires facing the old trauma and everything it evokes.

Dissociation in the brain

Dissociation involves a "dis-integration of the right brain", says Schore (2012: 83). It can happen during trauma, and afterwards due to dissociated emotional fragments that remain in implicit memory. The right brain's capacity to integrate external stimuli from the environment with internal stimuli from the body, moment to moment, is diminished, the subcortical survival reaction of immobilising preventing the cortex from fulfilling its normal integrating function.[6] Affect regulation gives way to affect dysregulation in the form of very low arousal; mind, body and feeling come apart at the seams.

The breakdown in integration is especially between the right hemisphere and right subcortical areas, Schore believes, which results in a "collapse of the implicit self" and of both subjectivity and intersubjectivity (2012: 83–84). Our felt sense of what's happening disappears, as does our sense of self and other, and our capacity for social engagement. There's a loss of frontal lobe functions that integrate past, present and future. This can happen in reaction to even mild interpersonal stress: we go into a parasympathetic state characterised by shame, hopelessness and helplessness, where safety and trust disappear. The pattern can become chronic.

A factor in the right subcortical areas (including amygdala and brainstem) that trigger dissociation may be that their integration with the cortex above was never very well developed because of early attachment trauma. Therefore, whatever top-bottom integration there is fails under stress. Dissociation can happen in an infant's brain before the frontal lobes are myelinated and before the corpus callosum has developed sufficiently to co-ordinate the hemispheres (Schore 2012).

If the terror of a traumatic experience becomes a dissociated fragment, when we recall explicit memory fragments of the event, the brain's capacity to trigger fear may be shut down, brain imaging shows (van der Kolk 2014). There is some narrative but no feeling.

Disconnected hemispheres

If we're prone to dissociating, we may have a "functional superiority of the left hemisphere over the right," with unusually fast inhibition of the right when the left is activated, says McGilchrist (2009: 236). There's a "relative hypo-function of the right hemisphere", reflected in our mind being cut off from body and feelings (2009: 235). So when we're not dissociating, our left hemisphere may inhibit the right in order to avoid further dissociation, but when we do dissociate, the 'dis-integrated' right brain hijacks everything from a subcortical survival place. How much left hemisphere bias amongst people generally might stem from underlying dissociative experiences?

While dissociating, traumatised people have been found to have more activation in their right hemispheres in brain imaging studies (Schore 2012). The rest of the time their left hemispheres may process verbal stimuli perfectly well, but right hemisphere functions such as perception of prosody may suffer. In studies where they're asked to sustain focused attention amidst negative emotional stimuli, they've been found to have difficulty in "coordinating activity within the right hemisphere" (2012: 161).

Dissociation in the body

As the body immobilises and the mind dissociates, the dorsal vagus brings on a shutdown state in which muscles lose tension – the floppy part of 'floppy immobility' – according to Porges (2017). Blood pressure drops, heart rate and breathing slow down, as if we were 'feigning death'. Sympathetic enactments can be in awareness such that the experience can be processed, but in dissociation there's little or no body awareness because activity in the right insula dwindles (Levine 2010). We *feel* dead inside. The failure of the right brain to integrate somatosensory and vestibular (balance) signals creates a sense of detachment from the body (Schore 2012). At its most extreme, this leads to an 'out of body' experience.

Dissociation stemming from early attachment trauma means we're prone to reacting to interpersonal stress with low arousal and shutting down (Schore 2009). Our body then lacks vitality, evident in our movement, gestures and lack of energy for engaging wholeheartedly in life. We may have little sensation in the body generally, or in certain areas of the body; sometimes this manifests on one side of the body, and sometimes in the upper body or the lower body.

Dissociation in childhood

If dissociation begins with early attachment trauma, it can lead to mental health problems (Schore 2012). The right brain-body ensemble is prone to collapsing in the face of stressful family or social settings, unable to keep inner and outer worlds in sync. The implicit self implodes, social engagement falters, we feel empty inside. We grow up as children unaware of the pain our parents inflict upon us, oblivious to our suffering. We desperately need someone to point out what's really going on, which is often the therapist's task later in life. When we finally realise what's been happening, our world turns upside down in a positive way.

It may be that most dissociation in the therapy room stems from early attachment trauma. Van der Kolk mentions research showing that dissociation is learnt early on through experiencing "maternal disengagement and misattunement", while abuse and trauma later in childhood or in adolescence doesn't seem to lead to dissociative symptoms in young adults (2014: 121). The child grows up not feeling real inside and not engaging fully in life. Therapy has to address the consequences of failures in early parental mirroring and attunement which aren't obviously traumatic (or evident to anyone outside the family), but which may be more damaging than later traumatic events. A typical scenario is the neglected child who cries and screams and then collapses and dissociates.

Since trauma and dissociation cause dis-integration in the right brain, they will clearly be particularly damaging if they happen repeatedly during the early stages of neural development when attachment and affect regulation take centre stage. If right brain development goes well in the early years, the risk of chronic dissociation resulting from later trauma is probably lower because the child has a stronger right brain foundation and is better able to seek support to help him recover.

Dissociative phenomena

Dissociation can manifest in many ways, thanks to the interconnected but diverse nature of the right brain world. It can continue for years, and may start years after the traumatic experience (Rothschild 2000).

In a general sense, suffering dissociation means being somewhat detached from others, the world around us and our own bodies. Who we are, and our motivation for doing what we do, isn't entirely clear to us. "What's it all mean?" we wonder. When we're fully engaged in the experience of living, we're less likely to ask such questions.

Here are some typical phenomena that point to dissociation ...

Disorientation

Trauma can leave us feeling disoriented and, if we don't recover, the disorientation may continue. It's possible to feel disoriented much of the time, whether in time or space – "where am I?" I once saw a man who arrived very early for sessions which, without a waiting room and receptionist, can be a nuisance. After first feeling irritated with him, I came to appreciate that time was problematic for him. He lacked the normal orientation in time that most people have, so he made sure he was on time by arriving early and waiting on the stairs outside my flat. I needed to cut him some slack, and he became less disoriented as therapy progressed. Some awkward aspects of clients' behaviour have to be accommodated rather than challenged.

Depersonalisation

Trauma can leave us prone to our mind going blank, not knowing what we're feeling. We stare blankly, perhaps talking about traumatic events but without feeling anything. This is the outward manifestation of the freeze reaction, with little brain activity when it happens in a brain scanner (van der Kolk 2014). In therapy, the energy drains out of the room and the therapist struggles to stay awake; the right hemisphere is all at sea, while the left speaks in a disconnected manner, not very meaningfully. My experience of depersonalisation was of needing to be alone for a while to recover my sense of self, which implies early attachment problems.

Derealisation

There's a lack of a sense of the reality of the phenomenal world and of one's own reality – "I don't feel real", "this isn't really happening to me". It's another low arousal right brain state, in which the left hemisphere may plough on for a while but in a way that seems disconnected and unengaging.

Out of body experiences

It's common during traumatic experiences to dissociate to the extent that we experience ourselves as outside our body, as if watching what we're doing. This stems from a breakdown in the integration of somatosensory and vestibular signals in the right hemisphere (Schore 2012). And it can happen when we try to recall a traumatic memory – "I was looking down at my own body while reliving the accident".

Dissociative identity disorder

In this, the most severe form of dissociation, "whole personalities become separated from consciousness", says Rothschild (2000: 65). Often linked to chronic and sadistic child abuse, it's reasonable to imagine that the more severe the early trauma, the more severe the later dissociation may be. DID may point both to the fragility of the human brain and its capacity for adapting to extreme interpersonal realities (Cozolino 2010).

McGilchrist thinks EEG studies point towards "right hemisphere dysfunction coupled with relative left hemisphere overactivation" (2009: 406). Having multiple personalities has nothing to do with differing personalities in either hemisphere – for one thing, people with DID often report many more than two personalities. Instead, the multitude of dissociated personalities suggests a role for the left hemisphere's capacity to separate and categorise, perhaps reflected in the personalities' different outward appearances and the DID brain's ability to keep them separated. The separation may also be linked with very low activation in the orbitofrontal cortex (and its integrative functions) found in DID (Schore 2012).

Trauma and dissociation in the therapy room

Therapists are told they should work differently with trauma in order to be effective and avoid re-traumatising their clients, so our assessment of whether trauma is present is significant. I hope a neuroscience-based perspective can help us agree on some aspects of trauma and dissociation.

First, we might distinguish left-right issues of emotional wounding and developmental delay from top-bottom ones of trauma and dissociation. In practice, people often present with a mixture of the two, but it helps to tell the difference, so we know what we're working with at any moment.

Second, trauma presents along a spectrum of severity. It can accumulate in a person's life – one unresolved trauma leaves us at greater risk of further trauma. In general, the earlier, more severe and more prolonged trauma is, the more damage it does (Cozolino 2017).

Third, we can "expand our notion of trauma from the catastrophic events of adulthood to the everyday interactions during childhood that we depend on for our survival", as Cozolino suggests (2017: 322). Instead of considering trauma as one phenomenon, we might distinguish:

- *trauma in adulthood:* one or more events of which the client has at least some narrative memory
- *trauma in childhood:* one or more events of which the client usually has at least some narrative memory

- *early attachment trauma:* a damaging dynamic in the attachment relationship laid down in implicit emotional and somatic memory.

Fourth, therapy is often harder than we think it will be because early attachment trauma means the client's ability to maintain social engagement is compromised. The trauma is likely to be enacted in the therapeutic relationship, which may or may not survive the enactment.

Fifth, defences can be distinguished from dissociation. Psychological defences must be challenged, but challenging dissociation only makes matters worse. Defences have to be respected as well as challenged, for they may protect against dissociation.

Finally, we can replace repression with dissociation in our understanding of trauma. Instead of digging and confronting, we create an atmosphere that allows a re-associating of fragmented memories and feelings.

So how do we work with trauma and dissociation in the light of neuroscience? One answer: we aim to re-integrate body, feeling and mind, staying within the window of tolerance where possible, as we help clients to piece the fragments together. In the absence of trauma, such integration may take care of itself, but when it's present, it probably won't. This is a big subject, so I'll briefly mention some aspects of practice.

Felt sense

Encouraging the client to consult his felt sense ("notice how all this feels inside just now") develops his capacity to stay grounded in his right brain-body ensemble while engaging with the therapist. His sense of feeling safe or unsafe, of what feels right and what doesn't, helps him stay in polyvagal safety, pace the work, and feel sufficiently in control of the process. Trauma damages our sensitivity to our inner experiencing which needs restoring. The therapist can support this by letting him lead the process ("let's talk about that when you feel ready"). She can tell him it's OK to feel numb inside (there's a reason he does), it doesn't matter if he can't say what's happening inside (words will come later), and if he feels too anxious then it's time to pause.

Social engagement

The therapist's social engagement system has some power to draw the client out of immobilisation and fight-flight (Porges 2017). Polyvagal theory enables us to see why, as van der Kolk says, "a kind face and a soothing tone of voice can dramatically alter the entire organisation of the human organism" (2011: XVI). The therapist can be sensitive to the client shifting into danger or life threat, and offer cognitive explanations of these states so he understands what's happening and what to do about it.

Affect regulation

Trauma can only be processed within the window of tolerance, but therapy requires that "at some point the threatening dissociated affect must be activated", says Schore (2012: 92). When it is, and the client is overwhelmed with emotion, the therapist can help to make it tolerable. She can shift from the story to supporting him with the emotion ("it's OK, breathe through the tears", "of course you're furious!"). When affect regulation improves, right brain networks linking the orbitofrontal cortex downwards into the cingulate, insula and amygdala mature (Schore 2012). These networks are sufficiently plastic to respond to a good therapeutic relationship.

The body

Trauma erupts bottom-up in the brain, so therapy can work bottom-up with bodily experiencing as well as top-down with understanding. The client must, as Levine says, learn to embrace "the 'living' experiential body" and his instincts that reside there (2010: 37). He must move from shutdown into mobilisation to regain his capacity for fight or flight, feeling his fear and distinguishing it from immobilisation. In sensorimotor language, he becomes aware of sensations such as trembling, tingling and the heart racing, along with related 'action tendencies' such as muscular tension in the limbs (Ogden et al. 2006). Working with the body doesn't have to mean getting out of the chair: noticing the felt sense, breathing, gestures, posture, and impulses to move are all grist to the mill.

Avoid re-traumatising

When traumatic fragments are re-experienced, the client must be helped to recover before the session ends. But rushing headlong into trauma stories or overwhelming emotion can leave him feeling re-traumatised, exacerbating symptoms and increasing the degree of dissociation (Ogden et al. 2006). "A little is a lot", as my biodynamic trainer used to say. The key is to use the frontal lobes to integrate whatever fragments are in awareness as the process unfolds. Re-traumatising is a common complaint about therapy, and experiential training in trauma work is required to avoid it.

Beware interpreting

Interpretation is worse than useless during enactments or while the client is re-experiencing trauma or dissociating (Schore 2012). The therapist risks shaming him with remarks he's unable to take in; instead, emotional support is needed. Cognitive understanding can come later, once he's back in his window of tolerance with access to his frontal lobes and both hemispheres.

Talking about trauma

Talking about traumatic experience weaves a narrative with a context, integrates emotional, behavioural and cognitive aspects, and helps to avoid further dissociation (Cozolino 2010). But talking "should give way to the unspoken voice of the silent, but strikingly powerful, bodily expressions as they surface", says Levine (2010: 45). The therapist can guide the client through these top-down and bottom-up aspects of recovery, encouraging him to slow down when over-arousal drives his talking, to stay grounded when emotion wells up and dissociation threatens, and to remain present by avoiding long silences.

Traumatic memory

The attention therapy places on the client's past can start an unfolding process of old neural pathways firing and fragments of explicit memory returning ("I'd forgotten I remembered that"). There's no need to hunt for memories, lest fantasy takes over and the client becomes confused about what really happened. A narrative can be constructed, but typically there's never a complete story. With early attachment trauma, there's no explicit memory anyway, but implicit memory can be evoked by the therapeutic relationship itself and by using the imagination ("imagine how you felt as a baby held by your mother"). Feelings and sensations may be evoked that link with implicit emotional and somatic memory.

Enactments

Dissociated fragments of the client's experience can suddenly erupt from his right brain, such as verbal attacks and threats to quit therapy abruptly (Schore 2012). Even kindness can be a trauma trigger since, as van der Kolk points out, "the promise of closeness often evokes fear of getting hurt, betrayed, and abandoned" (2014: 211). The client, for example, may tell the therapist she's useless and he won't come again. Enactments enable the therapist to respond to the client's early attachment trauma that he can't articulate. She finds herself immersed in the experience, having to *with*stand it before *under*standing it. Merely following the client's flow isn't enough, as enactments involve affect dysregulation.

A striking example I recall was a man who, after some years of a good working relationship, suddenly accused me of not being present and threatened to quit. He had been a premature baby, separated from his mother after birth, which was later compounded by his father preventing his mother from comforting him when he cried at night. It seemed as if this early trauma was re-enacted with me as he protested, saying he wasn't coming again, while I very obviously wrote his next appointment in my diary. He did come, and after a few weeks his hostility subsided and we were able to make sense of it.

Dissociation

Even more challenging than enactments are clients who dissociate in the room. The most severe manifestation of right brain dis-integration results in the safety of the therapeutic relationship evaporating. Schore thinks dissociation is "the major counterforce to the emotional-motivational aspects of the change process in psychotherapy" (2009: 127). The client may go silent and stare blankly at the wall, or he may disconnect from his body following hyper-aroused fear. The therapist must help him re-connect with something: what he sees in the room, the feeling of squeezing a rubber ball in his hand, the smell of scented oils, for example. A cognitive understanding of dissociation can counter the disorientation and shame, and aid recovery. He can learn to give attention to his body, re-discover fight or flight impulses, and thereby re-establish a sense of mastery (Ogden et al. 2006).

Conclusion

Trauma and dissociation are major impediments to neural integration, and many people who enter therapy bring unresolved trauma, much of it from their early years. Their poorly integrated right brains need healing in a therapeutic relationship, their left hemispheres unable to do this unaided.

Whilst there are some excellent post-qualification training courses in working with trauma and dissociation, these topics are not always taught sufficiently on initial therapy trainings. Trauma should surely be included from the outset, particularly since students on placements are often exposed to severe trauma – this stressful situation isn't healthy for either the client or student therapist.

How much human behaviour is driven by unrecognised, unresolved trauma? Whilst we *can* have a healthy connection with our body, maintain social engagement with our fellows and use both sides of our brains, for much of the time we don't. We get into conflicts we can't resolve, we don't listen to our bodies, our emotions run riot. Our left hemispheres defend against old trauma and dissociative states lurking in our right brains that sometimes overwhelm us. We may know how to live with the after-effects of trauma, but many people don't know the process of recovery and healing. Therapy has a big role to play in our world.

Trauma underlies many mental health conditions, so we'll examine the most common ones in the next chapter.

Notes

1 Another kind of freezing precedes fight-flight: being energised and tense, heart pounding, ready and able to act, as when a child waits fearfully for parental demands (Ogden et al. 2006). Porges places freezing under danger, alongside fight-flight, in the polyvagal hierarchy (2011).
2 Floppy immobility is also called 'feigned death' (Ogden et al. 2006).
3 'Default mode network' is a term for a number of brain areas that are active when the brain isn't engaged in any particular task, i.e. they're inactive *during* tasks (Cozolino 2017).
4 'Metabolism' essentially refers to brain activity.
5 A factor here may be epigenetic changes. Cozolino says "most scientists now think that early experiences are converted into the neurobiological and biochemical structures of our brains via the transcription of specific sections of our genetic code through a process called epigenetics" (2017: 305).
6 The right anterior insula in particular, with its link to internal bodily stimuli, is inhibited in dissociation (Levine 2010).

Chapter 8

Mental health matters

Introduction

The words 'mental health' are usually followed by another word such as 'problem' or 'services' – signifying mental *ill* health. This chapter explores not only what neuroscience has to say about common mental health disorders but also some ideas about mental *good* health and healing in therapy. I'll also touch on sleep and insomnia, which are often symptomatic of our state of psychological health.

There's a yawning gap between neuroscience and psychopathology in that the diagnostic psychiatric categories lack biological markers. Whilst the use of biomarkers is growing rapidly in medicine, "psychiatry ... doesn't currently have a single blood test or biomarker to its name", according to Bullmore (2018: 107). Porges's view is that "although virtually every mental disorder is assumed to be biological and is often considered to involve genetics or brain structures, decades of research searching for an elusive biomarker or biological signature has been far from impressive" (2017: 74). There are merely some correlations between psychiatric conditions and neural abnormalities.

An explanation for this gap is ventured by Ramachandran: "what is missing ... is what might be called 'functional anatomy' – to explain the cluster of symptoms that are unique to a given disorder in terms of functions that are equally unique to certain specialised circuits in the brain" (2011: 320). Reasons for the lack of 'functional anatomy' may include the difficulty equating neural networks and firing patterns with particular psychological functions. The brain may simply be too complex to do this. Another issue is that brain imaging is better at measuring cognitive activity than affective activity, partly because it's difficult to be emotional while lying in brain scanners, unable to move (Panksepp 2012).

The way diagnostic categories are created may not help either. The neurologist Oliver Sacks makes an interesting observation about the description of psychiatric conditions: they reduce the patient to a list of diagnostic criteria and fail to paint a picture of his world, and "will be of little use in helping us to bring about the synthesis of neuroscience with psychiatric knowledge that we so need" (2017: 194). He thought the old way, with detailed phenomenological observations embedded in narratives that read like novels, would be more useful. Perhaps they give us a *feel* for the condition, bringing the right hemisphere as well as the left to bear on the diagnosis.

Diagnostic categories can imply clearly defined conditions, but often they're umbrella terms for a cluster of problems (our left hemispheres attempting to organise nature's complexity and chaos?). Nevertheless, they're reference points for thinking about particular phenomena and informing ourselves in assessing people for therapy. The therapist can ask herself "can I work with this person?" as well as "can I work with this mental health issue?", while including any diagnosis as contextual information.

Causal and predisposing factors

What causes mental health disorders, or predisposes people to develop them? I'll briefly name some factors here, some of which relate to themes from previous chapters.

Genetics. The evidence for genes causing mental health disorders is weak, but they may predispose people to them, especially where there's stress and trauma. Although science is finding genes that can be linked with some conditions, including schizophrenia and autism, this doesn't offer a means of predicting them in individuals because no one genetic 'defect' can account for more than a tiny proportion of all cases of these conditions (Seung 2013). The psychologist Oliver James argues that genetics explains a little rather than a lot about why people suffer most mental illnesses (2016). Whilst psychological traits run in families, this may be due to patterns of early maltreatment passed down the generations.

Trauma. There's substantial evidence linking psychosis to trauma from sexual, physical and racial abuse, poverty, neglect and stigma (Timini 2013). In fact, the only diagnosis that doesn't correlate with trauma is bipolar disorder (Fisher 2017). The conclusion must be that the more adversity suffered in childhood, the more probability of developing mental illness later on (James 2016).

Insecure attachment. Schore thinks there's "compelling evidence ... that all early-forming psychopathology constitutes disorders of attachment" (2003: 24). The polyvagal angle is that psychopathology concerns a lack of safety due to "either a person's inability to *inhibit* defence systems in a safe environment or the inability to *activate* defence systems in a risky environment – or both", says Porges (2011: 12–13).

Poor affect regulation. Poor mental health in infancy is expressed in "prolonged, frequent, and intense episodes of affect dysregulation" and negative emotions, according to Schore (2012: 239). Panksepp suggests that what we conceptualise as psychiatric disorders are really "sustained emotional storms" (2009: 25).

Hemispheric imbalances. A lack of integration between the hemispheres has been linked to psychosis, psychosomatic conditions, affective disorders and anxiety (Cozolino 2010). McGilchrist believes the most common pattern in mental health issues is the "hypofunction of the normal right hemisphere, and an exaggerated reliance on the provisions of the left" (2009: 407).

Gut bacteria. A relatively new area of study is the effect of intestinal bacteria entering the blood and crossing the blood-brain barrier. Imbalances in these bacteria may be linked to mood and psychiatric disorders, although this could be a correlation rather than a cause (Perlmutter 2015),

So let's look at some common mental health disorders – remembering the old adage that sometimes it's where the cracks are that the light gets in. I've already covered much of the background to this subject under the rubrics of stress, anxiety and depression, and of trauma and dissociation. The foreground concerns specific psychiatric diagnoses, or 'psychopathology'.

Schizophrenia

This is an umbrella term for "a family of conditions that can be manifested in different ways in different people", says LeDoux (2003: 272). The brain becomes less integrative and more chaotic, reflected in the behaviour of the person suffering with schizophrenia.

It's a 'neurodevelopmental disorder' in which the brain veers off its normal trajectory of growth from the outset (Seung 2013). The causes are thought to lie in a combination of genetic and environmental factors, genes alone neither predicting nor explaining it, and it may start in the womb with malnutrition or viral infection. Given its severity, we might expect its roots to lie in very early development, leaving the child predisposed to struggle in later neural development, particularly with the demands of adolescence, and especially if circumstances go against him.

The key neural issue may be a breakdown in the right hemisphere's global attention and the way it guides the left's focused attention, as its ability to sense the whole of a situation diminishes (McGilchrist 2009). The result is a lack of normal and necessary inhibition across the corpus callosum. Many phenomena of schizophrenia may result from each hemisphere's mode of functioning intruding into the other's very different mode. The left is relatively over-active, the right under-active. The problem in the right lies in the frontal lobe which mixes up self and other, and lacks social brain capacities. But something must be amiss in the right brain as a whole, which no longer functions as an ensemble with the body.

Despite the right hemisphere's under-activity, it may nevertheless intrude into the left. This can manifest as feelings of dreaming while awake, difficulties distinguishing reality from unreality, and delusions as the left hemisphere interpreter tries to make sense out of nonsense (Cozolino 2010). One form of delusion is auditory hallucinations, and the hemispheric imbalance means that the 'voices' are experienced as coming from outside the self.

On the front-back axis, the usual predominance of frontal lobe activity over posterior lobe activity is reversed, leaving the person at the mercy of environmental stimuli and internal associations that distract him (Goldberg 2009). The dysfunction in the frontal lobes disrupts the normal top-down control of perceptions, their capacity for perceptual mapping failing to organise incoming sensory signals. The external world implodes in on the person in a "wildfire of sensory stimulation", says Greenfield (2017: 136).

Biochemically, schizophrenia is associated with abnormal dopamine functioning. It involves the SEEKING system being grossly over-stimulated by dopamine, leading to psychotic fantasies (Panksepp 2012). Excessive dopamine in the frontal lobes makes thinking run wild, and facilitates people seeing causal links between things where in reality there are none.

The breakdown in neural integration with schizophrenia means that depth therapy isn't generally recommended as sufferers aren't equipped for the stress it entails. They can, however, benefit from support and brief counselling to help them cope with their condition.

Bipolar disorder

Compared to other psychiatric conditions, this is thought to be more genetic and less related to early trauma; although James argues that there *is* evidence of childhood maltreatment (2016). McGilchrist thinks the genes involved give rise to "unconventional alignments of functions within either hemisphere", and may have been conserved in evolution because they confer benefits such as creativity (2009: 12). Ramachandran makes a similar point, adding intelligence into the mix and describing bipolar as a possible side-effect of bad combinations of such genes (2011).

There's little clear neuroscience on bipolar disorder.[1] But there are signs of over-activity in the left hemisphere during manic episodes and of over-activity in the right during depressive ones (McGilchrist 2009). Ramachandran sees an extreme form of "spontaneous 'flipping' between the hemispheres and their corresponding cognitive styles", and between their biases of "manic or delusional for the left, anxious devil's advocate for the right" (2011: 271–272).

In my experience, people with bipolar may find they can manage the condition better if they learn to listen to their body and felt sense. It's not a magic bullet, and some discipline is needed.

Borderline

This category made little sense to me during my training. But when, with certain clients, I experienced the emotional battering of unwarranted flattery, extreme sensitivity to minor misattunements, verbal attacks and abrupt endings, I began to get a feel for it. The border, whether in borderline 'traits', 'states' or 'personality disorder', is with psychosis. Borderline states reveal the effects of early attachment trauma on the right brain-body ensemble which is prone to regressing to the world of the infant where survival is at stake and raw emotional systems, especially FEAR and RAGE, are unleashed without being tempered by anything cortical. The result is emotional stress for the borderline person, and for anyone they're in a relationship with.

Borderline states reflect the inner world of the very young and very frightened child. Early attachment was experienced as "traumatic, emotionally dysregulating, and possibly life threatening", says Cozolino (2010: 281). Other people can appear hostile and threatening in a sort of traumatic flashback to infancy. The right hemisphere reacts to real or imagined criticism and abandonment with fear and rage, and therefore has difficulty maintaining stable relationships. "The feelings that are experienced by borderline people evoke the intensity and terror of a helpless, uncared for baby", observes Gerhardt (2015: 189). They can go into a nonverbal state of horror, as if falling into a void, which they may have done when not safely held as babies – a form of dissociation.

Social situations can be a red rag to a bull for borderline people's sympathetic nervous system, throwing them outside their window of tolerance as dysregulated arousal of PANIC/GRIEF triggers feelings of insecurity (Panksepp 2012). They're prone to polyvagal danger and life threat states, their nervous system unable to maintain the vagal brake on sympathetic arousal that enables trust (Porges 2017). Their social stress may stem from an unusually small hippocampus and amygdala (a smaller amygdala doesn't equate with less fear and stress), leading to difficulties with affect regulation (Porges 2012). The frontal lobes are insufficiently developed to maintain emotional inhibition and impulse control. For much of the time, borderline people may have dominant left and under-active right hemispheres, but when emotionally aroused they can flip into intense right brain activity (McGilchrist 2009).

The amygdala was primed in early attachment experiences to react with fight-flight to any signs of abandonment, whether from facial expressions, eye movements or words (Cozolino 2010). Chronically high cortisol compromises the hippocampus's ability to control the amygdala with reality-testing ("am I *really* being abandoned again?"). Serotonin levels tend to be low because of insufficient good early bonding, leading to difficulty being soothed and containing emotions, and a risk of depression. Compromised development of the insula and anterior cingulate means difficulty sensing boundaries (an old girlfriend sometimes complained that I was in her 'aura' despite our being in separate rooms – I told her to kick me out, which usually resolved things). Finally, the insula may associate experiencing the bodily self with disgust, shame and the pain of rejection, a hangover from the infant having repeatedly seen disgust or anger in his parent's eyes.

Borderlines in therapy

The untempered right brain world has to be enacted and worked through, which is challenging for both parties. The emotionally stressful nature of the work means that, as with young children, there must be clear boundaries, patience and flexibility (Cozolino 2010). If the client, however mistakenly, perceives signs of being abandoned by the therapist, it may trigger "a kind of post-traumatic flashback of life-threatening proportions", says Cozolino (2006: 264). I once worked with someone who became furious whenever I momentarily closed my eyes to sense how to respond to him, accusing me of not being fully present. I wondered whether his right hemisphere became genuinely fearful, or his left simply seized on the concept of presence as a stick to beat me with – fear or rage.

Narcissism

Many of us are a little borderline at times, and even more of us can probably find ourselves somewhere on the spectrum of narcissism. It took me a long time to understand the concept properly – perhaps it was too close to home. What has helped is the experience of listening to people in my therapy room who make me feel as if I might as well not be there.

Narcissism starts a little later in development than borderline, but may overlap with it. There's less enactment of the infant's right brain world, and a more stable right brain-body ensemble foundation that allows the left hemisphere to dominate and avoid the right's felt sense. Whereas the borderline is prone to flipping into right hemisphere overwhelm, the narcissist is prone to defending against anything uncomfortable from the right.

The narcissist has a left-right divide. The left hemisphere interpreter hides a false self that tries to keep the feeling world of the right at bay (Cozolino 2010). When it succeeds, his sense of self-importance inflates, and when it doesn't, he collapses into feeling empty. The right provides a poor emotional complement for the left's outgoing social activity. Narcissists are people who weren't mirrored properly in childhood because their parents' own emotional needs trumped their ability to attune to them.

Narcissism starts early in life as "a dysregulated self-in-interaction-with-a-misattuning-other", says Schore (2003: 24). There's insecure attachment and poor self-esteem, which continues through life with the right brain's mapping of self and other reflecting the parent's skewed mapping. When attuned to mother, a young child may feel omnipotent as he learns to move and exercise autonomy. But sometimes mother disapproves of what he's doing and the attunement ruptures. A lot can go wrong here: she may have over-stimulated him in the first place, she may not repair the misattunement quickly, and she may leave him mired in unbearable shame. My mother thought that punishment and shaming were the way parents teach children to behave – "the children have got to learn" was her motto, as if we were incapable of learning by being told something.

In early childhood, mirroring gets reversed (Cozolino 2010). Instead of the parent sensitively mirroring the emotional world of the child's social brain, the child reacts to the parent's need for affect regulation and attunement. Everything is back to front, leaving the child in a vulnerable place in his right brain, though prone to left hemisphere grandiosity when he successfully mirrors his parent and makes things right again between them.

The child of narcissistic parents doesn't experience relating emotionally as safe, and therefore may not experience the world as safe (Stauffer 2010). He searches for meaning in life, since his relationships don't feel meaningful enough. The inner world of his right brain carries anxiety and fear and a sense of emptiness, so he feels unworthy of love, his body reflecting this in a tight diaphragm and rib cage. A relationship may fill the emptiness, but he fears love turning to criticism.

The skewed sense of self and other leads the adult narcissist to try and manage his emotional ups and down on his own (Gerhardt 2015). Sometimes he feels he can achieve great things, other times he fears that others will destroy his efforts. His right hemisphere repeats the misattuning self-and-other dynamic of his infancy, and the fear of collapse impedes his learning that others, unlike his parents, *can* attune to him and ease his shame. The left-right divide becomes a split between head and body in which he avoids his felt sense.

Another pattern is narcissistic rage that starts in infancy. Separation from mother can lead to sympathetic hyper-arousal that the child can't regulate alone (Schore 2003). He may develop a pattern of explosive self-fragmentation and aggressive behaviour, instead of a parasympathetic self-fragmentation and implosion triggered by shame. Maybe the parent sometimes over-stimulated him and then failed to calm his high arousal and bring his grandiose affect back to earth, while neglecting him at other times.

Narcissism in therapy

While the borderline's right brain and inner world is enacted in its raw state, those of the narcissist are kept hidden from view. So the narcissistic client may find relationships hard work. He may be unable to let the therapist care for him, or soothe himself. When distressed, his social brain may expect criticism rather than support. Learning to listen to his felt sense, without interpreting it, builds the foundation for an emerging sense of a *real* self.

A manifestation of narcissism is the client sending the therapist to sleep due to the lack of arousal in his right brain. The focus is on him in the room, and not only does he habitually avoid certain feelings evoked in his right brain, he also lacks the sense of there being someone else to relate to. So he does all the work himself, talking as if the therapist weren't there. He may oscillate between positive feelings ("I'm feeling good, I don't want to stir anything up today") and negative ones where he becomes demanding ("you've got to help me today"). The therapist may not feel she's connecting with him, and her energy may ebb away. Patience is needed to get through to something real in him.

The narcissistic client learns to feel loved in therapy through interacting with the therapist's consistently warm and reflective presence. He learns to expect good feelings from the therapist instead of criticism. His rib cage and diaphragm relax as he feels loved rather than hungry for love (Stauffer 2010).

Obsessive compulsive disorder

Sometimes I leave my house and can't remember locking the front door. I can't find the body memory of having locked it, though it must be there somewhere because if I return I find the door locked. There's a disconnect somewhere in my brain. My client with OCD has it much worse than this, so maybe there's an OCD spectrum. According to Panksepp (2005), the rituals are an attempt to keep fears at bay, but he's unsure whether FEAR or PANIC fuel OCD. Perhaps it's an unholy combination of both, feeling threatened and fearing abandonment, hence its power.

If OCD involves a left-right split, it's a big one. People with OCD can be desperate to stop their compulsive actions, yet completely unable to. Does the fearful right hemisphere not connect with the routine action of the left, or was the left hemisphere anxious about something else and suppressing the right's signalling about the present moment? McGilchrist (2013) thinks OCD is part of the "sticky rigid functioning" typical of the left hemisphere, which keeps checking the door is locked, while the right fails to register it.

On the top-bottom axis, the neural network thought to be implicated in OCD links the orbitomedial prefrontal cortex with a subcortical area, the caudate. This network involves "the primitive recognition of, and reaction to, contamination and danger", says Cozolino, and it becomes locked into a feedback loop of activation that is "highly resistant to inhibition" (2010: 345–346). Improvement of OCD symptoms correlates with lower activation levels of both cortical and subcortical ends of this loop. It's the right caudate that's the culprit, suggesting that OCD may be about the right brain being locked into a fearful state (Watt 2003). OCD implies a scary childhood.

Neurochemistry-wise, the frontal lobes lack sufficient serotonin to inhibit and calm subcortical areas, creating the mental rigidity (Goldberg 2009). But there's enough dopamine to power the loop, and dopamine, as Panksepp says, is "a highly addictive brain chemical that fuels repetition compulsions" (2012: 142).

Therapy for OCD

OCD can be treated with behavioural therapy where the compulsions are tackled head-on, with ordinary therapy where a reduction of anxiety may diminish them, with SSRI antidepressants that reduce anxiety, or even with brain surgery targeted at the caudate and cingulate (Marsh 2014).[2] Brain imaging studies that show lower activity in the orbitomedial prefrontal cortex and caudate correlating with improvement of OCD symptoms have been demonstrated for both therapy and SSRI treatment (Cozolino 2010).

But OCD can prove hard to treat, and working with feelings or with interpretation is generally counter-productive. An alternative approach devised by psychiatrist Jeffrey Schwartz aims to teach OCD clients to reframe their compulsion as 'my OCD', caused by an imbalance in their brain, rather than as the content of the compulsion (e.g. locking the doors), and then to immediately re-focus their mind on a pleasurable activity for at least 15 minutes (Schwartz & Begley 2003). Doing something, rather than thinking about something, helps to shift gear.

Addictions

The best thing to be addicted to is other people, since drug abuse is "a substitute for necessary mammalian social interaction", according to Sue Carter (2012) – who practices social engagement by being married to Stephen Porges. So addictions have something to do with love and relationship problems. If we can't be comforted by people, we may turn to other things to restore our internal equilibrium and feel better (Gerhardt 2015). Our nervous systems can learn to depend on many things, despite their negative consequences: substances like alcohol or cocaine, activities such as gambling or shopping. These serve two functions: generating feelings of pleasure, albeit temporarily, and self-medicating away stress, anxiety and depression (Sapolsky 2004).

Marc Lewis, a neuroscientist who overcame his own battle with drug addiction, describes drugs as "a neural mistake ... an attempted shortcut to get more of what you need by condensing 'what you need' into a single, monolithic symbol" (2012: 305). But one thing can't be everything. Drugs narrow our sense of meaning in life and limit what feels good to taking the drug for relief, which then constrains what we do. Addiction carves ever deeper ruts in neural pathways, compromising the brain's adaptability.

On the left-right axis, McGilchrist thinks there are reasons to link addiction with under-activity in the right frontal lobe (2009). The left frontal lobe may decide to resist the addiction, but it needs the right to co-operate with good affect regulation and social engagement; however, the right is prone to being overwhelmed by emotional impulses from subcortical areas. Left is responsible for the denial that's common with addiction.

Dopamine looms large in addiction. Anticipate something pleasurable – drinking, smoking, using, for example – and it's released in the reward system. Experience something pleasurable, and it continues to be released. But when the experience ends, dopamine levels drop, sometimes below the baseline level where we began, starting the downward spiral of addiction (Sapolsky 2004).

Endorphins interact with dopamine to fuel the 'wanting' in addiction. They create feelings of liking something which increase the flow of dopamine, creating more desire for it.[3] It's "dopamine's flame of desire, unleashed by the *ahhhh* of opioids, that causes animals to repeat behaviours that lead to satisfaction", says Lewis (2012: 135). Liking leads to wanting. The downside is that pathways linking subcortical reward networks with the frontal lobes are strengthened each time the addictive something is consumed, leading to the compulsion to repeat the experience. The synaptic sculpting of addiction is a perverse form of neuroplasticity.

Addiction is also about loss of self-control. We need the anterior cingulate, between subcortex and frontal lobes, to resist temptation (Lewis 2012). It needs support to do this, the sort that a relationship and a support network can provide. Without these, it can't take the strain, and our self-control goes. Addicts may work harder than non-addicts to keep their balance, but in vain if the anterior cingulate is unsupported and we lose our sense of self and of our place in the world.

Tolerance, withdrawal and relapse

Addictive things can lead to tolerance, the state where "you need increasing amounts of the stuff to get the same anticipatory oomph as before", explains Sapolsky (2004: 344). The more dopamine that's released when we experience pleasure – and addictive substances can release a lot – the more the neurons on the receiving end compensate by becoming less sensitive to it. Then we have to consume more substance to release more dopamine to have the same impact next time. The explosions of pleasure that come with addictive things evoke strong habituation, and then we're less attracted by the more modest rewards of worthier activities. We become hungrier for what we're addicted to.[4]

Withdrawal is hard because it's stressful. Cortisol secretion is high and depletes dopamine levels (Sapolsky 2004).[5] There's a simple way to raise them again, of course: relapse is easy. Other stresses in our life tend to encourage relapse, and we've already moved from *wanting* the drug to *needing* it, from seeking the pleasure of consuming it to avoiding the bad feeling of its absence. And even when we're in control of our addiction, we can find ourselves in a context, particularly a social one, where cortex and hippocampus respond by triggering the dopamine release that anticipates the drug. This is why the principle 'once an addict, always an addict' is realistic.

Working with addictions in therapy

"There are ... only a few things that work" in combating addiction, says Lewis (2012: 305). Nevertheless, the brain always has some more plasticity somewhere, so filling one's life with feelings and meanings rich enough to compete with the synapses of addiction is needed. Understanding how the brain is vulnerable to addiction may help.

Depth therapy is one thing that can work with addictions and, because of the link with the absence of love and social interaction, group support can be a good complement. Other things that work are a healthy relationship and a good circle of friends – so long as they don't involve too much of the addictive substance to tempt the addict.

Eating disorders

Eating should be simple. The body signals hunger via neural (vagal) and biochemical (peptide) routes to the hypothalamus, which informs the cortex. We can then choose to eat. When the gut's full, it signals fullness; likewise, the hypothalamus informs the cortex, and we can choose to stop eating. Eating is usually pleasurable, and we can enjoy the company of others at the table.

In practice, it's not so simple. Into the brain-body mix come parental battles with children about what they eat, the atmosphere around the family dining table, cognitive stuff about diets and healthy eating, how we want our body to look, how we feel as we sit down to eat, and so forth. Our brains have to sort all this out, and eating disorders are sometimes the outcome.

The frontal lobes (orbitomedial prefrontal cortex in particular) handle conscious decisions about eating, but with eating disorders less conscious subcortical urges may rule. For example, the pleasure of eating includes the release of endorphins (Wilson 2014), which can mask other feelings and lead to compulsive dopamine-fuelled reward-seeking to repeat the experience – the same dynamic as with addictions.

The social engagement system is implicated in eating disorders since eating is often a social activity. Emotional and relationship issues that compromise polyvagal safety underlie eating disorders; these issues may have their roots in unresponsive parenting in early childhood (Knox 2011).

People with eating disorders may have a distorted sense of the size and shape of their body, perhaps due to a conflict between a rigid idea of their body in their left hemisphere and the dynamic body image in their right, or maybe because the body image itself has become distorted.

Dieting can lead to a vicious circle whereby the more we try to control what we eat with our left hemisphere, the more body signals to our right hemisphere disrupt our intentions. Suppressing right to left signalling may be the next step. Baumeister and Tierney point out that dieting means ignoring body feelings and involves a catch-22: we need willpower to diet, but we need glucose in the bloodstream to have enough willpower – and an easy source of glucose is sweet food (2012). They recommend delaying eating what you want rather than not eating at all, because the anticipatory dopamine-fuelled pleasure this provides reduces the need to binge.

Anorexia

As well as starving themselves, anorexics numb their feelings and their "need to be delivered from the contradictions and ambiguities of embodied existence", says McGilchrist (2009: 405). Brain imaging studies reveal an over-reliance on the left hemisphere at the expense of the right when engaging with others. Distortions of the whole body image in the right parietal lobe imply a troubling affective experience. Embodied experience may be dissociated following trauma, with the anorexic craving to be cut off from their feelings, lacking empathy and emotional depth.

Anorexics have raised pain thresholds because of the way the vagus from gut to brain modulates sensory experience (Porges 2011). This may link with the endorphin release that accompanies the experience of starvation and gives the anorexic a high – endorphins quelling both physical and emotional pain. Reward networks may support further starvation with dopamine release (Wilson 2014), implying a motivated state and a tendency to an addictive pattern.

Anorexics often have a hyper-sensitive stress response and high levels of cortisol (Gerhardt 2015), so they don't relax easily. Starving oneself can itself raise cortisol levels. The roots of all this may lie in patterns of affective and somatic regulation formed in infancy. Anorexics may use the addictive high of starvation to mask unbearable feelings that stem from not having felt safely cared for in early childhood. They often have difficulty with anger, and they control their emotions by distancing themselves emotionally from others.

Bulimia

Bulimia is an attempt at affect regulation by purging oneself of bad feelings. Most bulimic people are "bewildered by their emotional feelings and have great difficulty describing them", says van der Kolk (2014: 98–99). The effect of binge eating followed by vomiting can cause the vagus to inhibit pain signals, leading to a higher threshold for pain; the bulimic then becomes accustomed to the pattern (Porges 2011).

Compulsive eating

We can eat to mask emotional pain, and this can become addictive (Gerhardt 2015). It probably involves endorphin release following the 'comfort' of eating, and then motivational dopamine to seek further edible pleasure, which can lead to cravings.

Cozolino thinks compulsive eating reflects an adaptation to early trauma (2010). The frontal lobes struggle to control what we eat and how much. I used to over-indulge on sweet creamy desserts but was cured long ago during a residential workshop on 'Life, Death and Reincarnation' in which imagination and drama let rip. Following a massive catharsis, the compulsion disappeared, to my astonishment, and I was able to control my indulgence. Let's say my frontal lobes were liberated by the release of bodily tension.

Obesity

Many of us inhabit a world where too much food is available, while our genes may hark back to our evolutionary past when it was scarce and tell us to keep eating. We need our frontal lobes to manage the situation, but obese people have under-active ones and are therefore prone to behaving recklessly (Greenfield 2017). Their immediate sensory experience of enjoying their food trumps their knowledge of the longer-term consequences. Under-active frontal lobes correlate with poor decision making, and physical inactivity correlates with neural inactivity in them.

Some people may be born with a tendency to obesity due to poor nutrition while in the womb. According to Gerhardt, there's a "mismatch between the expectations of an undernourished foetus programmed with a predisposition to store fat, who becomes a baby and toddler unprepared for a world awash with cheap sugary and fatty fast foods" (2015: 18).

Attention deficit disorders

Attention deficits mean a short attention span and being impulsive and easily distracted. Unlike other diagnoses, this one is actively sought by parents for their children and by adults for themselves. ADD is an elastic but genuine diagnosis that comes in a number of flavours, sometimes with hyperactivity added in (ADHD), according to Goldberg (2009). The attention deficit can be selective, in that attention drifts away from tasks lacking instant reward but returns with activities the person finds interesting.

Attention is fundamental to the differences between the hemispheres, and McGilchrist thinks ADD reflects the sensory stimulation of the modern world in which the left hemisphere constantly grasps at things and the hemispheres are unable to sustain attention together (2013). Support for McGilchrist's view comes from Goldberg who suggests a possible "lateralised ... brain dysfunction" (2009: 134).

Goldberg also describes the condition as a "mild dysfunction of the frontal lobes" (2009: 202). Attention is a loop-like process involving the frontal lobes, posterior lobes and brainstem, and a problem anywhere along this loop can produce a form of ADD. There's damage to neural or biochemical pathways linking frontal lobes with the brainstem; attention can be disrupted in different ways due to their complexity, and their functional diversity compounds this. The hyperactive form may be associated with dysfunction in the orbitofrontal (lower and middle) area and its links with the brainstem, hence the emotional volatility it brings, while the non-hyperactive form is generally associated with the dorsolateral (upper and side) area.

Panksepp links the condition to the lack of enjoyable rough-and-tumble play for many modern children (2009). Play is fundamental to brain development, and he recommends this kind of play with its movement and interaction with other children to reduce ADD impulsivity.

Medication for ADD, such as Ritalin, is a stimulant for the frontal lobes and may work by boosting dopamine and noradrenaline levels to enhance attention while reducing motor movements and agitation (Cozolino 2010).

Sleep and insomnia

How well we sleep is a good indicator of our autonomic state and mental health. As therapists, we can enquire about the quantity and quality of our clients' sleep, and the answer we get tells us something about the true state of their inner world.

Sleep happens in repeating 90-minute cycles through the night (Jarrett 2015). Each cycle takes us through stages: shallow sleep, deep or slow wave sleep (the largest proportion), and finally REM (rapid eye movement) sleep where most dreaming happens and the brain becomes quite active. The difference between being awake and sleeping lies in the arousal level of the cortex, but the REM stage is the exception due to higher cortical arousal (LeDoux 1999). Around an hour before we wake up, stress hormones begin to rise again, and these play a role in bringing sleep to an end (Sapolsky 2004). Having 'a good night's sleep' is mainly about the deep part of the cycle when the stress response shuts down and the sympathetic nervous system gives way to the parasympathetic.

It seems we need sleep so our bodies and brains can restore their energy supplies. Awake, the brain consumes 25% of our overall energy (Sapolsky

2004). Slow wave sleep in particular is needed for energy restoration. Bodily wounds heal more quickly, white blood cells (part of the immune system) are made, reserves of hormones are replenished, and waste products are removed from organs including the brain (Claxton 2015). REM sleep is thought to involve consolidating memories and solving problems from the previous day. In doing this, "the brain is also attending to its own organisation during sleep, especially during . . . REM sleep", says Claxton (2005: 314). It sorts out what information it wants to keep and what it wants to discard.

During sleep generally, the frontal lobes are less active so that inhibitions are relaxed, fantasy takes over, and a wider range of brain activities rise to the surface when we dream (Claxton 2005). During the REM stage, the right hemisphere seems to be more active than the left, especially the temporal and parietal lobes (McGilchrist 2009). There is evidence for lateralised differences during sleep from the animal kingdom: some birds keep one hemisphere awake if they're on the edge of their group so they can respond to signals from their outward facing eye (Sapolsky 2004). It's also known that some birds can fly, and dolphins can swim, while one hemisphere sleeps.

Insomnia

Stress reduces both the quantity and quality of sleep. There's a vicious circle: stress disrupts sleep, particularly restorative slow wave sleep, and sleep deprivation is a stressor (Sapolsky 2004). The shallow sleep stage dominates, so we wake more easily.[6] The more we lack sleep, the higher our stress hormone levels – the reverse of what happens when we sleep well. And the higher they are, especially CRH in the brain, the more our reserves of neural energy are depleted, learning and memory decline, and "all sorts of fear, anxiety, and arousal pathways in the brain" are activated (2004: 236). Some of the vicious circle is the brain arousing the body which then keeps the brain alert.

There's another dimension to insomnia – the gut microbiome (Perlmutter 2015). Many cytokines (small proteins) are important for inducing sleep and enabling deep restorative sleep. When cortisol levels rise, gut bacteria inhibit their production, so if your gut bacteria are disrupted, you may lack sufficient quantities for a good night's sleep.

Mental health

And so to mental *health*. Dan Siegel likes to regale his audiences of therapists by asking how many were taught what it actually means: few raise their hands, so he's making a valid point.

What do we think constitutes mental health, and how do we recognise it in someone? We probably have an implicit sense based on relational phenomena that reflect co-operation between the hemispheres: the person makes us feel safe, and enables us to have a sense of who they are and where they're coming from inside.

Mental health begins at the beginning of life. Schore thinks its earliest expression reflects "the adaptive ... functioning of the right brain, the neurobiological locus of the emotional self", so it also reflects the quality of attachment relationships (2012: 237). The right brain learns to regulate both good and bad feelings, to cope with stressful moments, and to alter bodily states as needed. The right brain-body ensemble takes shape and learns to maintain a sense of self both when we're alone and when we're with others.

Siegel suggests some hallmarks of mental health, all of which are outcomes of secure attachment (2007):

- *somatic regulation:* shifting easily between arousal and relaxation
- *affect regulation:* living within our window of tolerance, and experiencing life as meaningful
- *calming excess anxiety:* dampening unwarranted fear reactions
- *empathy:* being able to imagine another person's mind and feelings
- *insight:* self-awareness, and understanding what makes us do what we do
- *intuition:* not always having to think everything through logically.

He adds to this list *morality:* reflecting on the ethics of our behaviour in relationships with others and with society.

Neural integration

Mental health is, surely, rooted in neural integration. Cozolino certainly believes it is, claiming that "psychological health is related to the proper balance of activation, inhibition, and integration of systems biased toward the left and right hemispheres" (2010: 110). This begs the question of how we might assess such integration. If Siegel is right that neural integration flows from attuned relationships (2007), the reverse is probably true too, and we can sense a person's capacity for attunement.

Siegel also suggests a number of 'domains of integration' in the brain that each of us may achieve in varying degrees (2010). These include:

- *horizontal integration* of the hemispheres, bringing creativity and richness to living
- *vertical integration* of cortex and subcortex, which is disrupted by trauma
- *narrative integration* whereby we make sense of our lives by creating stories that weave together the autobiographical memory of the right hemisphere with the narrator function of the left

- *state integration* that allows us to shift easily between opposing needs such as closeness and solitude, autonomy and interdependence
- *interpersonal integration* that enables us to sense another's inner world as well as our own.

I'm happy to go with Panksepp's view that weaves together affective and cognitive dimensions: "mental health ultimately means that an individual . . . has integrated his or her life in such a way that the emergent self-structures, deeply affective, can steer a satisfying, cognitive course through future emotional jungles of lived lives" (2009: 6–7).

Healing in therapy

What aspects of neurobiology might underlie the beneficial effects of therapy? Seung says "curing mental disorders is ultimately about repairing connectomes", which means changing synapses (2013: XIV). But the question is: which synapses where in the nervous system need to change? We may already have found much of the answer: synapses that enable the frontal lobes to modulate posterior lobes and subcortical areas, and synapses that enable both hemispheres to contribute to whatever we're doing.

Cozolino reports studies suggesting that successful therapy may trigger genetic expression in ways that reduce stress, improve learning and enable healthier relationships (2010). He thinks the therapist's caring and encouragement may improve the production of neurochemicals, especially dopamine and serotonin, that reinforce plasticity. The bottom line is that "compassion, warmth and love have the power to change our brains" (2006: 315).

Schore thinks healing involves the therapist's ability to facilitate the client's emotional experience (2009). Much of it happens nonverbally outside awareness in neural mapping of implicit models of attachment and self-image. The frontal lobes come to regulate the autonomic nervous system more effectively, through top-down pathways from the right frontal lobe to the amygdala and hypothalamus.

Without engaging the right brain-body ensemble, healing can only be limited. The 'healing touch' involves the client trusting the therapist's capacity to resonate with his emotional pain. Panksepp supports the use of experiential approaches that get past the client's cognitive defences into his somatic experience, believing "this area could constitute a major neuroscience contribution to the therapeutic enterprise" (2009: 24).

Healing points us towards better neural integration, and this suggests using not only cognitive interventions such as interpretation, but also encouraging affective processes that arise in the right hemisphere: working with the body, felt sense, emotion, the therapeutic relationship, and the deep archetypal forces of the psyche. It means creating a genuine emotional engagement, and blending affective and cognitive responses in a dialogue that feels meaningful to both client and therapist.

How do we know when the client's neural integration improves? Maybe we sense it. The dialogue flows more easily and fruitfully; the relationship feels more engaged and more multi-faceted. Each person's integration is their unique neural life, so it's better just to sense it and describe it than to try to specify criteria for it.

Placebo effects

Richard Kradin, a doctor and psychoanalyst, claims therapy itself is a placebo with a success rate of between 30 and 60%, the higher figure being because depression and mild anxiety respond particularly well to placebos (2016). The placebo response is a way the nervous system seeks to feel better and restore good health, in mind and body. It works through implicit memory of earlier states of well-being, possibly from early in life (despite adversity then), being triggered and the client shifting from his current bad feeling back into them, bringing measurable physiological changes. Factors that promote the placebo response are the therapist's confidence that the client can heal, the client's hope and expectation, and his trust that the therapist won't shame him – all of which work below the surface of awareness.

Conclusion

Sometimes I feel my work with a client has been helpful, sometimes I don't, and sometimes I'm unsure and hope that it has. My left hemisphere interpreter may reassure me ("this person may be disgruntled with me, but he's in a better place now"). Whatever *his* interpreter says explicitly, I may speculate about changes at an implicit level. Ultimately, who knows whether there's been healing? But it's rewarding when both of us feel that things have changed for the better and we part on good terms. However, occasionally, instead of healing, we accompany someone in his suffering, knowing that in his case deep healing is unlikely.

Mental health is also emotional health, which comes with healthy relationships. Everything about it points to the value of secure attachment from the outset as the basis for the developing nervous system, particularly the right brain-body ensemble. This means parents need supporting to care for their children. There's an overwhelming argument for bringing mental health resources to bear in the early stages of life to reduce the need for them at later stages. Parents need supportive communities around them, and should never have to feel isolated in looking after young children. Perhaps child-rearing shouldn't be seen as a nuclear family affair. This point is fundamental, yet collectively we seem to have lost sight of it, and governments sometimes seem to be creating the conditions for worse mental health in the future.

Notes

1 Other possible neural correlates of bipolar include unusual arrangements in pathways linking the frontal lobes with limbic areas, especially the amygdala, and extreme fluctuations in dopamine transmission – up for mania, down for depression (Wikipedia 2017).

2 Interesting to note that a study in the 1980s showed that both therapy and SSRI antidepressants reduced over-activity in the *right* caudate cortical-subcortical loop system in OCD patients (Watt 2003).

3 Endorphins and dopamine interact so that liking leads to wanting in the subcortical *ventral striatum* (Lewis 2012).

4 'Sensitisation' means that less substance generates stronger cravings (Doidge 2008).

5 Baumeister and Tierney put the same point this way: "during withdrawal, the recovering addict is using so much willpower to break the habit that it's likely to be a time of intense, prolonged ego depletion, and that very state will make the person feel the desire for the drug all the more strongly" (2012: 31).

6 An interesting lateralisation point: Craig says slow wave sleep starts most often in the left insula (2015). This reflects his view that the left hemisphere triggers the parasympathetic nervous system. Might it also mean that an over-active left hemisphere at bedtime may be poor at triggering slow wave sleep?

Chapter 9

The mind-body connection

Introduction

Although our left hemispheres may see mind and body as separate, we all experience their connection: how thinking about something can evoke feelings in our body, and how pain and illness can affect our mental state. Combining our intuitive knowing with neuroscience allows us to address some interesting questions. Can thinking different thoughts change how we feel in our bodies? What happens in our body if we suppress our emotions? Can stress and trauma lead to illness?

'The body knows best' is an article of faith for many, a belief that's hard to argue against. Many people believe passionately in 'the wisdom of the body', some even stretching this into the notion that the body knows better than the brain. Nevertheless, this subject often appears cloaked in mystery, subject to more imaginative thinking than real understanding. There are some fascinating books on aspects of it, but seemingly no comprehensive account of the whole of it.

Anatomy is a good place to start, uncontroversial and well charted. But then we find acupuncturists with meridians, acupressurists with pressure points, craniosacral therapists with craniosacral fluid, body therapists with subtle energy fields, meditators with chakras, and so forth. Why does each profession rely on their own theoretical base when they're all working with the same human body?

I'll weave various threads together here to attempt a broad overview of the subject, drawing on the work of both neuroscientists and body psychotherapists. The right brain-body ensemble idea gets a fuller explanation, and the ingredients of the felt sense become clearer. There is much for therapists to ponder. Should we all work with the body? Do we need to get out of the chair to do so? And why is paying attention to bodily feeling generally a good move?

Mind-body questions

The intuition that the body has a mind of its own, distinct from the mind in our heads, has a long history. "My great religion is a belief in the blood, the flesh, as being wiser than the intellect", wrote DH Lawrence in 1913 (1979: 503), and body therapists from Wilhelm Reich onwards have placed their trust in the 'bodymind' over the 'headmind'. Does this poetic truth find a modern reflection in the left hemisphere and right hemisphere minds?

Since right hemisphere contributions are more background than left hemisphere ones, yet we often feel their effects in the body, it's easy to imagine that those contributions must arise from a mind in the body. After all, right hemisphere phenomena such as the felt sense contrast starkly with more familiar left hemisphere cogitation. So people project the wonders of the right hemisphere's wholistic functioning into the unsolved mystery of the body and its contribution to mental life. They're not entirely wrong to do so, since the body belongs to the right brain-body ensemble. But by understanding the differences between the hemispheres, including our bias towards a left hemisphere perspective (even if we extol the superiority of the right!), the philosophical arguments over the 'mind-body problem' diminish.

Does the body have a mind of its own?

Yes, but only up to a point. There are nervous systems in the walls of the intestines and the heart, but they're linked with the brain, not separate from it. They're important to our well-being, but neither constitute a mind in the body capable of generating a separate consciousness. The notion that the body has a mind distinct from the brain's mind probably arises because the right brain generates emotional arousal, outside awareness, that we then experience as sensation in our bodies.

It was once thought that glands in the body had minds of their own, secreting hormones without receiving signals from the brain. But the pituitary gland in the brain, controlled by the hypothalamus, regulates the glands in the body, so the brain is the 'master gland' (Sapolsky 2004).

Is the mind in the body as well as in the brain?

Again, yes, but only up to a point. The brain itself is in the body in that the central nervous system extends down the spinal cord. Where there's nervous system, there's something we may call 'mind'.

Candace Pert, the neuroscientist who discovered endorphin receptors, claimed in *Molecules of Emotion* that the mind is in the body as well as the brain (1997). Her argument was that peptides, the molecules in question, are found in both body and brain. She then boldly asserted that "the body is the unconscious mind!" (1997: 141). Given that the body belongs to the right brain-body ensemble, there's some truth in this.

A more nuanced perspective comes from Damasio who paints a detailed picture of the relationship between body and brain (summarised below). The well-being of the body is a priority for the brain such that "the brain is the body's captive audience" (1996: 159–160). Nevertheless, "I am not saying that the mind is in the body", but rather "the body contributes more than life support" by contributing "a content that is part and parcel of the workings of the normal mind" (1996: 226).

What we call 'mind' is a brain-based phenomenon, but one with the body as its starter topic.

Do body and mind function as one or do they interact?

David Bohm, a British physicist, distinguished the 'explicate order' of named objects from the 'implicate order' that underlies it (1983). We're familiar with the former, in which mind and body are separate and interact with each other, but find the latter, in which "everything is enfolded into everything", mysterious (1983: 177). In the implicate order, mind and body are ultimately one, a single organism, so they don't interact.

For Damasio, body and brain (the basis for mind) form "an indissociable organism", and this organism "interacts with the environment as an ensemble" (1996: 88). When we see and hear and touch, we don't differentiate between mind and body. Nevertheless, within this ensemble, "body and brain are engaged in a continuous interactive dance" (2010: 96). Eyes, ears and limbs send sensory signals to the brain, while the brain orients and moves them where it wants.

The left hemisphere view allows us to unravel the details of the interaction of mind and body, while the right hemisphere view enables the sense of their being an ensemble. McGilchrist thinks the two hemispheres see things differently precisely because of the right's greater connectivity with the body. Right says "I *am* my body", left says "I *have* a body" (2009: 67) – two quite different perspectives, both valid. The right hemisphere, at least, is relaxed about having contrasting perspectives.

So, body and mind form an ensemble, but within this ensemble body and brain interact with each other. To unravel the mind-body connection mystery, we must examine their interaction. At the level of the nervous system and its anatomy, we find both sensory and motor nerves, signalling in either direction.

Body-oriented neuroanatomy

For a useful discussion of mind-body matters, we must begin with anatomy.

Nerves and nervous systems

We've already met the *central, peripheral, autonomic, sympathetic* and *parasympathetic* nervous systems (Chapter 2). To these, we can now add two more parts of the peripheral nervous system:

- the *somatic nervous system* that links muscles with the central nervous system for voluntary control of bodily movement
- the *enteric nervous system* in the intestinal wall that handles digestion, and which can function autonomously.[1]

And a reminder of some of the sorts of nerves within these nervous systems that we've already met ... *motor nerves* go from brain to body, triggering movement in limbs and organs, while *sensory nerves* go in the reverse direction from body to brain, signalling the body's state back to the brain.[2] Sensory nerves outnumber motor ones because sensory feedback from the body is diverse and complex, while motor messages from the brain are relatively straightforward. The *vagus nerve* is primarily sensory, with 80% of its fibres letting the brain know what's happening in the body. The other 20% are motor nerves that, inter alia, slow the heart and stimulate the gut.

Bodily innards

Viscera is a collective noun for a lot of bodily flesh. It embraces (Damasio 2010):

- the major organs: heart, lungs, gut, liver, pancreas
- mouth, tongue and throat
- glands: pituitary, thyroid and adrenal
- ovaries and testes
- skin, bone marrow, blood and lymph fluid.

The *internal milieu* is "the bath that all body cells inhabit and of which the blood chemistries are an expression", as defined by Damasio (2010: 94). Think hormones and peptides.

Bodily systems

Nervous systems are not the only 'systems' in the body.

The *endocrine system* refers to glands and the hormones they release to circulate in the blood to help the body do the things it has to do. Hormones shape how we feel.

The *lymph* (or *lymphatic)* system is a network of vessels running alongside blood vessels throughout the body. The vessels collect colourless lymph fluid in connective tissue (connecting organs to other tissue), filter it through lymph nodes, and return it into the bloodstream.

The lymph system is part of the *immune system* that defends us "from the biological warfare waged against us by alien organisms", in Bullmore's description (2018: 27). Alien organisms include viruses, germs, bacteria and more. The immune system comprises cells found everywhere in the body and brain, most of them white blood cells. Some of these cells are *macrophages* which 'eat' bacteria, taking fragments to lymph nodes to show to *lymphocytes* to tell them what the enemy looks like.[3] Lymphocytes produce antibodies that help macrophages fight infection, macrophages secrete proteins called *cytokines* that circulate in the bloodstream looking for other macrophages to bind to and enlist their help.

The immune system is like an ecosystem; Maté calls it a "floating brain" (2011: 175). It's a good example of mind-body ensemble functioning: immune responses in the body affect the brain which itself can trigger them in the body. We don't feel its workings directly, but we certainly feel the sickness states it generates.

Brain areas linked with the body

Some key brain areas have dealings with the body. From the bottom upwards (see Figure 9.1) …

The *spinal cord*, where much of the central and peripheral nervous systems meet, has its own neurons and therefore something of a life of its own. It tweaks the body signals that become pain, and it sometimes acts

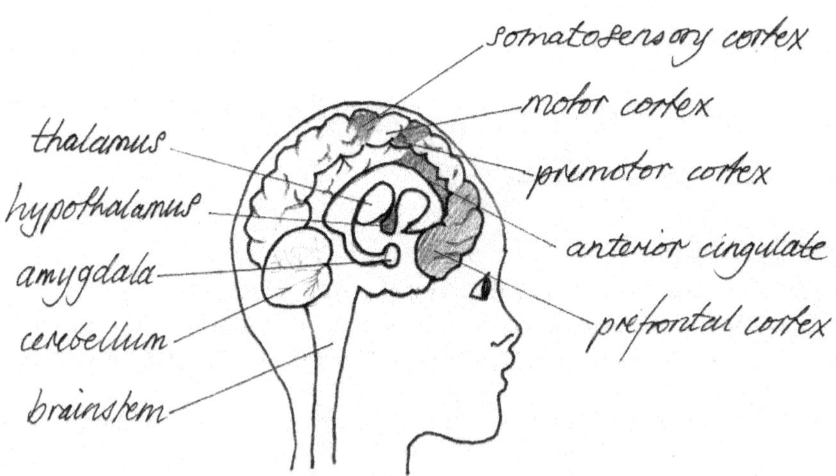

Figure 9.1 Brain areas particularly linked with the body: brainstem, cerebellum, amygdala, hypothalamus, thalamus, somatosensory cortex, motor cortex, premotor cortex, anterior cingulate and prefrontal cortex. The insula, not shown, sits next door to the anterior cingulate, hidden behind cortical areas

off its own bat with reflexes such as jerking your leg when the doctor taps your knee. By not referring upwards, reflexes are super-fast.

The *brainstem* is where the spinal cord "pokes up out of its bony sheath of vertebrae, enters the skull, and grows thick and bulbous", says Ramachandran (2011: 17). It regulates autonomic things like breathing and blood pressure, and is a bad place to have a brain injury or stroke – we can survive without some cognitive functions, but not without autonomic regulation.

The *cerebellum* sits behind the brainstem, co-ordinating movement, balance and posture with sensory signals.

In the limbic system, the *amygdala* and *hypothalamus* are big players in generating stress and anxiety in the body. Body signals then feedback to them, potentially making matters worse. The *thalamus* filters and relays sensory signals to brain areas that need them.

The *insula* receives body signals from the brainstem (via the thalamus) and organises them like a map of the body, which makes it an important contributor to how we feel inside.[4] It's lateralised, the right insula being dominant for our "visceral awareness of subjective emotional states", says Schore (2012: 83). Such feelings begin in the brainstem, but the insula elaborates them and links them with cognition (Damasio 2010).

Interlinked with the insula is the *anterior cingulate*, which becomes "active in parallel with the insula when we experience feelings", says Damasio (2010: 118). It weaves together emotion, feeling, attention and working memory so that, with the insula, it's key to the felt sense. It must be important because it lights up in many, "almost too many", brain imaging studies, says Ramachandran (2011: 295) – perhaps because it's associated with attention and will (or maybe because it likes being in brain scanners).

The ultimate destination of body signals is the *somatosensory cortex* in the parietal lobes.[5] Signals here are also organised like a map of the body, and particular neural columns and particular neurons within them respond to specific areas of, for example, skin. The more nerve endings in a body area, the more somatosensory cortex there is to map it; lips and genitals are well-provided for. The maps of the body's surface are in the contralateral somatosensory cortex in either hemisphere, but the map of the *inside* of the body is biased to the right somatosensory cortex. This is a dynamic map combining signals from muscles and skeleton with those from viscera to form an "integrated body sense" (Damasio 1996: 66) – a close relation of the felt sense.

The results of mapping and processing in the somatosensory cortex go to the *prefrontal cortex* which mixes them with signals from elsewhere so we can be aware of our felt sense and of what's happening in our body. It enables us to contain our emotional reactions: "the frontal cortex does all this disciplining of you by inhibiting that frothy, emotional limbic system", says Sapolsky (2004: 229).

Motor cortex is found in areas of the frontal lobes; it initiates movements of arms and legs (in the contralateral hemisphere). *Premotor cortex* is where we plan movements before making them, so we can imagine a movement without actually moving.

With this anatomy on board, we're equipped to delve deeper into the relationship between body and brain.

Body-brain dialogue

A body that moves needs a nervous system to co-ordinate sensory perception with the movement of limbs, breathing and blood circulation; it can't function without a brain. Conversely, a brain can't function without a body to inhabit – where would blood, oxygen and sensory signals come from? The hypothetical idea of studying a 'brain in a vat' without a body to accompany it is a non-starter.

The brain is 'body minded' (Damasio 2010). It must ensure the survival of the body it inhabits, so it's well informed about it. Everything that happens in every nook and cranny of the body is signalled to it. But it can also bypass the body in the cause of speed and energy efficiency by concocting neural images of emotional body states based on past ones – 'as if' feelings. However, the body will interject eventually. In their interactive dance, thoughts generate emotional states in the body, and the body changes the neural landscape from which thoughts arise. Damasio goes further: "neurons … need inspiration from the very body they are supposed to prompt" (2010: 90).

Body mapping

The brain absorbs the world by mapping it, and it absorbs the body likewise. In fact, the body is the central object of brain mapping. Damasio is eloquent: "the human brain is a born cartographer, and the cartography began with the mapping of the body inside which the brain sits" (2010: 64). Everything is mapped: the five senses, the movement of muscles and limbs, the configuration of the body in space, the state of the viscera (including the contraction and dilation of arteries) and internal milieu.

Body mapping starts in the brainstem and is refined in the insula and somatosensory cortex. The body's state constantly changes, so the mapping is in constant flux. Unlike the maps humans make, the brain's maps are dynamic. Although the mapping of the body's overall structure is inevitably stable, that of the viscera and internal milieu mean that "the body is permanently re-created in brain activity", says Damasio (2010: 93). The result is that the left hemisphere maintains the more stable representation of the body (such as the body I like or dislike), while the right hemisphere image is based on the dynamic mapping of our somatic experience (McGilchrist 2009). The right hemisphere is dominant for our 'whole body' awareness.

When body mapping reaches the prefrontal cortex, an increasing level of abstraction occurs, with more awareness and reflection. And when we become aware of bodily feelings, thinking about them can replace here-and-now awareness, the left hemisphere joining in the body party and taking over the show. To keep our bodily feelings integrated with our awareness, we must keep sensing them freshly.

Interoception

Dynamic body mapping enables interoception, the sense of the body from within. Interoception is distinct from *exteroception* (our five senses) and *proprioception* (where our arms and legs are in space). It's a relatively slow process, partly because interoceptive body signals travel along unmyelinated pathways, unlike proprioceptive and motor ones. When you move your body to hit a tennis ball, you have to be quick, but when you contemplate your inner state you can take your time.

Bud Craig, a neuroanatomist and author of *How Do You Feel?*, broadens interoception to cover the brain's mapping of *all* body tissue (Craig 2015). It enables the brain to manage energy efficiently and maintain homeostasis. The insula integrates interoceptive signals from all over the body, giving rise to our awareness of "emotional and social feelings, like pleasure, anxiety, trust, and anger" (2015: XIII).

Interoceptive awareness varies for each person (Craig 2015). Awareness of our heartbeat, for example, correlates with our general level of somatic awareness, with how intensely we feel emotions, and with how well we read our own and others' feelings. Another correlation is with making better decisions based on subtle environmental cues. Good news: interoceptive awareness can improve with practice.

The key area for interoceptive awareness is the anterior insula (Craig 2015). Body signals are mapped in the posterior insula and then combine with other feeling signals in the anterior insula to form what Craig calls "the global emotional moment" (2015: 200). This sounds like the felt sense – of the whole situation, in the here-and-now. Our *experiencing* of bodily and emotional feelings arises in the anterior insula with the help of the anterior cingulate. This is the root of the brain's extraordinary capacity to synthesise a mass of body signalling so that we can express our feelings to others who also have bodies and feelings ("I had a bad stomach but feel OK now, though I'm a bit nervous about my lecture tomorrow").

Interoception is biased to the right brain. "The activation and the size of the right anterior insula cortex are uniquely related to subjective awareness of interoceptive feelings", says Craig (2015: 204). This may explain why we can be unaware of what's happening in our body. We use the mind as a screen to hide the inner goings-on of the body, presumably so that our left hemisphere can focus attention on the outer world (Damasio 1999). But when we turn attention within, we see through the screen into the right hemisphere's world. Noticing our breathing ups the activation of the right insula in particular (Craig 2015).

Why is it that turning attention to interoceptive awareness can shift painful feelings? For example, noticing our breathing can reduce anxiety. A hypothesis: when left turns to right and stops inhibiting its signals, hemispheric integration improves, enabling mind and body to complete emotional cycles.

The body in the brain

As well as dynamic body mapping, there's also a stable body image in the somatosensory cortex that's partly innate. This is demonstrated by some strange neurological conditions that shed light on the mind-body connection. Patients with these conditions experience their problem in their body, but the explanation for it lies in the brain. In effect, we have two bodies: the physical one and the mapped-in-the-brain one.

Ramachandran is a good story-teller here (2011). Patients with a stroke in one hemisphere are often paralysed in the opposite side of their body. But when the stroke is in the right hemisphere, a small minority deny their left side paralysis (*anasognosia*), and an even smaller minority deny ownership of their left arm (for example), claiming that it belongs to someone else, such as the doctor (*somatoparaphrenia*). The arm no longer feels like *their* arm, because of damage in body mapping areas of the right insula and somatosensory cortex. The brain will go to extraordinary lengths to resolve internal conflict, and concludes that the absence of the usual feelings of ownership means the arm belongs to someone else – never underestimate its talent for mangling reality! Left hemisphere strokes don't lead to denying ownership of the right arm, because mapping the viscera is biased to the right hemisphere.

Another phenomenon is *body dysmorphia* (or body dysmorphic disorder), where someone has a wildly inaccurate perception of part of their body that distresses them and which they try to hide (Jarrett 2015). Whether or not the body mapping itself has gone awry, the body sense that enters awareness generates anxiety.

Body and brain change each other

Darwin was onto the two-way interaction between body and brain a long time ago:

> When the mind is strongly excited, we might expect that it would instantly affect in a direct manner the heart ... when the heart is affected it reacts on the brain; and the state of the brain again reacts

> through the pneumo gastric [vagus] nerve on the heart; so that under any excitement there will be much mutual action and reaction between these, the two most important organs of the body.
>
> (cited in Porges 2011: 22)

Today we know more about the nature of the interaction. In Damasio's account, the brain tells the body "what to do to maintain its even keel" and "how to construct an emotional state", while the body tells the brain "this is how I am built and this is how you should see me now" (2010: 94). Rather than just bossing the body around, the brain "hosts conversations" between them, writes Claxton (2015: 66).

Let's explore each direction of the interaction in turn.

How the brain changes the body

The brain initiates emotional changes in the body after evaluating sensory signals about the outside world. It may seem that the changes start in the body, but only because affect regulation in the brain happens outside awareness. The brain has two routes for initiating change in the body: the *electrical* route of neural pathways that move limbs and adjust bodily organs, and the *chemical* route of hormone release, the HPA axis being the prime example.

Just because the brain initiates changes in the body doesn't mean we can control them. Autonomic changes are triggered unconsciously – sexual arousal, for example – and can cause us embarrassment. The brain controls where in the body gets more blood or less blood. The brainstem regulates sleep, waking and bowel movements. Of course, the brain can be divided, one part of it triggering these bodily things, the other wishing it wouldn't.

Other examples of the brain changing the body are electrical changes in the skin, registered in lie detector tests, in response to statements we hear. Jung's word association tests are another example.

Simultaneously, the brain also changes itself and the way it's influenced by the resulting body signals (Damasio 2003). So when the amygdala and brainstem pitch the body into anxiety, they also tweak body mapping, cognitive mode and what we remember. The result is that anxiety in the body is matched by anxious thinking and anxious memories.

How the body changes the brain

The body also uses neural and chemical routes to tell the brain what's happening. The neural route includes sensory signals from viscera and muscles that feed into body mapping. The chemical feedback includes hormones and peptides released by organs into the bloodstream; this is registered in the hypothalamus en route to the cortex.

Damasio describes the picture the brain receives from the body as a continuous "multimedia documentary" (2010: 94). The documentary covers all sorts of things: blood flow, temperature and acidity level at different locations, the presence of toxic molecules, and so forth. The information is both quantitative (e.g. blood sugar levels) and qualitative (e.g. relaxation or tension of muscles). So how we're feeling at any moment is based on many things in the body.

In the dance of body and brain, "the body can change the brain's landscape and thus the substrate for thoughts", says Damasio (2010: 96). Feeling and thinking can be changed. For example, when we're anxious, signals from our anxious body reinforce our brain's anxious landscape. But if we slow our heart, whether by fair means such as mindful breathing, or foul such as beta-blockers, its changed signals to the brain help us to feel less anxious and think less anxious thoughts.

The body can also influence the brain via the immune system and inflammatory processes. Whilst the blood-brain barrier protects the brain from toxins in the bloodstream, it's now known that the immune system can signal across the barrier and affect the brain (Bullmore 2018).

Somatic regulation

The body, assisted by the brain, has to maintain some equilibrium amidst the up and down cycles of living. Somatic regulation involves things like the control of heart rate and digestion, and the release of hormones in the body.

The autonomic systems for regulating the body and its arousal level are biased to the right hemisphere (McGilchrist 2009). The qualifier to this is that while the sympathetic nervous system is more governed by the right, the parasympathetic is more governed by the left. This fits the broader hemispheric picture: the sympathetic is important for regulating heart rate and blood pressure in response to new and emotional situations, whilst the parasympathetic produces the sort of relaxation that comes with doing familiar and emotionally undemanding things. So, for example, when we're stressed, we can sometimes relax by doing a familiar and repetitive activity we find 'therapeutic'.

Let's examine some features of somatic regulation.

Homeostasis

Homeostasis means the viscera and internal milieu staying on an even keel by "having an ideal body temperature, heart rate, glucose level, and so on", says Sapolsky (2017: 125). Stress, and the anticipation of stress, disrupts our homeostatic balance, and the stress response is meant to get us through things and restore it. Organs need homeostatic regulation in order to recover and maintain their health (Porges 2017). Homeostasis is best understood as a feedback system that oscillates either side of a set point, with extreme stress in one direction and deep rest in the other.

The body doesn't do homeostasis of its own accord. "The brain executes homeostatic compensations on behalf of the whole organism, and 'we' benefit from them, effortlessly", explains Damasio (2018: 59). It happens through both neural and chemical routes.

Peristalsis

Smooth muscles in the intestinal walls "march to their own drum and produce digestion and nutrient absorption with little or no interference from you", says Damasio (2018: 59). This is peristalsis, managed by the enteric nervous system during parasympathetic states, which the brain can stop by triggering sympathetic arousal.

Biodynamic therapists believe peristalsis is accompanied by 'psycho-peristalsis', a means of self-regulation to digest emotional stress (Boyesen 2006) – explained below.

Emotional cycles

These play a big role in somatic regulation. An emotional charge builds up with sympathetic arousal, is expressed and discharged, and then subsides so we wind down with the parasympathetic and return to our homeostatic baseline, which feels good (Schaible 2009). Completion means we're genuinely ready to 'move on'. We have an innate tendency to complete these cycles, and doing so makes us feel alive.

But the cycle may stop in midstream if we're emotionally 'blocked'. This can start in infancy since babies need attachment support to go through the full cycle which may not be forthcoming. As Schaible says, "a hostile or abusive family climate prevents the child from finding a healthy balance of arousal and calm" (2009: 36). Emotional blocks mean that homeostasis isn't fully restored.

Emotional cycles need to work on three levels to be complete (Southwell cited in Boyesen 2006):

- the *mental* level of awareness of the feelings involved
- the *physiological* level of tense and relaxed muscles
- the *vegetative* level of psycho-peristalsis.

When the natural capacity for regulation on these levels is blocked, neurosis develops.

An example of completing an old, blocked cycle ... I remember lying on a biodynamic massage table and late in the session spluttering "I don't deserve to have your help" to my therapist, a feeling I hadn't been aware of before then. Deep sobs welled up for a while, and then I relaxed into peacefulness.

Emotional issues in the body

If you believe that stress, suppressing emotion, and one's attitude to bodily feelings affect well-being and health, here are some ways this can happen. They all involve problems with somatic regulation.

Heart issues

The poetic heart, revered by therapists and everyone else, has something to do with the physiological heart, which can 'close' with loss, disappointment and anger: chest muscles tighten, leaving less space for it, explains body therapist Kathrin Stauffer (2010). This is natural, and patience and resilience are needed to bear the emotional cycle so that it completes. When it does, we're able to let go, and the heart 'opens' again as chest muscles relax.

While the brain raises and lowers heart rate, the heart has its own neural networks for co-ordinating its muscles and synchronising heartbeats. A nervous system in your heart might suggest a source of intelligence wiser than the one in your head, but Sapolsky bluntly disabuses us of this notion: "your heart is just a dumb, simple mechanical pump, and your blood vessels are nothing more exciting than hoses" (2004: 41). But don't be disappointed: the heart is at the core of the ensemble working of brain and body. It both reflects our physiological and emotional health, and affects it. If something is amiss, we feel it.

Heart rate variability concerns variation in the time gap between heartbeats (Porges 2017). Because the heart links with the autonomic nervous system and the vagus, it doesn't beat at a constant rate; more variability equates with better cardiac health. A happy, healthy heart is flexible and adaptable, and patterns of variability can demonstrate coherence or chaos (Watkins 2017). Coherent patterns correlate with positive feelings like love and gratitude, and with good cardiovascular health. Chaotic patterns correlate with anger and frustration, and poor cardiovascular health. Love feels good, anger doesn't. To make your heart rate variability more coherent, breathe rhythmically.

The body has more capacity for blood than actual blood. So blood vessels dilate (open) as they fill up in response to need and close as they empty out. Adrenaline causes them to expand and the heart to beat faster with sympathetic arousal; for example, when we're angry and our face goes red. Blood vessels have receptors to sense what's happening and signal it to the brain.

Blood pressure is the resistance to blood flow from the periphery. It's regulated by the vagus and correlates with how relaxed we are (Stauffer 2010). Chronically high blood pressure is an inflammatory process in blood vessels that points to cardiovascular disease. It suggests excessive sympathetic arousal linked to unresolved fear or anger; we may have difficulty with parasympathetic 'letting go', winding down and digesting our experience.

Restricted breathing

Constriction and tightness in the chest are part of many people's experiencing when they explore body sensations. They reflect the state of the diaphragm and chest muscles.

The diaphragm is a big muscle below the lungs that regulates breathing. It's usually controlled autonomically from the brainstem, sometimes consciously from the somatosensory cortex. We can use it to breathe shallowly or hold our breath, which is the main way we (unconsciously) control the intensity of our emotions to avoid feeling overwhelmed (Stauffer 2010). So our breathing reflects our emotional state. When stressed or threatened, we may restrict our in-breath with sympathetic fight-flight arousal. When the stress or threat is over, breathing returns to its normal rhythm, but the less aware we are of our breathing, the more likely it'll be restricted for longer than necessary.

Holding our breath is part of the startle reflex and can become habitual. With a history of insecure attachment, simply engaging with another person may disrupt our breathing. Also, as air goes in and out of our lungs it passes our vocal chords, so breathing and speaking are interlinked, and our talking carries implicit messages (Stauffer 2010).

Breathing links with the heart. As we breathe in, there's a little sympathetic arousal and heartbeat speeds up. As we breathe out, the parasympathetic nudges the heart to slow down.[6] Hence some breathing techniques encourage a longer outbreath. The larger the variability in heartbeat between breathing in and out, the better (Sapolsky 2004).

Anxiety and hyper-arousal can cause excessive breathing in and the heart beating too quickly: we gulp air in and don't exhale properly, which can lead to hyperventilating and light-headedness. We can also suffer from not breathing in enough – shutdown and very low arousal.

Biodynamic therapists believe the diaphragm is the 'royal road' to emotional suppression, which the brain initiates and the diaphragm enacts. Gerda Boyesen, the Norwegian physiotherapist who founded biodynamic therapy, called the diaphragm "the gateway to the unconscious" because of this (2006: 132). A tight diaphragm muscle means we don't breathe deeply and only express surface emotions. We have too little oxygen in our blood, and lack energy. An unconscious fear of old, painful feelings may leave us unable to relax our diaphragm; we may experience a vague emotional pressure which leaves us agitated or depressed. When our diaphragm does relax, deeper emotions arise, and the emotional cycle completes.

Gut issues

The enteric nervous system in the intestinal walls manages peristalsis, the movement of food through the gut. Parasympathetic relaxation starts digestion, sympathetic arousal stops it. This nervous system has some 100 million neurons (small beer compared to the brain's c. 100 billion). It links with the brain via the vagus, most of which comprises sensory nerves to the brain, hence your stomach's ability to make you feel good or bad.

Having a 'second brain' in your gut doesn't mean that wisdom arises from your body rather than your head. Michael Gershon, the neurobiologist associated with the enteric system, says it reveals more about bowel disorders than philosophy (1999). And Panksepp is clear that, whilst it's important in understanding emotional reactions and psychosomatic conditions, the emotional systems in the brain are more important (2005). Nevertheless, it plays a big role in the body's influences on the brain and therefore on how we feel.

'Gut feelings' are generally held in high esteem.[7] They may seem to arise independently from the brain, but they probably start outside awareness in the right brain with emotional reactions to situations and then play out in the gut. The resulting feedback to the brain can influence its evaluation of situations as basically good or bad – another example of ensemble working.

Emotional reactions may affect the gut by interrupting parasympathetic peristalsis and healthy digestion with sympathetic arousal. "Anxiety reduces peristaltic mobility and blind rage stops it", says body therapist Monika Schaible (2009: 39). Digestive problems may ensue. Furthermore, peristalsis includes *psycho-peristalsis*: lymph fluid containing left-over stress hormones that accumulates in the intestinal walls drains into the gut as it contracts (Boyesen 2006). Insufficient parasympathetic relaxation, reflecting incomplete emotional cycles and unresolved stress, can mean insufficient psycho-peristalsis; excess lymph fluid and stress hormones create a pressure in the intestines that makes us feel unwell.

Conversely, massage or other methods of relaxation can trigger positive feelings as this fluid drains into the gut. Pressure eases, stress is 'digested', and old emotional cycles are completed (Schaible 2009). Biodynamic therapists put a stethoscope on their clients' stomachs to hear the cacophony in the gut and use it to guide their massage treatments. When you meditate and your tummy rumbles, psycho-peristalsis may be draining excess fluid (don't be embarrassed!). This sometimes happens in therapy too.

Muscle tension

Muscles come in two varieties. *Striated muscles* attach to bones and have characteristic 'bands' visible under a microscope. Our body moves when we contract one connecting two bones at a joint, which means tensing it. Afterwards, all being well, it relaxes. *Smooth muscles* belong to the viscera and are found in the walls of arteries, intestines and bronchi. When smooth muscles in artery walls tighten their grip, for example, blood pressure rises. One exception: the heart has striated muscles, but the signals it sends to the brain nevertheless go to areas dedicated to viscera rather than movement.

We're better off controlling our emotions with our frontal lobes than with our muscles as they're less likely to get 'stuck'. Chronically tense striated muscles may have restricted movement, and are a way of holding stress in the body. They embody fight-flight impulses where the arousal cycle hasn't completed, and imply a state of readiness for further attacks and fight-flight states. Wilhelm Reich, the original body psychotherapist, described chronic muscle tension as 'body armour' (Eiden 2009).

Frozen fight-flight impulses lead to tight (hyper-tonic) muscle tissue. If too much energy is held in muscles, they may become slack (hypo-tonic) instead, and then they're unable to contract and move. Both tense and slack muscle tone interferes with posture, mobility and aliveness (Schaible 2009).

Psychosomatic issues

An important question about the mind-body connection is whether psyche can make soma ill – and vice versa. Where brain and body function as an ensemble, it's reasonable to imagine both are possible, as Jung thought:

> A wrong functioning of the psyche can do much to injure the body, just as conversely a bodily illness can affect the psyche; for psyche and body are not separate entities, but one and the same life.
>
> (1986: 3)

Making a distinction between illnesses with physiological and psychological causes is problematic. Panksepp thinks the effects of the emotional systems on the body mean that "the division between emotional and physical disorders narrows to the point of extinction" (2012: XIII). This implies that all illnesses may have a psychological element, while no illness is purely psychological in origin. But the psychological element may be the straw that breaks the camel's back. Asthma, heart disease, ulcerative colitis, back pain and tension headaches all have a link with emotional suppression (Claxton 2015). Add to this list other intestinal problems, abdominal or chest pain, and breathing problems, all of which link with poor affect regulation (Landale 2009).

Psychosomatic illness, therefore, isn't a straightforward concept (Stauffer 2010). To be psychosomatic, it should originate in psychological distress rather than infection or injury, and the distress should be largely hidden – suppressed or dissociated – rather than expressed emotionally. It's time we understood how 'somatisation' might work.

It may be tempting to interpret an illness as being psychologically meaningful, but which hemisphere is speaking when we do this? The left with its interpreter, possibly dogmatic, or the right in an unfolding way that makes intuitive sense to the ill person? Interpreting physical symptoms in therapy can be done jointly in the therapeutic dialogue, rather than relying on the therapist's 'expert' opinion or looking them up in a book. And experience tells us that psychological transformation and expressing authentic emotion don't necessarily make an illness go away.

How might psyche and soma interact to cause or contribute to illness? The stress response and the immune system may be involved, as we'll see. Porges (2017a) thinks trauma can leave the nervous system in a chronic state of readiness for ongoing threat, and polyvagal theory offers a plausible model for gastrointestinal disorders in particular. The hemispheres may play a role, as psychosomatic disorders involve a lack of integration and balance between them, claims Cozolino (2017). People suffering them tend to have few dreams, a difficulty articulating their feelings, and exhibit a lack of symbolic thinking – all suggesting poor hemispheric integration.

Stress and illness

Stress itself doesn't make us ill, but "the relentlessness of human stress, the long-term disruption of homeostasis ... increases our risk of disease", says LeDoux (2003: 279). Sapolsky describes what happens when the stress response is repeatedly activated for psychological reasons:

> no single disastrous effect, no lone gunman. Instead, kicking and poking and impeding, here and there, make this a bit worse, that a bit less effective. Thus making it more likely for the roof to cave in at some point.
>
> (2004: 70)

The kicking, poking and impeding can result from an over-activated cardiovascular system and chronically high blood pressure, which increase the risk of arteries clogging up (atherosclerosis), heart attacks and strokes. It can also result from excess cortisol suppressing the immune system, making us more prone to succumbing to infection and less capable of fighting back having succumbed (e.g. catching a cold when we're stressed).

Some disorders involve the *under*-secretion of cortisol, including chronic fatigue syndrome, fibromyalgia and rheumatoid arthritis (Sapolsky 2004). Cortisol, of course, helps us recover from stress as well as deal with it; low cortisol, associated with unresolved trauma, therefore implies poor recovery from stress.

Can stress be a factor in cancer? Sapolsky offers a sensible caveat: "once we recognise that psychological factors, stress-reducing interventions, and so on can influence something like cancer, it is often a hopeful, desperate leap to the conclusion that such factors can control cancer" (2004: 178). Since stress can worsen an illness like cancer, it can *seem* to be the cause, but this isn't necessarily the case (Stauffer 2010).

Psychoneuroimmunology

This mouthful of a term embraces psychology, neuroscience and immunology.[8] It weaves mind and body together via the immune system (Bullmore 2018). The brain and immune system were once thought to be kept separate by the blood-brain barrier, but cytokines (immune cells) in the blood supply to the brain have been found to send signals through the walls of blood vessels. This means that the mind can become 'inflamed', the brain having its own immune response.

So here's another way psychological influences can contribute to illness. Sapolsky thinks "the brain has a vast potential for sticking its nose into the immune system's business" (2004: 144). When we're stressed, cortisol briefly activates the immune system but then suppresses it, so it returns to baseline and avoids over-shooting into autoimmunity (in which an overactive immune system attacks the body it's meant to protect). With severe and sustained stress, immunity can be suppressed *below* baseline, and therefore stress "can increase the likelihood, the severity, or both of some immune-related diseases" (2004: 171). Nevertheless, it's unclear just how much chronic stress makes us more prone to getting ill or unable to fight off illness once we have it.

The psychoneuroimmunological picture can be confusing. While stress generally suppresses the immune system, chronic emotional stress can overactivate it. Stressful life events and situations, such as bereavement, poverty, debt and social isolation, can trigger the immune system, macrophages pumping more cytokines into the bloodstream and inflaming clogged-up arteries, making heart attacks and strokes more likely (Bullmore 2018). Is the contrast with a suppressed immune system explained by the low cortisol scenario?

In the other direction of soma affecting psyche via the immune system, cytokines help us fight illness by triggering fever, loss of appetite and the need to sleep more (Maté 2011). But they can also enter the brain and bind to receptors on neurons, causing changes in mood and behaviour that lead to excessive or chronic fatigue, which may be more intense versions of normal sickness behaviours and feelings.

A significant point that's emerged recently is that the immune system may be changed by childhood trauma, as if it 'remembers' the trauma and is therefore prone to reacting to both adulthood infections and social stresses with disproportionate inflammatory responses that can trigger depressive symptoms (Bullmore 2018). Furthermore, 'burn-out' symptoms may correlate with more activated macrophages, leaving the person prone to more extreme immune reactions to further stress. Possible routes for this to happen: stress-related adrenaline sending a danger signal to macrophages so they react as if the body were infected, and activated macrophages being less responsive to the calming effects of cortisol.

Van der Kolk echoes this (2014). Changes to immune cells and their 'memory' following trauma can make the immune system over-sensitive to threat, such that it's prone to mounting a defence when none is needed. Trauma means that the body as well as the brain has a problem with feeling safe. "Stressful experiences ... have a negative effect on immune function" (2014: 240). Fortunately, there's also evidence that resolving trauma can improve it.

Autoimmune disorders

The immune system can make mistakes, causing illness instead of protecting against it (Bullmore 2018). Lymphocytes sometimes mistake the body's own proteins for alien invader proteins and start an immune response against them, manufacturing antibodies against friendly proteins. It's as if "one part of the immune system thinks the body is under infectious attack by the antibodies produced by another part of the immune system", says Bullmore (2018: 56–57). The immune system fights with itself, macrophages churning out cytokines that cause inflammation. This can continue for years because the immune system isn't good at dealing with threats from itself.

Autoimmune disorders include allergies, rheumatoid arthritis, ulcerative colitis, lupus, multiple sclerosis and possibly Alzheimer's (Maté 2011). The damage can be to joints, connective tissue or organs – which include eyes, skin, nervous system, and the brain itself.

Given what we know about psychoneuroimmunology, trauma may play a role in autoimmune disorders. Van der Kolk thinks he's observed such a link (2014). But this doesn't necessarily mean that trauma *causes* autoimmune disorders.

Inflammation

This is what happens when the immune system tries to heal an injured part of the body so that it swells up and becomes red and painful (Bullmore

2018). The injury triggers an inflammatory response that sends more blood into the wounded area; swelling results from lymph fluid getting through leaky blood vessel walls to attack alien invaders.

The destructive forces of inflammation must be regulated so they don't damage healthy tissue: some neuropeptides promote inflammation while others inhibit it (Sapolsky 2004). The nervous system is involved in their release, hence psychological factors can affect inflammation. Cytokines can also inhibit inflammation or promote it (which they do when we have flu, so our body aches and we feel depressed afterwards).

We can have too much or too little inflammation. Stress, whether physical or psychological, suppresses inflammation when cortisol suppresses immunity, and anti-inflammatory drugs play on this mechanism (Sapolsky 2004). But chronic stress can manifest as inflammation in joints, connective tissue and organs. Chronic high blood pressure that damages arteries causes an inflammatory response. The normal state of the gut is one of controlled (by neuropeptides) inflammation as it's on the front line of dealing with foreign material (Maté 2011). If chronic stress tips the balance so that gut inflammation gets out of control, the result can be inflammatory bowel disease.

Gerhardt discusses the low cortisol scenario from early stress and trauma (2015). If the child doesn't learn to express distress and anger effectively, he becomes chronically stressed and high cortisol can flip into low cortisol – which means his stress response fails to suppress his inflammatory response. The result can be chronic inflammation which provides "fertile ground for all sorts of more life-threatening diseases such as heart disease and cancer to flourish" (2015: 116). This low cortisol scenario may be present in the excessive inflammation in joints, connective tissue, organs and the gut described above.

So psyche can affect inflammation in the body and thereby contribute to physical illness. In the other direction, soma to psyche, "your body's state of inflammation … can have a direct effect on how you feel, and what you think about", says Bullmore (2018: 21). And this can reach the level of the changes to mood, thinking and behaviour that amounts to depression.

Pain

The brain, not the body, decides if something hurts. Australian physiotherapists David Butler and Lorimer Moseley, authors of the illuminating *Explain Pain*, say all pain is produced by the brain, and it's all real (2013). It's there to protect us, not to make us suffer. Receptors (peripheral nerve endings) in skin and tissue react to damage such as cuts and heat by firing 'danger' signals to the spinal cord where neurons relay the signals to the brain.[9] When it receives these danger signals, the brain decides whether to translate them into pain.

Let's assume danger results in pain. Different receptors, neurons and pathways signal acute and persistent danger: fast (myelinated) pathways for acute so we move, slow ones for persistent so we can heal (Sapolsky 2017). The fast pathways lead to sharp pain but are soon inhibited, so the 'ouch' is dulled. The slow pathways lead to throbbing pain and keep firing. Tissue damage can lead to inflammation which, though meant to heal, makes the receptors more sensitive and affects neighbouring areas so that they hurt too.

The brain responds to danger signals by releasing neuropeptides that make spinal cord neurons on slow pathways more sensitive, so they fire more strongly and for longer than receptors do (Bloom, Nelson & Lazerson 2001).[10] Enhanced sensitivity can mean that what was hurting now hurts more, and what didn't hurt starts to hurt (Butler & Moseley 2013). Persistent pain usually involves danger signals being amplified in the spinal cord to encourage us to act on them. Endorphins counter amplification and the sensitivity ends "once the damaged structures are under control, and/or you fully understand what is going on", say Butler and Moseley (2013: 75).[11] Less anxiety means less pain.

Danger becomes pain

Danger signals arrive in the brainstem and are sent onwards and upwards. The insula generates the *sensation* of pain, the anterior cingulate the *emotion* that accompanies it (Ramachandran 2011). The brain decides we're 'in pain' and we don't distinguish the sensation from the agony. "The brain is not a mindless pain-ometer, simply measuring units of ouchness", explains Sapolsky (2004: 193). In generating painful feelings, it interprets danger signals contextually.

The fast/slow distinction continues in the brain (Bloom et al. 2001). Fast pathways lead to the insula and produce sharp pain to warn us. Slow pathways lead to the anterior cingulate and produce nagging pain that makes us miserable so we don't ignore the injury, and to the amygdala – when the brain decides we're in pain, it arouses the FEAR system (Panksepp 2012). The brain also changes its cognitive state so we prioritise protecting our body (Damasio 2010).

Also, the brain area for a damaged body area may grow and overlap with other areas for other body areas (Butler & Moseley 2013). This is cortical 'smudging', and the nearby body areas become more sensitive too.

Sensitisation, chronic pain and trauma

After an injury heals, pain may persist because the brain thinks a threat remains (Butler & Moseley 2013). The cingulate's capacity for generating agony means that further emotional stress can mean further pain. The brain can generate pain from internal stimuli, without any bodily stimuli (Bloom et al. 2001). Old pain has primed it to protect us, and the cingulate doesn't distinguish emotional from physical pain.

Sensitisation can mean that other body signals, such as touch, are interpreted as danger and trigger pain (Butler & Moseley 2013). We may experience stabs of pain unrelated to anything we're aware of. Fearful thoughts can maintain and magnify pain, especially if we don't understand how pain works. Persistent pain can become chronic pain: the central nervous system becomes so sensitised that we may develop fibromyalgia, chronic fatigue, repetitive strain injury or back pain. Tissue damage is no longer the real issue.

What may be the issue is old trauma making the brain vigilant for further threats. Combined with tissue damage at some point, this can lead to chronic pain. Porges thinks polyvagal theory provides a model for linking trauma with chronic pain: traumatic experiences can leave the nervous system in a chronically vigilant state (2017a). The best way for the brain to protect the body is to make it hurt. But healing old trauma and understanding pain may help to alleviate chronic pain.

Touch

Touch is the "mother of all senses", proposes Schaible (2009: 32). It's the first sense to develop in the womb, and after birth our psychological and neurological development depend on it. So there's plenty of scope for evolution-supported pleasure, as well as for problems if we're not touched enough or in a way we like.

Loving touch and holding are even better than breast milk for healthy neural development (Schaible 2009). There's evidence that they help more cortisol receptors grow in the hippocampus, so infants have lower cortisol levels and more ability to cope with stress. Being well held allows muscles to relax, breathing to deepen, and feelings of safety and support – a healthy parasympathetic response.

Skin is a sensory organ with some 20 different sorts of receptors for different aspects of touch, such as temperature and vibration, light and firm touch (Carter 2009). Having our hand gripped feels very different from having it stroked. Different receptors mean different pathways to the brainstem and thalamus and different cortical destinations. *Firm touch* pathways go to the somatosensory cortex and enable us, for example, to manipulate objects (Cozolino 2006). *Light touch* pathways go to different neural columns in the somatosensory cortex, and also to the insula, anterior cingulate and orbitomedial prefrontal cortex, to enable communicative emotional touch and soothing.

The involvement of the insula enables us to distinguish our own touch from others' touch, starting in babyhood so we recognise our mother's touch. Light touch triggers oxytocin release and bonding responses, and endorphin release for feelings of well-being. Blood pressure drops, the immune system is stimulated and autonomic regulation and cardiovascular health are supported (Cozolino 2006).

Touch in therapy

Therapists can 'touch' their clients with their sensitivity and their voice, and many therapists never physically touch their clients for fear of invading their boundaries. However, there are states of deep distress where people can't be reached by words, the sort of distress an infant might experience. Occasionally I have the feeling that it would simply be wrong *not* to offer a hand to hold – at these times the 'mother of all senses' is needed. Of course, the client can say no. Working with touch requires experiential training to learn the required sensitivity.

The body in therapy

The somatic and affective dimensions of therapy are as important as the cognitive, maybe more so. The mind can be changed with new ideas, but the client may feel that nothing has *really* changed inside. Going deeply inside involves immersion in his bodily experience, and real psychological transformation is experienced on a visceral level. Engaging the body is a bottom-up intervention to accompany top-down talking therapy, increasing the opportunities for integration. Restricting ourselves to top-down work only may be limiting what we can do by half.

Do therapists have to get out of the chair to work with the body? Doing so changes the dynamic and brings fresh air into the room. But there's much we can do to work with the body while remaining in the chair. This requires experiential training, and we must first delve deeply into our own bodily experience to be properly prepared for accompanying our clients into *their* inner depths.

Sensing the body

The body can be observed from outside via posture, gesture and other aspects of body language. 'Going inside' to sense the body from within relies on interoception. It fires up the right brain-body ensemble and brings the person into the here-and-now, shifting the client out of their usual talking self. It helps to grow the right frontal lobe's capacity for affective and somatic regulation. Noticing the depth of one's breathing is an obvious place to begin.

Interoceptive awareness comes more naturally for some than others. Thanks to the right brain's tendency to rekindle old trauma in the body, many people are understandably averse to it. But everyone can appreciate that bodily awareness is a good thing, and neuroplasticity means that anyone can improve their interoceptive capacity with practice, noticing feelings and sensations, and reflecting on their possible meaning.

Working with the felt sense means encouraging the client to notice how he carries situations in his body, such as a tight chest or a burden on the shoulders ("take a moment to sense how all this feels in your body just now"). Or, to notice the place in his body where an emotion arises from ("can you sense a place in there where your tears come from?"). Or, inviting him to pause to sense the felt background of his talking ("let's pause a moment so you can sense this whole business inside").

Everything the therapist wants her client to do, she can do herself: sensing her own bodily experiencing, her somatic countertransference. She can also develop her sensitivity to her clients' somatic communication, including breathing patterns and skin colour changes.

Completing emotional cycles

From a body perspective, completing cycles of emotional arousal that have stopped midway in the past is key in therapy. Once completed, the psyche reaches a new state of balance and integration. And from a whole person perspective, the more ways we have of helping cycles to complete the better, whether based in talking therapy, body therapy or anything else.

Engaging the right brain-body ensemble

A neuroscience perspective implies that, whatever we do, we must engage the right brain-body ensemble – and for this, therapist and client must form a good working partnership. We can engage with the body indirectly via aspects of experience rooted in the right brain: relationship patterns, family systems, childhood, imagery and transpersonal experience. All of these imply the body and have emotional power. The therapeutic relationship is a particularly effective avenue for changing the right hemisphere and the balance with the left: it's immediate and visceral.

Grounding talking therapy in the body

Therapeutic dialogue can be grounded in the body. Interpretations can be checked by noticing whether they *feel* right or not, the left hemisphere consulting the right. Both therapist and client can talk from their felt sense of the topic being discussed (right), and not rely solely on their mental filing cabinet of familiar stories and concepts (left). And when dialogue feels meaningful to both, the body is implied.

Other ways to ground talking therapy in the body are to address the client's eating and exercising habits, and to encourage body practices such as yoga and tai chi to complement therapy.

Conclusion

We have some answers to the questions posed at the beginning of the chapter. Suppressing emotion can have negative effects on the body which can be hidden from self and others. Ongoing stress, and trauma, can contribute to illness. Paying attention to bodily feeling can evoke bottom-up emotional catharsis that might never happen with top-down interventions. And therapists of any persuasion can work with the body by drawing attention to the felt sense and pointing to whatever's meaningful in the therapeutic dialogue.

The 'wisdom of the body' involves the brain as well the body, thanks to the right brain-body ensemble. Furthermore, we needn't always separate brain from body – one implies the other. The body belongs to the psyche whether we deliberately include it or not. But when we do separate them in order to understand them, we see that often, but not always, it's the brain that initiates and the body that influences.

Do therapists need training in anatomy and physiology? I think there's a good case for this, but such training must be kept in proportion so that it doesn't crowd out experiential learning and psychological understanding.

Therapists' remit is generally to intervene via the mind; our remit to intervene via the body is more limited. So whatever the importance of the body to the mind, our normal way in is via the mind. Even if a problem seems to be more in the body than the mind, it may still be the easiest way in. But mind can lead directly to body, and body can be a gateway to more of the mind.

In the next chapter, we'll explore the role embodiment plays in aspects of mind we engage with in therapy.

Notes

1 The enteric nervous system "alters the gut environment and manages digestion by controlling the acidity, fluidity, secretions of digestive fluids, and mechanical contractions of your gastrointestinal tract", says gastroenterologist Emeran Mayer (2018: 102).

2 Two more terms are *efferent* and *afferent:* efferent nerves are motor nerves from brain to body, afferent nerves are sensory nerves from body to brain. An easily confused bit of scientific nomenclature!

3 Lymph nodes are found in many places in the body: clustered in the armpits, the groin, the neck and all along the midline of the thoracic and abdominal cavities (Bullmore 2018). Immune cells also meet up in lymphoid tissue in the tonsils and adenoids and gut, and in the spleen, bone marrow and the thymus gland.

4 The organisation of body signals into a map of the body in the insula and somatosensory cortex is called *somatotopic* (think topography).
5 Somatosensory cortex divides anatomically into SI and SII areas. SI looks after tactile and vibratory sensations, SII feelings of pain and pleasure – SII is more closely associated with the insula and therefore body sense (Damasio 2003).
6 Speculating ... breathing techniques can be evocative, and the sympathetic-parasympathetic oscillation implies bilateral stimulation – could this have similar effects to the bilateral stimulation of EMDR?
7 Maybe we should be careful with 'gut feelings' – George W. Bush famously followed his when he decided to invade Iraq.
8 Even longer terms for the same thing are 'psychoendoneuroimmunology' (PENI) or 'psychoneuroendocrinoimmunology'. There's also 'neuroimmunology' and 'immunopsychiatry' – essentially the same subject.
9 The whole process is called 'nociception' – the perception of danger, beneath awareness – and the receptors in skin and tissue that send danger signals are called 'nociceptors'. 'Nociception is neither sufficient nor necessary for pain', say Butler and Moseley (2013: 32). Others refer to these receptors as 'pain receptors', but pain is made in the brain not in the body.
10 The neuropetide in question is called substance P (Bloom et al. 2001). P for pain? Surely not so simple!
11 The endorphin release happens in the pituitary gland in the brain and directly in the spinal cord (Sapolsky 2004).

Chapter 10

Engaging the mind

Introduction

Can we engage the mind while staying connected with the body? The mind can seem to be separate from body and feeling. We say "you need to get out of your mind and into your body", which is sometimes a good idea, and "stop thinking and get into your feelings", as if one precluded the other. This duality is often blamed on Descartes and his maxim 'I think therefore I am', for which he gets a lot of stick – scapegoated, perhaps, for our own struggle to reconcile thinking with feeling.

Neural architecture sheds light on the question. It offers us the premise of having one brain but two minds, one in the right hemisphere background, enmeshed with the body, the other in the left hemisphere foreground, standing apart from the body; working separately and working together. Hence, we may be 'of two minds' about something as the hemispheres slug it out, and then 'of one mind' when they unite.[1]

Let's explore how 'the mind' can both obstruct psychological transformation and participate in it. In therapy, we don't want to merely re-arrange the mental filing cabinet, we want to *really* change minds. And we need to think with the felt sense.

What is the mind?

I rather concur with Claxton who says "after more than a hundred years of scientific psychology we still struggle to give an overall account of this mysterious organ of intelligence" (2015: 23). Neuroscientists often describe the brain's mental activity in terms of processing information and computing everything. They must be wedded to their computers, for whatever the brain does, it surely doesn't 'compute'. There must be more to a mind that can be creative and imaginative.

We can conceive of the mind as a process rather than a thing, as McGilchrist does: "a way of being, more than an entity" (2009: 20). Damasio veers towards process when he says minds are a "flowing combination of actual images and recalled images in ever-changing proportions" (2010: 71) – neural not visual images. Mind as process suggests we don't switch it on to 'use' it but engage with it while it's firing of its own accord anyway. Greenfield highlights the notion of mind as a resource at our disposal, "something continuously available yet something you need not necessarily be accessing all the time" (2017: 7). Much of it must be processing things in the background, away from the foreground mind that tries to figure things out. Thoughts come to us when we're doing something else, clarity dawns after we've rested. I've been stuck umpteen times while writing this book, yet the next day my mind has found a path through the jungle.

The relationship of mind and brain

Whether mind and brain are the same thing is debated endlessly. If they're not, we enter dualist territory, so neuroscience generally thinks they are. Panksepp, for example, thinks "they are really one and the same thing" (2012: XIII). His mind is essentially affective in nature, a bottom-up process that leads to the top-down control we're familiar with. If mind and brain *are* largely synonymous, then mind must be affective as well as cognitive, much of it unconscious, and at least half of it directly embodied. We can correct our bias towards our conscious, cognitive mind.

Whether or not mind and brain are precisely synonymous, the brain is involved whatever our minds do and whatever we do with them. Understanding the brain may help us understand our minds. McGilchrist suggests we call the mind "the brain's experience of itself", so the brain lends its structure to the mind (2009: 19).

Do two hemispheres mean two minds?

If the brain lends structure to the mind, we can play with the one brain, two minds hypothesis. As discussed in Chapter 3, the left hemisphere works in an ordered sequence, naming and categorising the things it focuses attention on, while the right plays with whole experiences, as when an image (inner and visual) or a dream unfolds. Left is a rationalising mind in the more conscious foreground, while right is a feeling bodymind in the less conscious background.

We have no direct sense of two minds at work, but we can see the distinction when, for example, we get stuck trying to solve a problem and later witness a solution arrive unexpectedly. With one mind we say "I can't see it, I'm stuck", with the other we say "er ... something's just occurred to me ...". And whereas the foreground mind may anxiously inhibit its partner and dig a deeper hole for itself, the background bodymind shares its fresh idea so both can co-operate in making the solution explicit. Two distinct mental processes, one bringing frustration, the other possibilities.

The embodied mind

Minds can be embodied, especially the right hemisphere 'background bodymind' – perhaps there are degrees of embodiment. Damasio thinks the foundations of our minds lie in brainstem areas responsible for mapping bodily feelings, including those of pain and pleasure, which form "the primordial constituents of mind, based on direct signalling from the body proper" (2010: 76). Because of this, the "ebb and flow of internal organism states ... constitutes the backdrop for the mind" (1999: 30). Before the mind can become disconnected from the body, it's first embodied – a bottom-up perspective. Embodiment is not something to be achieved, it's something to be experienced when we overcome our top-down bias.

This doesn't mean that the mind *is* the body. Rather, mind is infused with body, unable to cut off from it even if we *feel* disconnected from it. Equating mind and body surely misses the point about embodiment. Also, it allows no scope for the hypothesis, that makes sense of our experience, of a right hemisphere that's embodied and a left hemisphere that stands aside from the body.

Embodiment is not just for the foundations of the mind, leaving the upper echelons free to depart from bodily influence. Our conceptual systems draw on our embodiment. George Lakoff (a linguist) and Mark Johnson (a philosopher) explain how "our common embodiment allows for common, stable truths" that we need to live and work together (1999: 6).

The critical mind

Most of us experience a critical mind that attacks us inwardly, leaving us feeling bad ("I'm no good", "I'll never get this right"). Also known as the inner critic and superego.

Some writers link it with the frontal lobes. Sapolsky says "the frontal cortex is the nearest thing we have to a superego" (2004: 229). McGilchrist thinks the critical mind is a front-back issue, not a left-right one (2010). This implies the frontal lobes as regulators of our wilder selves, telling our posterior lobes what's OK and what isn't.

Cozolino, however, sees a left-right dynamic (2017). He places the phenomenon in the right hemisphere, the hemisphere that's "the worrier, the critic", and "biased toward negativity" (2017: 430). Our critical voices are "remnants of voices of parents and tribal leaders" from our evolutionary past that "supported group coordination, cooperation, and cohesion", and that we experience as aspects of ourselves (2017: 430).

Having dealt with many inner critics, my own and others', I'm not persuaded by these explanations for this powerful psychological phenomenon. When I hear someone's critical mind speaking, I hear their left hemisphere saying something non-specific and repetitive that cuts them off from their felt sense in the right hemisphere. It looks like a pre-emptive strike against the self to dodge someone else's critical attack. It evokes bad feelings in their right hemisphere, and suggests a left-right constellation to maintain the psychological status quo. However, when I hear someone putting the critical voice aside and listening to their felt sense, the right hemisphere responds with vulnerable feelings, suppressed emotion, and fresh associations.

A hypothesis for the critical mind's origins ... without an empathic connection between our felt experience and another person (that unites the hemispheres), we become anxious, encouraging the inner critic to wade in to protect us.

Attention

Engaging the mind means turning our attention to something, since we can't attend to everything. The brain receives more sensory signals than it can bring into awareness, so attention acts as a filter (Kandel 2007). When we do something automatically because it's familiar, we still need *some* attention (Goldberg 2009). If I talk to my passenger while driving the car, my attention may be largely with our conversation, but if I pay no attention to driving, I'll be in trouble. I can divide my attention.

Attention is not just another cognitive function. McGilchrist describes it as "a relationship ... that brings into being a world" (2009: 29). Where we turn our attention changes the nature of our experiencing. By attending to someone else, we become more like them in our behaviour and in how we think and feel, and "the attention we pay to anything also determines what it is we find" (2009: 133).

Attention in the brain: top-bottom

The top-bottom axis sheds light on the voluntary and involuntary aspects of attention. Goldberg suggests considering attention as a set of stage lights in the brainstem that are controlled by the frontal lobes (2009). The stage they illuminate is in the posterior lobes, occipital for vision, temporal for hearing, parietal for the body. Top-down pathways from the frontal lobes to the brainstem facilitate voluntary control of attention, while bottom-up pathways from brainstem and thalamus facilitate involuntary shifts of attention triggered by external stimuli. So attention is a team effort across the brain. When there's a conflict for my attention, such as when I'm torn between my own thoughts and listening to you, the anterior cingulate, linked to body and emotion, helps decide where my attention goes (Siegel 2007).

Focused and global attention: left – right

The left-right axis explains the difference between focused and global attention (McGilchrist 2009). The evolutionary origins of this arrangement are illustrated by the example (Chapter 3) of a bird focusing attention to find grain in the soil while maintaining global attention in case of lurking predators. McGilchrist thinks this is at the root of lateralisation in brain evolution. They're such different forms of attention that they had to be kept apart in the brain; while being predators, creatures must avoid being prey lest they become evolutionary toast. The human mind uses the spotlight of focused attention to make things and grasp things, and the broad sweep of global attention to absorb music, other people, and the ever-changing world around us.

McGilchrist elaborates on the role of the right hemisphere. It attends to our peripheral vision, and only this hemisphere "can direct attention to what comes to us from the edges of our awareness" (2009: 40); this is true whether the sensory signals come from left or right eyes or ears. Because of the original predator-prey dilemma, it "guides the left hemisphere's local attention", changing its focus when needed (2009: 43). So it's dominant for exploratory movements of attention, while the left focuses on whatever's the priority. Learning new skills and having novel experiences engages the right in particular.

The right hemisphere's global attention is primary: first we take in the whole ("that's a table", "this feels like an argument"), then we focus attention on something about it ("it needs cleaning", "I didn't say that!"). Right can therefore re-orient left's focused attention. Although we mainly notice what's in our focused attention, our global attention is where the power to change our mind lies.

We tend not to notice our brain's binding of the two forms of attention. But if you stop reading at this point and look out of the window, or close your eyes and sense how you feel in your body, you may notice the change of mental gear and of what captures your attention ...

Attention in therapy

Where do we place our attention in the therapy room? The client focuses attention on what troubles him, perhaps trying to figure out why he behaves as he does. Part of the therapist's job is to engage his global attention by pointing to what lies at the edge of his awareness: unexpressed feelings, what's happening in his body, his felt sense of what he's talking about. Interventions such as experiential exercises can bring open attention to the inner world of his right hemisphere to balance focused attention in his left.

The therapist can interweave both kinds of attention. With focused attention on the content of the dialogue, she can also have global attention to the process: the nonverbal communication, her own feelings, and what arises in her mind. In my psychosynthesis training, we were taught to have 'bifocal vision' for both foreground detail and the background 'bigger picture'. We can hold both focused and global attention simultaneously, thanks to our divided brain.

Consciousness

We engage the mind and turn attention to the edge of awareness in order to allow new things into consciousness. This can become a confusing topic, partly because 'consciousness' means many things to many people. What I mean by consciousness here is allowing aspects of our experience into awareness. What can neuroscience tell us?

Consciousness is a minefield for neuroscientists who dare to research it, says Damasio, since it involves consciousness exploring itself (2010). Having traipsed through the minefield, he concludes that it's "the part of mind concerned with the apparent sense of self and knowing", and "an indispensable ingredient of the creative human mind" (1999: 27–28). This suggests its importance to the work of psychological transformation.

Consciousness is close to *wakefulness* – what happens when we wake up – but the two can be separated (Damasio 1999). For one thing, we're either awake or we aren't, whereas consciousness comes in degrees which, for example, are assessed in coma patients by doctors. It's also close to *awareness*, but neuroscience distinguishes the two since we can be conscious but aware of a little or a lot. However, for our purposes, we can probably put consciousness and awareness in the same general basket.

Consciousness in the brain

We may see consciousness as a 'higher' function, but an evolutionary perspective suggests a bottom-up process. For McGilchrist:

> consciousness is not a bird ... coming in at the top level and alighting on the brain somewhere in the frontal lobes – but a tree, its roots deep inside us. It reinforces the nature of consciousness not as an entity, but as a *process*.
>
> (2009: 221)

The same bottom-up view underlies Damasio's proposal that we think of consciousness in layers (1999):

- *Core consciousness*, rooted in the brainstem, gives us our sense of self in the here-and-now. We need this layer to bring our mind into the present moment.

- *Extended consciousness*, more cortical, dependent on memory and enhanced by language, allows us to have an elaborate sense of self with a past and a future. We need this layer for our identity.

In practice, we sometimes lose touch with core consciousness and need to be reconnected with it through meditation or focusing. Perhaps Goldberg is in such need, as he believes consciousness and the frontal lobes have evolved together since any aspect of mind can be made conscious, and the frontal lobes are the convergence zone where everything comes together (2009). But where things come together may not be where they start.

We might conclude that becoming conscious of something requires us both to be 'in the moment' and to pause for the elements of experience to converge in a new constellation.

The feeling of what happens

Damasio links consciousness with emotion and body (1999). That it can't be separated from emotion is evident in brain injury patients for whom emotion stops when consciousness stops. Neural mapping of the whole body underlies "the feeling of what happens" when we engage our senses, and is the beginning of consciousness (1999: 26). Such a feeling precedes the interpretations we make about it – experiencing comes before verbalising. So consciousness amounts to "the feeling of a feeling" based on "the universal nonverbal vocabulary of body signals" (1999: 30–31). This sounds like the felt sense: the feeling of what's happening inside in the moment, a feeling without a clear label, as when we say "something doesn't feel right . . ." and pause to sense what it may be.

Ocean waves, currents and depths

Very little brain activity enters consciousness, perhaps as little as 1% (McGilchrist 2009). We can't grow more consciousness to make this 2%, but we can grow the range of things that make it into the 1% zone when needed.

Let's return to Claxton's metaphor of waves breaking on the ocean surface of awareness (2005). Below them lie the hidden undertow of currents of neural activity (implicit memory, neural predictions, emotional triggering etc.) that affect our conscious experience outside awareness. Running with the metaphor . . . breaking waves bring thoughts, feelings and so forth into awareness; a felt sense of their undercurrents underlies them, everything is integrated. We can also look further afield to the edges of awareness and see waves breaking we hadn't noticed before, exploring the sense of what happens around them; everything is integrated. In the depths beneath the waves, it's too dark to see anything – it's all unconscious and always will be. And: sometimes a rogue wave breaks unexpectedly on the surface, not fitting the pattern of other waves, a dissociated fragment of experience. It erupts from we know not where, from no felt sense. If we're curious about it, a process of unfolding and integrating may begin. (Warning: the metaphor may not be perfect).

Conscious experience may be just one manifestation of all the brain activity going on beneath the surface. That all sorts of things happen outside consciousness isn't in doubt: the drama of our dreams takes place without it, for example. Perception needn't rise above the surface. But allowing things into consciousness has advantages for, as Jung says, "the reason why consciousness exists, and why there is an urge to widen and deepen it, is very simple: without consciousness things go less well" (1986: 29).

Consciousness and lateralisation

Consciousness can look like the beam of focused attention since, as McGilchrist says, "conscious processing tends to go on in the left hemisphere" (2009: 187). However, relatively little of what the left hemisphere does is in consciousness, as the 1% estimate of conscious brain activity makes clear. So we can't just put consciousness in the left and everything that's unconscious in the right.

Perhaps when something enters consciousness, involving both hemispheres, it can then be absorbed into the left hemisphere's routine capacities. It can return to consciousness whenever needed. How to drive your car, for example. But something else that's never really entered consciousness sits in the right hemisphere background at the edge of awareness, available to global attention, waiting to be noticed by the left's focused attention. My tendency, on occasion, to try to dominate a conversation, for example.

Consciousness in therapy

Therapy hinges on things entering consciousness that have previously not made it there. Instead of searching for presumed 'unconscious' feelings and memories, we can watch the ocean waves more closely. The right hemisphere can *seem* to be 'the unconscious' since it's the source of much that has previously eluded our focused attention, and of dissociated trauma fragments. But there are no depths we can safely dive to; allowing unconscious things to enter consciousness is a process that requires both global and focused attention, both hemispheres. Left looks to right to see more of the ocean.

For example, the client knows he sometimes puts people's backs up, but he doesn't understand why this happens. He sees the big wave breaking, but not the undercurrents. If he stops trying to explain it and starts exploring his felt sense of what happens, he may become conscious of some undercurrents. His left hemisphere consults his right, and a process of unfolding awareness begins. Maybe he glimpses an old anger he was suppressing.

Cognition

According to cognitive science, cognitions are mental representations of aspects of the world or of ourselves, and the mind works by manipulating such representations. But things may not be so straightforward. Francisco Varela, a neurobiologist who promoted dialogue between science and Buddhism, challenges this view of cognition. He argues eloquently that:

> cognition is not the representation of a pregiven world by a pregiven mind but is rather the enactment of a world and a mind on the basis of a history of the variety of actions that a being in the world performs.
>
> (Varela, Thompson & Rosch 1993: 9)

It can be understood as 'embodied action' rooted in the individual's history of embodiment and the body's sensorimotor capacities. Cognition is therefore personal, and "all cognition brings forth a world" (Maturana & Varela 1987: 29).

Embodied cognition

Varela's view of cognition suggests a right hemisphere perspective of interconnected minds and bodies, in contrast to a left hemisphere one of detached representations of the world. If we have only the left hemisphere's view and omit the body, a disconnect may arise between mind and body (Porges 2017). But if cognitions remain anchored in the body, we have their context and history, and they will evolve as we reflect on our lived experience. This may be what nature intended for, as Watt argues, "evolution appears to have created a seamless integration of homeostasis, emotion, and cognition" (2003: 91).

Perhaps there are two kinds of cognition. One is embodied, integrates the hemispheres, and reflects how we really are in the world. The other is a more limited kind associated with a left hemisphere that lacks the contribution of the right and the body, either temporarily due to stress and suppression of feeling, or more permanently due to dissociation in the right brain.

Cognition and emotion

We've already seen that affect is primary – implying that cognition is secondary. Cognition should regulate emotion, but our emotional reactions have a habit of arising first, and then we try to control them. And whether we like it or not, as Gazzaniga says, "emotions colour our cognitive states almost moment to moment" (2016: 79). Cognition may be an evolutionary enhancement on raw emotion. Watt, for example, thinks it evolved to make our enactment of emotional tasks, such as selecting a mate and gratifying our attachment needs, more effective (2003).

On the other hand, cognitive networks may sometimes fire with a degree of independence from emotional ones (LeDoux 2003). My left hemisphere may be able to ignore the emotional signals of my right so it can focus on cognitive tasks. However, this only works up to a point. My emotional state colours my cognitive one, my feelings may interrupt such that I attend to them rather than my task, and any disconnect between my cognitive and affective capacities will exact a price on what I achieve, through its disruption of neural integration (Cozolino 2017).

Reflecting on our feelings is itself a cognitive process since, as Damasio points out, "feelings are just as cognitive as any other perceptual image" (1996: 159). Noticing feelings and naming them are examples of cognition.

Cognition and the hemispheres

We may tend to ascribe everything cognitive to the left hemisphere, but the right is also cognitive, though in a different way. "Our two cerebral hemispheres have such different cognitive and emotional perspectives on the world", thinks Panksepp, that words delude us as much as they inform us (2005: 302). The left is better at constructing an account of things, lying if necessary, while the right reveals our intimate secrets. Right is needed for expressing deep emotions, while left will express superficial ones if left to its own devices.

The left hemisphere's style is sequential, so it likes to take things apart and put them together again one by one (McGilchrist 2009). By contrast, the right hemisphere's cognitive style is one of seeing something come into focus as a whole; the left hemisphere can then help to make explicit what's implicit in the whole. This is the essence of 'focusing' (Gendlin 1996): we feel something (the felt sense) but lack the words to articulate it, then we get a 'handle' on it, and finally the feeling shifts – "ah, now I see what this is about".

Another view comes from Schore (2012). He refers to 'primary process cognition' generated by the right hemisphere. It develops in infancy, is fused with affect, makes quick, unconscious evaluations of self and other, and finds expression in nonverbal communication. 'Secondary process cognition', by contrast, is generated in the left hemisphere, develops later in childhood, is language-based and more conscious, and concerns facts. In normal conversation, we use both forms of cognition – explicit content and implicit nonverbal communication. They may be integrated, or they may conflict with each other.

Working cognitively in therapy

Whether we call ourselves cognitive therapists or not, much therapeutic work is cognitive. We work with the foreground mind on attitudes and beliefs, and on what the client thinks about his feelings. The more embodied his cognition (e.g. "I'm uncomfortable around anger"), the more effective this is.

However, cognitive work may be insufficient if we don't also work affectively. We can do so by working experientially with emotion and the body, and with what arises spontaneously from within. Vice versa, working emotionally must be balanced with cognitive work, since our core emotions are universal givens with typical expressions, whereas our cognitions are more personal and dependent on our history.

Can I change my thoughts to change my mind? Up to a point, yes. I can catch a negative train of thoughts ("I'll never get this book finished") and deliberately think something different ("I *can* finish it"). But it works better if I feel whatever feelings accompany these thoughts and imagine the positive outcome so I have a felt sense of it.

Interpretation

Interpretation is a cognitive approach to engaging the mind and probably all therapists, not only psychoanalysts, do it in some way. It aims to get underneath the explicit mental level to reach the implicit backdrop, to make what's unconscious conscious. Interpretations may point to an aspect of the client's experience he's unaware of. They need to be on the mark and well-timed; if they land well, the client will pause and reflect. The therapist gets past the client's left hemisphere interpreter by naming a defence that previously kept painful things at bay – left-right and top-down inhibition are paused, and the client may become emotional. The hemispheric bias shifts from left to right for a time as greater self-awareness unfolds from the right hemisphere.

There are pitfalls to bear in mind (Schore 2009). If the client is emotionally aroused, then empathic support may be needed instead of an interpretation that his mind is in no state to reflect on. And if he's acting out, interpretation is useless and may worsen the enactment.

Thinking

Therapists want their clients to think, but in a reflective way, and not too much. What can neuroscience tell us about thinking?

We usually contrast thinking with feeling, but from the brain's perspective the real contrast is with acting. For it to think about acting without actually doing so is a spectacular evolutionary achievement. Brains have evolved to link thinking and feeling seamlessly and quickly with behaviour, but they can also inhibit movement and action. This allows us to do more thinking and thereby refine our options: think before you act.

Thinking may seem like something we *do* consciously, but most thinking *happens*, outside awareness. In fact, most mental processes we call 'thinking' happen without consciousness and without language (McGilchrist 2009). That we don't need language to think is evident when we have a thought we struggle to articulate. Deliberate thinking in words can fill our awareness, but we're unaware of the background processes that serve up fresh ideas. And I sometimes suspect my cat is thinking ...

Thinking and the brain

Conscious thinking tends towards the left hemisphere while unconscious background thinking, that may lead to original thought, tends towards the right (McGilchrist 2009). We need both because if we try to make all our thought processes explicit, the quality of our thinking deteriorates as we get stuck in the left hemisphere's surface view of the matter. "Both thought and its expression originate in the right hemisphere", says McGilchrist, and then the left hemisphere joins in (2009: 189).

The quality of our thinking may reflect serotonin levels in the brain. Serotonin inhibits over-excitable neurons and "makes the thinking process more relaxed", according to Lewis (2012: 81–82).

Thinking and the body

We associate thinking with our heads, but the body also plays a role. The right hemisphere links our visceral experience with our knowledge about the world, and the fact that thought is rooted in such experience allows us to have shared truths about the world (McGilchrist 2009). Just because we often disagree doesn't diminish the importance of these truths.

The 'body' here may mean what Panksepp calls the 'neurosymbolic' body in the brain – the brain's mapping of the body (2003). This mapping changes all the time. For example, when body energy is low because the immune system is highly active, thinking slows down – as you may notice when, for example, you have flu (Claxton 2015). The hormonal state of the blood entering the brain affects the quality of our thinking, as some of my female clients regularly remind me. And when my brain triggers anxiety in my body, its feedback contributes to my tendency to think further anxious thoughts.

Thinking and feeling

We may *think* we can think clearly while side-lining our feelings, but this is only partly true. Some explicit thinking may require inhibition of emotional signals from the right hemisphere, but thinking generally needs to be integrated with feeling, the hemispheres working together. Otherwise, we think in ways that are disconnected from the reality of other people and the wider world. Feelings could be said to orient our thinking to what's relevant in a situation.

Thinking can change the way we feel about something, and becoming aware of feelings can change our thinking. Both may be equally powerful.

Conceptual thinking

Concepts may seem to be rooted in the left hemisphere world of language, but McGilchrist says "we do not need words in order to hold concepts" (2009: 109). He follows Lakoff and Johnson who believe that "our conceptual systems draw largely upon the commonalities of our bodies and of the environments we live in", so that they're either universal or at least capable of crossing borders of language and culture (1999: 6). Thinking requires intuitive perception based on bodily experiencing, as well as concepts and knowledge. Otherwise, our conceptual systems become divorced from reality and therefore useless.

Psychotherapy theory, for example, must accord with our lived experience lest it bamboozle us with clever ideas. Once established, a theory is vulnerable to being supplanted by a better theory, since our lived experience evolves.

Reasoning and rationality

Reasoning involves the body since, as Lakoff and Johnson point out, "the very structure of reason itself comes from the details of our embodiment" (1999: 4).[2] Reason requires both hemispheres to work together, says McGilchrist (2009). Explicit reasoning and step by step argument lean to the left, while deductive reasoning (that infers individual instances from a general principle) leans to the right. He believes that "reason emanates from . . . the emotions, in an attempt to limit and direct them, rather than the other way about" (2009: 185).

Support comes from Damasio who thinks emotion, for better or worse, is integral to reasoning (1999). He has reason and emotion coming together in the prefrontal cortex, and points out that damage to somatosensory areas in the right hemisphere compromises reasoning as well as feeling.[3]

None of this need surprise us. Seeing what follows from an emotional appreciation of a situation is just as important when we think about it as arguing over what follows logically from an abstract idea (McGilchrist 2009). Therapists need their clients to think rationally about their feelings, as well as experience them.

Explicit and implicit thinking

Because we're aware of whatever's foreground in our minds, we may equate thinking with the explicit mental processes of the left hemisphere. But thinking also happens implicitly in the background, outside awareness. As Damasio says, "reasoning and creative thinking can proceed while we are conscious of something else" (2010: 72). What else would be the point of 'mulling things over'? Creative thinking doesn't happen by explicitly thinking something through in steps.

Furthermore, when we try to be explicit about how we arrived at an idea, we can get into a mess since it didn't arrive through an explicit process. If we over-analyse our thinking processes, we generally make poorer judgements because the implicit aspects of thinking involve the right hemisphere (McGilchrist 2009). At a certain point, they need the left as well to make them explicit.

A computer programmer I once saw told me how he enjoyed problem-solving to make software work, but dreaded the team meetings to explain how he arrived at his solutions. He didn't know! We have to trust our implicit thinking which, of course, may or may not lead to the best solution.

Understanding

The hemispheres take different routes to understanding something (McGilchrist 2009). The left builds up understanding from the parts, as if building a wall brick by brick. The right derives understanding implicitly from the felt sense of the whole wall; this may involve an illogical series of thoughts that contribute to forming a picture. The two sorts of understanding can combine. The left's understanding provides certainty and structure, the right's an embodied perspective and a reminder that what appears to be the truth is only ever provisional. Right tempers left's over-excitement.

For example, this book. I've amassed hundreds of computer files on neuroscience to organise the information. I also have a heap of little notebooks where I write thoughts that come when I feel I'm 'getting' something. Integrating the two kinds of understanding requires effort.

Problem solving

When we *try* to solve a problem, we can run into the limitations of explicit thinking. However hard we try, a solution evades us. Then we need to 'sleep' on it – literally, for sleep aids problem solving because "a morass of unhelpful facts are broken through to get to feelings" when we're asleep, says Sapolsky (2004: 231).

According to McGilchrist, the right hemisphere presents "an array of possible solutions", while the left "takes the single solution that seems best to fit what it already knows" (2009: 41). When we wake up with the solution to a problem, it's probably arisen in the right; the left hemisphere may be unsure about it, and the feeling differs from when we pick a solution that fits what we know.

Thinking in therapy

We want our clients to think, but in implicit as well as explicit ways. It's no use their straining their left hemispheres to puzzle things out: better to float ideas to see what stirs in the felt sense in the right. When we ask a question, we needn't demand an answer. We can encourage reflective thinking and mulling things over, during sessions and in-between sessions. The notion of 'psychological thinking', so helpful to making therapy work, is thinking that includes the right hemisphere world of feeling, relationship and imagination.

Language

Neuroscientists believe language has turbocharged the human brain to an evolutionary peak. Greenfield, for example, says it allows us to escape the here-and-now, remember the past and plan the future, and "indulge in scenarios that have never been" (2001: 75). With language, we can make novel associations between people, events and things.

Some people have reservations about language because it can trap us in a verbal world. In reality, it's a double-edged sword. We begin life without it, but from our second year onwards, as the left hemisphere enters a growth spurt, language infiltrates most of our experience and social behaviour. In Chapter 2, we saw how Stern describes its ambiguous effects in child development, both separating the child from his lived experience and enabling him to share it with others (1998). And so it continues through life: we can use language both to deceive others and detach ourselves from bodily experiencing, and to express ourselves authentically and enjoy social engagement.

Language facilitates communication between minds. Within our own minds, much happens without it. McGilchrist explains: "we make sense of the world, form categories and concepts, weigh and evaluate evidence, make decisions and solve problems, all without language" (2009: 107). Most of this takes place outside awareness, so neuroscientists may be over-egging the role of language.

Nevertheless, language is an embodied skill whose origins lie in "the empathic communication medium of music and the right hemisphere", claims McGilchrist (2009: 119). He continues:

> the deep structure of syntax is founded on the fixed sequences of limb movement in running creatures ... the very structures and content of thought itself exist in the body *prior* to their utterance in language.
> (2009: 119)

Language and the hemispheres

We associate language with the left hemisphere, the one that speaks most often. Speech is centred in Broca's area in the left frontal lobe, close to the motor area controlling grasp in the right hand (McGilchrist 2013).

What's interesting is the right hemisphere's contribution, thinks McGilchrist (2009). While the left focuses on one meaning of what's said, the right broadens it out into related meanings, hence its association with creativity.[4] Left places words in grammatical sequence and has more vocabulary and more complex syntax, which "extends vastly our power to map the world" (2009: 70). It deals in representations of things, their names, substituting signs for experience, and manipulating ideas and people. In contrast, right listens and makes sense of what people *really* mean, from context and emotional tone. Words can mean different things, after all, depending on the context. The right frontal lobe also enables us to use language with empathy, irony, humour and metaphor.

Talking therapy

The left hemisphere "may be more adept at lying and constructing a social masquerade" than being honest about our feelings, says Panksepp (2005: 302). So therapists obviously need to engage the right hemisphere, and can lead the way in using language to communicate openness and thoughtfulness. Speaking and our choice of words can come from the felt sense, which usually means slowing down the talking and allowing for pauses. We can also use language to connect with the client when he's in an uncomfortable emotional place and falls silent.

Intuition

The border between background and foreground minds is where intuitions form. Claxton describes it as "the kickings of the unconscious brain" that come into awareness, "those experiences that are somewhat conscious, but ill-informed, vague, allusive – and elusive" (2005: 268). Intuition needs time to become clear, and for us to decide what to do with it.

Intuition originates in the right hemisphere (McGilchrist 2009). We sense it implicitly, then make it explicit with our left hemisphere. It depends on the orbitomedial prefrontal cortex, with its links to the body, giving us a sense or a gut feeling that feels right (Siegel 2010). It results from unconscious background processing that brings something we wouldn't have arrived at by thinking deliberately and logically (Cozolino 2010). Intuition highlights the difference between the responses of left and right hemispheres to a situation. It can be a more effective mental process than conscious comprehension.

The brain extracts patterns from experiences to refer to in future. For Damasio, intuition is a "covert mechanism" in which it consults memories of somatic responses, positive or negative (1996: 188). Schore says something similar: "intuition depends on accessing large banks of implicit knowledge formed from unarticulated person-environment exchanges", working nonverbally outside awareness (2012: 122).

These explanations sound database-y (to coin a term), and the question arises whether intuition emerges *only* out of neural mappings of past experiences. It can seem to us that something more is involved; for example, when we do something new that feels right in an internally persuasive way. I've experienced this sometimes in new situations where, with reflection, I've had an intuitive sense of a way forward that turned out well. Was my brain simply drawing on patterns from the past without my knowing? Brains are inventive, and the right hemisphere is good on novelty. Maybe it has a talent for finding steps into the future.

Apparently 'complete' systems of thought, such as the left hemisphere likes to build, are ultimately incomplete (McGilchrist 2009). Their foundations lie in intuition, and the premises from which rational system-building begins must be intuited. But intuition doesn't stop, so the system of thought has to evolve. This might have a bearing on the theories underlying psychotherapy and psychoanalysis …

The intuitive therapist

During my training, intuition made me nervous. Some people were told they were very intuitive, which was lovely for them but obviously didn't include me. Then I discovered that intuition is a normal phenomenon of everyone's mind, especially when we relax and listen to our felt sense.

Intuition is obviously a valuable aspect of a therapist's skill. It implies doing more than responding to clients in scripted ways, and drawing on more than just our explicit thinking. Trusting our intuitive mind means trusting ourselves and our feelings, knowing that sometimes we'll make mistakes but must nevertheless take risks if we're to engage deeply with our clients.

The relaxed and receptive stance is conducive to intuition, as is the fact that sometimes we must respond to the client when we're unsure how to. Schore says intuition is "a complex right brain primary process, an affectively charged embodied cognition … especially in moments of relational uncertainty" (2012: 135). Somewhere in the background, we have our felt sense of the situation. We may have hunches, sudden insights and odd feelings we can't explain that turn out to be valuable. When the left hemisphere is stumped, we must turn to the right – something's happening there we can rely on.

Insight

Insight is close to intuition. What distinguishes it is that we feel stuck sometime before it comes. A solution appears suddenly out of apparently nowhere and we immediately sense its rightness, as when Archimedes leapt from his bathtub. Insights "explode into consciousness", in Claxton's description (2005: 227). Then we try to explain them, not necessarily successfully.

McGilchrist thinks the right hemisphere weaves together all the different aspects of a situation in the background and then "the whole suddenly breaks free and comes to life before us" in an 'aha!' moment (2009: 228). Insight happens when we're not focused on what it concerns, so the left hemisphere isn't involved, and is associated in particular with the right temporal lobe.[5]

Insight in therapy is sometimes considered to be the shift that brings transformation, but others see it as the *result* of transformation, such as Panksepp (2009). I go along with the latter view, but insight and a shift in the felt sense of the situation can seem to come simultaneously.

Imagination

Using our imagination means setting our mind free to roam where it will. The right hemisphere plays a big role, especially the right frontal lobe, but it takes both hemispheres to make imagination work for us (McGilchrist 2009).

If you imagine a sound or visualise something, your auditory or visual cortex lights up almost as they would if you were actually hearing or seeing it. Neuropsychiatrist Peter Fenwick points out that "as far as the brain is concerned, experiences which arise from the mind are just as real as those which arise from the outside world" (Fenwick & Fenwick 2011: 211). But the extent of perceptual activation is attenuated in imagination so that, in Claxton's words, the brain "produces a rather watered-down or bleached-out version of a scene" (2005: 275).

Using the imagination can be liberating for both therapist and client. The client may be unable to stand up to someone in his life, but he can *imagine* what standing up to that person would feel like, and then he may be halfway to doing so. Imagination can be grounded in the body and felt sense, and therefore in what's realistic. He can imagine his future and he can imagine his past, including his infancy before his autobiographical memory developed. And his imagination may be the doorway to unexpressed feelings.

For the therapist, her imagination is vital in reflecting on what it might be like to be the client, seeing things from his perspective and empathising with him.

Creativity

Creativity is a universal attribute of human minds. It's also an emotional experience. According to Panksepp, the SEEKING system "energises all human creativity" by motivating us to find new ways to solve problems and express ourselves (2012: 103).

When we relax and stop *trying* to do something, our attention broadens out and our left hemisphere engages with our right, says McGilchrist (2009). Creative impulses are more likely to arise in the right, the hemisphere biased for novelty due to its continually changing landscape as it weaves inner and outer worlds together moment to moment. Right tends to generate multiple responses to novel situations. But both hemispheres are needed for creativity, as things they previously kept separate must be united. Through sequential analysis, the left "forces the implicit into explicitness, and brings clarity" (2009: 207). Also, while the right tends to bin ideas that don't accord with experience, the left can entertain them.

As well as being an attribute of minds, creativity is also a learnt skill in that it benefits from our learning to tolerate conflicting thoughts, uncertainty, ambiguity and a degree of confusion. We do this by throttling back on hemispheric suppression and putting up with the discomfort. According to Claxton, "creativity depends on the brain's ability to modulate the strength and spread of its own inhibition" (2005: 271).

There's plenty of scope for creativity in therapy, where no one's watching over what transpires between client and therapist. Sometimes, the therapist finds herself in a place without any clear signposts and simply *has* to be creative.

Decision making

Nervous systems evolved to make decisions – about movement, for example. They learn, thereby enabling us to refine our choices over time, and they can do this unconsciously. Most decisions make themselves as we go about our daily lives, but some don't and we can't figure out what to do. Such decisions propel many people into therapy ("should I leave my partner?", "what direction should I take in my life?").

We may think we make decisions consciously, but many significant ones are made in the unconscious way the philosopher Daniel Dennett describes:

> our decision bubbles up to consciousness from we know not where. We do not witness it being *made*, we witness its *arrival*.
>
> (1984: 78)

An implicit process underpins the explicit one; without it, we don't make the decision unless we deliberately override our feelings. Everyone knows that making a list of pros and cons doesn't necessarily help.

We need our feelings since, as Damasio says, "emotion is integral to ... decision making, for worse and for better", although being *very* emotional can lead to making decisions we later regret (1999: 41). The implicit process involves somatic markers, the brain's implicit memory of what felt good or bad in our body in the past (Damasio 1996). Somatic markers improve decision making, working in the background. We may not know *why* we made a particular decision, though our left hemisphere can invent a reason to justify it. Our feelings provide a compass for making decisions – and conflicting feelings can block the implicit process.

Decision making in the brain

The implicit nature of decision making was demonstrated in a famous experiment by Benjamin Libet and colleagues in the 1980s (Frith 2007). Volunteers were asked to lift a finger whenever they felt the urge to do so, and to report when they had the urge. EEG equipment measuring neural activity not only found that the urge to lift the finger was experienced 200 milliseconds before the finger moved, but also that there was associated firing 300 milliseconds before the urge. When the volunteers thought they decided, their brain had already decided. Does this mean that free will is an illusion? Hopefully not – this phenomenon can also be interpreted as demonstrating the primacy of implicit processes in the right brain over explicit ones in the left (I'm speculating, as Libet made no distinction between which hemisphere was doing what).

There's certainly a front-back divide here as the associated firing was detected in the parietal lobe and the conscious urge in the frontal lobes. Our frontal lobes may think they're in charge, but they can't perform their 'executive functions' such as decision making without input from the posterior lobes. Nevertheless, Goldberg says "whether you are decisive or wishy-washy depends on how well your frontal lobes work" (2009: 100).[6]

Unless we force a decision, it's probably made in the right hemisphere with its wholistic processing and is then grasped and articulated by the left. Hence the experience of its arrival, and the value of consulting our felt sense when decisions don't make themselves.

Making decisions in therapy

Clients often come to therapy because they feel stuck on an important decision (for example, about a relationship). Therapists can help them explore the conflicting feelings causing the impasse in an attempt to align feeling with thinking. The inner conflict may point to unresolved experiences and emotional issues from the past; for example, insecurity triggered by wanting to end a relationship.

I've taught workshops on decision making based on the felt sense, and they're invariably thought-provoking. What's essential is that participants don't try to *make* a decision, but rather to explore the different feelings underlying the impasse. Sometimes a decision then makes itself, sometimes not.

Will and agency

In my psychosynthesis training, the two major aspects of psychological life were said to be love and will (Assagioli 1990). We have to find a balance of both in our lives – relationship and autonomy. What does neuroscience have to say about engaging our will?

We've seen how Libet's finger-lifting research brought into question the notion of free will, implying that it's the icing on a cake that's already been baked unconsciously. But McGilchrist points out that we can stop an impulse to move in its tracks, so at least our conscious minds have 'free won't' (2009).

Panksepp's three levels of neural control of emotion is a useful map here (2012). He thinks "free will" is "a tertiary-level neurocognitive function" that we use for planning and that "can only emerge from well-sculpted, deeply self-reflective, cognitive attitudes" (2012: 448). But there's no free will at the primary or secondary levels, so we can't will ourselves out of emotional turmoil or bad emotional habits (unfortunately). Exercising free will requires the cognitive mind engaging in self-reflection.

'Agency' is a close relation of will: it's "the technical term for the feeling of being in charge of your life", says van der Kolk (2014: 95). And it starts with interoception, which implies that we can't just will ourselves to feel we're in charge – it has to arise naturally from our embodied mind.

McGilchrist thinks there's a tendency for passivity to be linked with the left hemisphere and its love of routine, and independence with the right with its propensity for novelty (2009). However, left, with its purposefulness, would seem to be more about conscious will than right. But we may be over-identifying with the conscious aspects of will ("I will do X"), whereas genuine free will surely requires both hemispheres, and that means a more relative role for the left hemisphere. In Libet's experiment, "the conscious left hemisphere believes that it is an originator, whereas in fact it is a receiver of something that comes to it from elsewhere" (McGilchrist 2009: 191). Left may think it's in control, but really it selects from choices emerging from the broader world of the right.

When we find ourselves caught between two opposing choices, we may literally be 'of two minds'. The research on split-brain patients shows how one field of consciousness can accommodate two wills; for example, the man who embraced his wife with one arm and pushed her away with the other (Chapter 2).

Will has a bodily aspect in that we need sufficient blood sugar to exercise control over our feelings and behaviours. As Claxton says, "it takes a lot of energy to keep the prefrontal cortex pumping out all that inhibitory activation" (2015: 127).

Humour

When we feel safe and enjoy humour, the possibilities for social engagement expand. Panksepp says laughter is "rooted in the ancient PLAY systems that generate joyful social engagement", implying it's a fundamental emotional response that doesn't necessarily require "cognitive complexity" (2012: 367).

The right hemisphere, with its ability to understand meaning in context and as a whole, is essential for humour (McGilchrist 2009). It enables us to understand non-literal meanings, get a joke and enjoy irony, and tolerate uncertainty and ambiguity. Maybe this is why humour helps to defuse aggression and defensiveness, and to undermine the rigidities of conceptual thought. It brings the right hemisphere into a left hemisphere conversation in an unthreatening way.

Perhaps what we enjoy is the novel constellation of explicit and implicit meanings that humour sets up between the hemispheres, with the right finding an unexpected discrepancy in something presented by the left. Think of the *Two Ronnies* TV sketch set in a hardware store where shopkeeper and customer cross wires over the purchase of "four candles" or "fork handles"...

Humour can oil the wheels of therapy, bringing an element of PLAY into what leans towards the serious and emotionally painful. It creates social engagement where polyvagal danger may threaten, and helps both client and therapist relax into their bodies with both hemispheres available. Carefully used, humour builds trust.

Reflection

The capacity to reflect is required in therapy for both client and therapist to see themselves freshly. Reflection must be more than just thinking about ourselves rather than someone else. We need to look within to the inner world of the right hemisphere, which supports our left hemisphere in engaging with the outer world and sometimes conflicts with it, to sense what's happening there.

"We are keyed to action and not to reflection", say Maturana and Varela, yet reflection is "the only chance we have to discover our blindness" (1987: 24). Paradoxically, we may be blind despite looking outwards much of the time. "Every reflection brings forth a world", and then we may see both ourselves and the outer world more clearly (1987: 26). We allow a natural process to take place whereby new worlds unfold, and we feel alive.

Reflection doesn't just happen, it requires intention (Siegel 2007). Intending to attend to the inner world of the right hemisphere is a practice we can cultivate. We can learn to notice sensations, feelings, the flow of thoughts, the felt sense of a situation, and to 'stay with it', maintaining open attention to whatever comes.

For people who grew up experiencing secure attachment, reflection may come quite naturally, probably because their left hemispheres have less cause to suppress their right. Cozolino points out that attachment research has shown how securely attached children say self-reflective things, reflective parents have children who are reflective, and reflection correlates with the capacity to tell our story in a way that makes sense to others (2010).

Mindfulness

The practice of mindfulness develops the capacity for self-reflection. Siegel reports research showing mindfulness activating medial prefrontal areas which support both social attunement with others and internal attunement with self (2007). Secure attachment, mindful awareness and prefrontal brain function overlap, inner and outer worlds reflecting each other. The more attuned we are within ourselves, the more we're attuned to others, and vice versa. Prefrontal brain function, which dampens our emotional reactions and judgemental thoughts, includes integration with the anterior cingulate and insula, so that emotion and body are included.

Narratives

We love to tell our story. Doing so connects us to others and integrates neural networks (Cozolino 2017). It doesn't merely communicate what happened; it supports affect regulation when we're stressed, helps the frontal lobes co-ordinate mental functions, organises our self-identity, reduces anxiety, and integrates feeling with cognition and behaviour.

Story-telling begins with parent-child talk in the first year (Cozolino 2016). There's a link between the security of a child's attachment and the complexity of his narratives. But where parents carry unresolved trauma and overwhelming emotion, their own stories may lack coherence, which affects the child.

The coherence of our narratives is mediated by the right prefrontal cortex (Schore 2009). Narrative enables the left hemisphere's semantic processing to integrate with the right's emotional processing (Cozolino 2017). Gestures bring the body into the picture. Even when a story departs from the facts, the storyline, imagery and emotional expression knit together networks linking the hemispheres, and cortex with subcortex.

Therapeutic narratives

The client may tell stories he's never told anyone, and piece together new stories from fragments of memory. There's an inner urge to tell his life story in a way that fits his inner world of feeling and connects him with the therapist. Using narrative to weave cognition together with emotion, feeling and behaviour leads to better neural integration (Cozolino 2017).

Trauma leaves a lack of narrative coherence in its wake, and talking through it may repair things. Placing overwhelming feelings into a story puts them into perspective and makes them easier to understand. It's possible to construct a story that supports the integration needed to avoid further dissociation (Cozolino 2017). And when the client co-constructs a story with the therapist that resonates with his feelings, his inner world seems less crazy to him.

Some people begin therapy with stories so lacking in coherence that I don't understand them. We make a joint effort to piece things together ("so this happened, you felt X, and then you did Y"). Over time, I understand their stories better as their right hemisphere capacity for coherence grows. Therapy is an exercise in learning how to communicate what's happened and the effect it had on us.

Conclusion

The mind can both participate in psychological transformation and obstruct it. The model of a foreground mind and a background bodymind, correlating with left and right hemispheres, can help us understand how both phenomena happen, and offer clues to overcoming obstructions. Engaging the participative mind means meeting the criteria of embodiment, of grounding thinking in the felt sense, and of balancing cognitive with affective work. Then minds can be not merely re-arranged, but transformed.

If client and therapist turn their attention to what's meaningful for the client, the work should be therapeutic. In the next chapter, we'll explore what 'meaningful' means.

Notes

1 This is speculative; an alternative possibility is that such dilemmas may reflect two competing left-right constellations.
2 Lakoff and Johnson elaborate: "the same neural and cognitive mechanisms that allow us to perceive and move around also create our conceptual systems and modes of reason" (1999: 4).
3 Damasio says emotion and reason come together most in the ventromedial area of the prefrontal cortex (1999). Ventromedial sounds close to orbitomedial.
4 McGilchrist elaborates: "the right anterior temporal region is associated with making connections across distantly related information during comprehension, and the right posterior superior temporal sulcus may be selectively involved in verbal creativity" (2009: 41).
5 The area of the right temporal lobe particularly associated with insight is the anterior superior temporal gyrus (McGilchrist 2009).
6 The key area is the orbitomedial prefrontal cortex where cognition and subcortical emotional signalling come together (LeDoux 2003), giving us a top-bottom angle, the job of the cortex being to inhibit the inappropriate response rather than make the appropriate one (LeDoux 1999).

Chapter 11

Meaningful experiences

Introduction

We can engage our minds in ways that unlock their talent for finding meaning in experiences and for making life as a whole feel meaningful. We can have good experiences that happen spontaneously and have a transformative effect, and we can have experiences that feel bad at the time but which later become meaningful when we accept them and include them in our life narrative.

When an experience is meaningful, we feel more whole. Mind and body, feeling and thinking, unite. The sense of a renewed self probably correlates with better integration across the neural axes. The divided psyche becomes a more united psyche, as if left and right hemispheres have re-aligned themselves in a more co-operative constellation.

The experience of meaning unfolding in surprising ways points to the right hemisphere. First we experience it, then we think about it. The wholistic nature of the right brain makes it both personal and transpersonal in nature, embracing our past, our potential and our connection with the wider world.

Life should be a meaningful experience, but when it isn't, therapy may help. To be effective, therapy must feel meaningful. The client must discover fresh meaning in his life experiences. He may not be able to explain how his life now feels meaningful, but he knows implicitly whether it does or doesn't. The inner world of his right hemisphere is primary here, whatever his left hemisphere thinks or says.

So there are both meaningful experiences and the experience of life as a whole being meaningful. If I look back in my own life, I see an unhappy landscape in the past enlivened by meaningful experiences such as the revelation of discovering ancient Greek temples as an impressionable teenager and experiences of profound inner peace after learning to meditate while at university. Nowadays the landscape is a happier one, and my life usually feels satisfyingly meaningful. The best thing I ever learnt is how to sit with unwanted feelings so a fresh sense of meaning unfolds from them, left hemisphere giving way to right (many people learn this in infancy, but I didn't).

This is a big subject without obvious boundaries, so I'll discuss a few aspects that are particularly pertinent to therapy.

Making meaning

For life to *have* meaning, we need to *make* meaning of our experience. Making meaning is an implicit process rather than an explicit mental activity, connecting body with mind, and feeling with thinking. It starts early in life, as Trevarthen points out: "infants are ... meaning-making subjects with playful intuitions that require imaginative companions who will validate those meanings" (2009: 62). Making meaning requires relationship, and is central to a sense of well-being.

But meaning-making can be problematic. Parents may not validate their child's meaning-making, leaving him lacking in confidence. He may suffer painful and traumatic experiences that seem meaningless. He may make meanings from bad experiences that lead to further unhappiness; for example, the child who feels abandoned by an angry parent may erroneously interpret other people's anger towards him later in life as a rejection. And a common complaint is that despite having the trappings of a successful life – relationship, good job, money – life lacks meaning ("what's it all about?").

Knowing meanings and making meaning

There's a difference between knowing the meaning of something and making new meaning. Neuroscience sees deriving meaning as the brain interpreting the signals from our senses. For example, Kandel says neural pathways have "rules of guessing" that "allow the brain to extract information" from sensory signals and "turn it into a meaningful image" (2007: 296–297).

But this might be merely the unreflective way of assigning meaning to things. The brain must do this for, as van der Kolk says: "the mind cannot help but make meaning out of what it knows" (2014: 191). The fastest way is to think 'this equals that', and lump a new experience into a familiar category, without pausing to sense its uniqueness. For example, people unfamiliar with therapy sometimes think it's about giving advice or devising strategies to change behaviour. Their left hemisphere assigns a familiar meaning. We often repeat old meanings in a way that doesn't feel very meaningful.

However, making new meaning does feel meaningful. Psychologist Ed Tronick points out that "meaning is not one thing – one meaning"; rather, we experience a "flow of meanings" (2009: 87). And such a flow feels good, for "successful meaning making carries with it a sense of expansion and positive affects ... perhaps leading to a feeling of exuberance and aliveness, or an oceanic feeling of wellness" (2009: 88). When this happens with others, we feel engaged with them, while failing to evoke new meanings may leave us feeling disconnected and anxious. Making meaning, looking with fresh eyes to see what we haven't seen before, is an emotional process.

The different contributions of each hemisphere shed light. The right hemisphere enables us to understand what others mean because it appreciates meaning "as a whole and in context", according to McGilchrist (2009: 70). It deals with implicit rather than literal meanings, so it gets the moral of a story or the point of a joke. The left, however, trades in explicit meanings and, with its greater vocabulary and its capacity to play with ideas, it allows us to understand new ideas. It's good with existing meanings and grasping the meaning of ideas, whereas right is good with unfolding fresh meaning from emotional and social experiences. We need both hemispheres' contributions.

The process of making new meaning that feels right unfolds from our felt sense of a situation. At first, we may only *sense* the new meaning and be unable to articulate it ("ah, I've got it! Umm ..."). We don't just think what the meaning of something is, we sense what feels meaningful to us.

Gendlin says the felt sense contains the meaning we want to express; our meaning is implicit (1964). Instead of jumping to an explicit meaning that feels unsatisfactory, we can pause and wait for words to unfold from our felt sense – maybe they will, maybe they'll take their time. If the left hemisphere can let the right take the lead then, sooner or later, we get to say what we feel and what we mean. The right hemisphere senses implicit meaning in something, the left makes it explicit.

Making meaning in therapy

Therapy is a big meaning-making process. There are four hemispheres in the room, all of which need to participate. The therapist can facilitate meaning-making by embodying it and guiding the client to do likewise. Instead of the therapist telling him what things mean, hypotheses can be offered, and the client encouraged to make his own meanings. It's collaboration and teamwork, avoiding over-reliance on the therapist's interpretations (the psychoanalytic cliché) on one hand, and the therapist leaving it all to the client (the person-centred cliché) on the other. Therapist and client will make different meanings, and the task for both is to seek common ground. This is what makes therapy such stimulating and rewarding work.

The wholistic nature of the right hemisphere means that by exploring felt senses of implicit meaning, old wounds and unresolved traumas emerge from the background. For example, in discussing what a past relationship meant for the client, his unexpressed grief about its ending may suddenly well up. His felt sense is temporarily obliterated by emotion; the therapist puts meaning-making on hold and provides support. After the catharsis, a new felt sense constellates, and if client and therapist stay with it, new meanings will arise. What had previously felt unbearably painful becomes a meaningful experience, and the client's capacity for making meaning in future expands.

There are two ways to get to what's meaningful. One is to re-direct attention to the inner world of body and feeling, the other is to steer the dialogue towards meaningful content. How does the therapist know what's meaningful? She follows her felt sense, drawing on experience, intuition and knowledge. How does the client know what's meaningful? He feels it as an 'inner knowing'.

Imagery

Images put verbal minds into a different mode, whether we're contemplating art or seeing inner images. They have a way of feeling meaningful, surprising us, evoking feelings and triggering associations that our verbal minds might never make. Whilst thoughts and words can keep us in our explicit mind, images steer us towards the inner world of our background bodymind.

Pop psychology says the right hemisphere does images while the left does words, but this is simplistic. Both hemispheres process images, but in different ways. McCrone explains it thus: right looks after the "more global aspects" of an image, "the sense of where everything is and how things broadly connect", while left focuses in on particular elements within it (1999: 175). For example, imagine a large capital M composed of many little z's; we need our right to see the M and our left to see the z's.

The spontaneous 'bubbling up' of images in the mind probably happens in the right hemisphere, which then shares it with the left in the stream of inner world signals flowing across the corpus callosum (Cozolino 2017). This stream doesn't often enter awareness because left filters out signals from right in order to stay focused on the foreground. Hence images that do float into awareness can be fleeting and slippery, as are dream images when we wake up. There's also a front-back angle: imagery seems to be generated in the posterior lobes, at the anatomical junction of occipital, parietal and temporal lobes, before arriving in the frontal lobes (Greenfield 2017).[1]

When we turn our attention inside, eyes closed or unfocused, images may arise spontaneously, or we may deliberately visualise something. Imagery exercises involve activity in the insula and anterior cingulate, implying that body and feeling are involved (Cozolino 2006). They can evoke emotion, unexpected associations and memories in powerful ways, and are usually experienced as meaningful, sometimes profoundly so. It seems that we move into a state biased to the right hemisphere and benefit from its interconnectedness.

Symbols

A snake, the tree of life, the devil ... symbols are evocative images, full of meaning. That's meaning as in 'this feels meaningful', not meaning as in 'a green light means go'; Jung made a sensible distinction between symbols and signs (1978). The word 'symbol' is much used these days to mean a pictorial version of a word denoting something specific (e.g. 'click on this symbol'), which is a left hemisphere sign. A right hemisphere symbol, however, brings "an endless network of connotations", says McGilchrist (2009: 51). Contemplating a symbol can open up the depths of the mind that is one with feeling and body through the right brain-body ensemble – a meaningful experience.

Imagery and symbols in therapy

Suggesting to the client that he visualise a scene or invite an image to come inside can be a powerful intervention for getting underneath his talking and into his felt experiencing. There needs to be safety and trust for him to let go to his inner world, and timing needs to be considered.

When an image or a symbol arises, the befuddlement of knowing what it means suggests a right hemisphere experience (Fenwick & Fenwick 2011). Sitting with it and then drawing it before talking about it encourages holding the experience so that implicit meanings can come to mind. Trying to pin down an explicit meaning prematurely may encourage a narrower left hemisphere focus to take over, although this doesn't necessarily happen and the urge to talk may be overwhelming.

Dreams

Anyone who questions whether dreams are meaningful might like to explain why on earth the nervous system would put so much time and energy into a meaningless activity. The value of dreams is that they arise from a different mind than the one that demands to know what everything means. Dreams may be the best demonstration we have of the background bodymind and implicit processing, with bottom-up, back to front, and right brain biases. The fact that they often leave us perplexed doesn't render them meaningless.

The brain's extraordinary creative abilities are unleashed in our dreams. They can be better than going to the movies: my recent nocturnal activity has taken me cycling across Africa and watching one of my sources on the left-right axis in this book sailing a catamaran single-handed to win a yacht race (impressive, and two hulls!). They lead us into a more ancient world where we're closer to nature, but they nevertheless embrace modern accoutrements such as planes and cars (seemingly not computers or smartphones, fortunately). Damasio says dreams reveal "the depth of unconscious processing" that happens in the brain in which "the imagination goes wild and reality be damned" (2010: 178).

Dreaming in the brain

We dream profusely during rapid eye movement sleep, which was discovered by waking people up in sleep laboratories. REM sleep and dreaming arise from different mechanisms in the brainstem, but the two are usually well co-ordinated (Panksepp 2012). We also dream during non-REM sleep, but dreams with narratives are more likely in REM sleep. Whether we recall our dreams is another matter.

There's "evidence of a continuous thought process occurring during sleep", and dreams arise when this process reaches a certain level of arousal in the brain, according to Solms (2015: 138). Motor signals to the body are inhibited so the body doesn't enact the dream, although it may twitch (including the rapid eye movements). Dreams involve the senses, especially vision, sometimes hearing and touch, but never smell, and pain is usually suppressed. SEEKING arousal plays an important role, implying the dreamer's motivation.

During REM sleep, the frontal lobes are relatively inactive, hence the absence of reality-testing, while subcortical areas take centre stage and imbue dreams with emotion (Sapolsky 2004). Visual areas of the brain are particularly active. The normal front-back and top-bottom balance in waking life seems to reverse so that posterior lobes and subcortical areas are in charge. Dreaming appears to be a bottom-up process since it involves a fountain of acetylcholine being released in the brainstem to fuel higher subcortical and cortical areas (Greenfield 2017). In the cortex, the same junction of posterior lobes that generates imagery fires up; damage to this area abolishes dreaming.[2]

Neuroscience suggests that dreaming is more fundamental than being awake. The brainstem networks that generate REM sleep sit below those that wake us up, implying that REM sleep precedes waking in evolution and in child development (Panksepp 2012). Greenfield thinks REM-related dreaming may be the brain's default activity (2017).[3] We begin life with it: in late pregnancy, baby sleeps most of the time, and for half his sleep time he cycles regularly into REM, probably having embryonic dreams. This pattern continues after birth, the REM proportion of sleep time only declining to a quarter in adulthood.

Dreams may seem like a weird distortion of reality, but perhaps dreaming is the real basis of experience that waking life then modifies, as

Fenwick and Fenwick suggest (2011). Hamlet may have got it the wrong way around – the truth may be that "we dream perchance to wake" (2011: 213).

Dreaming leans to the right

Research evidence says the right hemisphere dominates in both REM sleep and dreaming (McGilchrist 2009).[4] A bias to the right may fit with dreams being more visual than verbal, the imagination running riot, their emotionality, and the idea that they speak an inner truth that contrasts with what we want to believe about ourselves. When we wake up, the left hemisphere wonders what the dream was about, and may reach for books on dream symbols to find the answer.

The interconnectedness within the right hemisphere may underlie the seemingly bizarre connections between dream elements. In REM sleep the brain makes more far-flung associations than when we're awake (van der Kolk 2014). An old repetitive dream of mine was of being on a plane that trundled along a road instead of a runway, resolutely refusing to 'take off'. Our imagination in dreams is of a different order than in active imagination exercises, perhaps because there's even less left hemisphere involvement and frontal lobe reality-testing.

Exploring dreams in therapy

The left hemisphere wants to know what a dream means, the right re-lives it and allows implicit meaning to unfold. Both client and therapist can accommodate both attitudes, perhaps leaning to the right's. Being interested in dreams has a value in itself, opening our left hemisphere to the inner world of the right, whether or not we discover their meaning. The therapist needn't put herself under pressure to interpret his dreams 'correctly'. She can embody curiosity and an open mind, and see what comes. Dreams sometimes offer signposts to the work.

Jung said that dreams compensate for our conscious experience:

> The relation between conscious and unconscious is compensatory ... When we set out to interpret a dream, it is always helpful to ask: What conscious attitude does it compensate?
>
> (1986: 66–67)

They become valuable when we put them alongside the context of the dreamer's waking life. The more the therapist learns of the client's life, the better placed she is to understand the context and help him make sense of the dream. Simply re-immersing oneself in the dream may not be enough to reveal meaning.

Gendlin points out that dreams can give rise to multiple meanings as we reflect on them (1986). If there's such a thing as a 'correct interpretation', it's the dreamer's body that signals it with a "yes, that feels right" felt shift – *Let Your Body Interpret Your Dreams* is the title of his book on dreams. We can allow the right hemisphere to take the lead in exploring dreams.

In a later article, Gendlin highlighted a way to explore dreams that draws out the inner conflict they often embody: look for the disagreement between the dream and the dreamer (1992). For example, I dream of being pursued by a character I want to get away from, but he gets closer and closer. Perhaps this is a hemispheric dispute in which the dreamer behaves like my left hemisphere persona, wanting to be in control and prone to anxiety, while the dream story disagrees, expressing my right hemisphere's emotional truth – I should face this inner character who's an aspect of me.

Transpersonal experience

Many people have experiences that take them beyond their usual sense of self and feel profoundly meaningful. They're often shy about reporting them ("I've never told anyone this before"). Such experiences get called transcendent, spiritual, mystical and religious; I'll settle for 'transpersonal'. We feel their significance when we have them ourselves, and we can sense their significance for others when we hear them describe theirs'.

When we feel moved by an experience that seems 'beyond words', it's likely to have arisen in the right hemisphere (Fenwick & Fenwick 2011). We may feel peaceful and filled with joy. Life becomes more meaningful, and we feel more connected with ourselves and with the world. Some people imagine they've gone 'beyond the brain', but it's more likely they've gone beyond their left hemisphere. The right experiences it, the left is unable to categorise it.

The right posterior lobes stand out in transpersonal experience (McGilchrist 2009). The following points have been reported:

- Research points to the right temporal lobe – for example, patients with temporal lobe epilepsy sometimes report having hallucinations with mystical or religious content (Nataraja 2008).
- The temporal lobes were targeted by magnetic stimulation emanating from a helmet constructed by Michael Persinger, a Canadian neuroscientist, which induces mystical experiences – although not when placed on his own head or that of Richard Dawkins (Blackmore 2017).
- The parietal lobes have been shown to go quiet in nuns and Buddhist meditators able to go about their spiritual practices while lying in brain scanners, and in the right parietal lobe this correlates with the self-other distinction dissolving, leading to unity experiences (Blackmore 2017).

- The right temporoparietal junction, where temporal and parietal lobes meet, is a key area – body signals meet other sensory signals in this area, and disturbances in it correlate with out of body experiences and the self-other distinction evaporating (Blackmore 2017).
- EEG research into meditation experiences show alpha waves associated with deep relaxation starting in the right hemisphere and spreading to the left until both hemispheres fire in sync (Nataraja 2008).

Unsurprisingly, there's controversy here, with sceptics such as Jarrett casting doubt on some of the conclusions (2015). For example, Persinger's research led to the notion of a 'God spot' in the right temporal lobe, but Jarrett thinks transpersonal experiences happen across networks linking parietal, temporal and frontal lobes, as well as the insula and caudate.

The front-back axis plays a role in transpersonal experience. McGilchrist says the left frontal lobe "brings distance, and allows the experience of the peaceful detachment from the material realm" (2009: 92). It can inhibit left temporal and parietal lobes, which are centres for language and sequential analysis.

The transpersonal in therapy

Therapy that includes the inner world of the right hemisphere tends to bring a transpersonal dimension. It may involve active exploration, eyes closed exercises that work with inner body awareness and imagery, and it may come about through an openness to archetypal themes underlying personal issues. Not everything the client faces is about mum and dad and his childhood; some of it is the challenge of allowing his individuality to unfold and find its place in the world – individuation.

Taking transpersonal experiences seriously brings therapy alive. Feelings of depth and meaningfulness are good for the soul, whatever one believes about their origin. They transcend the surface level of experience, implying a very different right-left constellation from those that get us through daily life. They give the client confidence that he has inner resources to overcome his difficulties and, if the therapist takes them seriously, more trust that his experiences will be accepted rather than judged.

Transforming the self

For therapy to bring about meaningful change, something about 'self' must transform. But what is the self that we explore, discover, realise and actualise – is it my 'real self', my 'authentic self', or my essence or 'soul'?

'Self' can mean many things, so let's go with what clients say. A common complaint is to be "out of touch with myself". A common resolution is to feel that "I've got my old self back again", or to have "found my real self". Such rough statements about self are meaningful – they give us a sense of what is meant. Such a self seems to be an implicit foundation of the psyche, affective and embodied. It's quite different from the anxious person who tries to work out what's wrong with him and how he should change.

Neuroscience views of the 'self'

For LeDoux, the self is "the totality of the living organism" (2003: 26). This comes from his book *Synaptic Self*, which implies that the essence of who we are lies in our synapses, the most plastic aspect of the organism. Self is the whole of me, but my synapses allow for "many aspects of the self to exist" (2003: 31).

Neuroscience sees the self as embodied. For Damasio, it's "a repeatedly reconstructed biological state" rooted in neural mapping of the body (1996: 226–227). This gives it both stability, as the body stays basically the same over time, and flexibility, as its emotional state is forever in flux. Brainstem areas generate feelings related to what's happening to us that are "primordial and indispensable components of the self" (2010: 76).[5] So the embodied self is a background process.

In Ramachandran's view, "our sense of being ... an embodied self seems to depend crucially on back-and-forth, echo-like 'reverberation' between the brain and the rest of the body" (2011: 151). He sees the self as a process from the bottom of the brain to the top, declaring that it's not a monolithic entity even if it thinks it is. So it's a fluid, rather than a unified, bottom-up process.

The bottom-up aspect is echoed by Panksepp who gives the "core SELF" the same capital letter treatment as the emotional systems because it's a "primary process of mind" (2012: 390). It consists of "deep subcortical processes that engender organismic coherence" as they map the visceral body, centred in the upper brainstem areas including the PAG (2012: 390). These SELF processes provide a "neural platform" for our felt experience which, along with the emotional systems, interacts with cortical processes to give us a "multi-layered existential self-awareness" (2012: 392–393). So the self comes in layers, with an emotional and somatic core deep in the brain fuelling our cortical experience of ourselves.

A subcortical self and divided cortical selves

The layered self may lead us to the divided self. Following McGilchrist, the "core of the self" has its roots in the subcortical layer, giving us our "fundamental sense of self" (2009: 221). Trouble arises in the cortical layer when the hemispheres run into conflict. While the right hemisphere, with its richer connectivity with the subcortex, maintains a coherent sense of self (unless fragmented in dissociation), the left hemisphere, with its capacity to suppress the right and stand apart, sometimes produces a disconnected self – a 'false self' detached from a 'real self'.

The false self may seem like a separate self, but other people can't be far away. For Ramachandran, the self "emerges from a reciprocity of interactions with others and with the body", despite its declarations of independence (2011: 152). And this points towards the right hemisphere for, as Cozolino says, "the experience of self is born in early relationships that shape the many layers of function biased toward the right hemisphere" (2006: 338).[6] The ground is prepared for potential conflict between a relational right hemisphere self and a separatist left hemisphere self. The former feels closer than the latter to my 'fundamental' sense of self.

Transforming the self in therapy

So-called 'peak' experiences can temporarily transform the client's sense of self; the feeling may not last, but their meaningfulness is never forgotten. However, what matters most is that therapy itself is a meaningful experience that transforms his sense of self in a lasting way. Such transformation may include experiencing more polyvagal safety in relationships, better affect regulation and a wider window of tolerance. It probably involves both hemispheres; it certainly involves the right brain-body ensemble. Sometimes there are incremental changes in the implicit background that the client scarcely notices: "therapy did nothing for me" his left hemisphere may say, yet his friends see that this time he hasn't ended his new relationship.

Transforming the self may begin in the left hemisphere with a new cognition; for example, understanding that grieving is a normal and necessary aspect of surviving the inevitable losses life brings. But whether initially cognitive or affective, the process must involve the right hemisphere and the embodied 'real' self. Then it will ripple through the client's interconnected right brain, which becomes a stronger foundation for his engagement with the world. This either happens or it doesn't – there's no in-between.

Profound changes in the client's sense of self may flow from integrating traumatic fragments in his right brain. Such fragments tend to undermine his core sense of self and lead to a divided self. With early attachment trauma, the development of the implicit self system is impeded and its capacity for integrating outer and inner sensory stimuli damaged (Schore 2012). The client's sense of self lacks robustness and fluidity, so he experiences difficulties in close relationships. As Schore says, "traumatic overwhelming emotional experiences dissolve this right frontal 'glue' function that integrates the self" (2012: 296).

The dramatic and cathartic experiences that people sometimes have in therapy and in groups are linked with the healing of trauma. When the fragmented self finds a pathway to wholeness, the experience is profound and meaningful. The self really *is* transformed.

'Self-actualisation' may be a process of left-right neural integration that counters the tendency to traumatic fragmentation and the avoidance of emotional suffering. Therapists can observe and comment from outside, but it's the client's sense of self, and what it enables him to do in life, that's at the heart of the matter. It reflects the overall constellation of the right brain-body ensemble.

Conclusion

The left hemisphere asks "how do I make my life meaningful?", and gets frustrated on finding no easy answer. The right hemisphere has a talent for making life *feel* meaningful, thanks to its implicit capacity for initiating meaning-making. Experiencing life as meaningless may be a symptom of a divided psyche in which the left hemisphere conflicts with the right and suppresses it excessively. In contrast, the natural ability to experience meaningfulness may reflect hemispheric co-operation and neural integration.

The inner world of the right hemisphere appears to be the source of meaningful experiences and meaning-making due to its capacity to adapt to novel situations, including those involving intimacy and emotional transparency. If we live from our felt sense of the here-and-now, in polyvagal safety in social situations, our inner life animates us. The range of experiences we find meaningful expands when we're open to their emotional impact. However, we need our left hemisphere to help us appreciate and share our meaningful experiences with others.

For therapy to be effective, the client must experience it as meaningful. It must help him make meaning of his life, including the painful and traumatic aspects. Meaningful experiences, whether in the therapy room or outside it, give him confidence in the inner world of his background bodymind. He can let go inside, giving up trying to 'make it happen'. When he experiences daily life as meaningful, he no longer needs to chase super-meaningful experiences that are inevitably followed by anti-climax.

Notes

1 An interesting question about imagery is whether the left hemisphere filtering happens between the posterior lobes or the frontal lobes or both.

2 Greenfield concludes that "the most plausible anatomical location for dreaming is therefore in the *interaction* between the frontal cortex" and this posterior cortical area (2017: 166).

3 There's a fascinating implication here. I always assumed that relationship was fundamental to everything in the brain, but REM sleep and dreaming, that precedes the experience of relating, may be even more fundamental; so the separate self precedes the relating self. I'm willing to sign up for this view.

4 McGilchrist's research evidence for right hemisphere dominance comes from EEG coherence data, and blood flow measurements showing greatly increased flow in the adjoining areas of the temporal and parietal lobes in the right hemisphere.
5 Damasio's brainstem areas that generate primordial feelings that feed into self are the nucleus tractus solitarius and parabrachial nucleus that map body state (2010).
6 But with the caveat of my point (in note 3 above) about the experience of self starting in REM sleep and dreaming in the womb.

Epilogue

Ways ahead

Psychotherapy, and indeed every field which begins with 'psych', may be at a turning point. To our personal experience of how our minds and bodies do what they do, we can now add our biology as a foundation for our understanding of psychology.

What will happen if therapy gets serious about neuroscience? As Cozolino points out, "psychotherapy came into being and survived for a century in the absence of a brain-based model of change" (2017: 379). It's come a long way without one, but we now have the outline of one, and a biological perspective can complement our psychological one. We must sift and summarise the many-headed monster that is neuroscience into a comprehensible body of knowledge that's digestible for non-scientists. Enthusiasts such as myself must promote understanding and encourage creative thinking, not dazzle people with science.

I hope this book is a useful contribution to the process. To bring our discussion to a conclusion, let me say something about how we might proceed.

Triangulation: psychological theory, personal experience and neuroscience

Psychotherapy theory has only had personal experience as a reference point until now. This has brought us a long way – Freud, Jung, Rogers and many, many more – thanks to the creative human mind and brain. Now neuroscience allows us to cross-reference psychological thinking with biological reality. The opportunity is for a synthesis of neuroscience and psychological theory.

What if neuroscience is no longer in its infancy?

Neuroscience may have come further in understanding the brain than many people appreciate, it's just that the dots are only now being joined up – the business of the hemispheres, for example. Has everyone been so immersed in their own specialist area that they haven't noticed the big picture that's been forming? Perhaps neuroscientists could benefit from talking more with therapists who, after all, develop an intuitive understanding of the nervous system. We do field work on it every day we sit in the therapist's chair.

Will therapy go hi-tech?

If therapy takes neuroscience to heart, will therapists send their clients off to have their brains scanned? Cozolino reports research studies suggesting that neuroimaging may be used in future to find brain areas with unusually high or low activation to help with diagnosis and choice of therapeutic approach, and may be repeated during therapy to fine-tune the work and measure outcomes (2017). In addition, new drugs derived from neuroscience research may aid the process of therapy, as may magnetic stimulation of depressed left hemispheres and manic right hemispheres.

Science fiction? Such developments will be interesting, but I'm sceptical, as I'm sure many therapists will be. Even if technical adjuncts to therapy become reality, their cost will restrict their availability. People see therapists in confidence and may not want a medical team involved. Neuroimaging conclusions might be hard to implement in the human encounter in the therapy room – and what if they confuse the client or conflict with what the therapist thinks? Effective therapy depends on personal qualities and experience, and hi-tech accoutrements might detract from these human aspects rather than help them. A sensitive and well-trained therapist's ear may in practice be better than any brain scanner at noticing the quirks in someone's neural functioning.

Integration is the aim

Therapy seeks a better integration of neural networks and psychological capacities, especially when these have been hampered by emotional stress and trauma. Cozolino says "no major form of psychotherapy has emerged with the stated goal of neural network integration" (2017: 410), but perhaps that's just as well. Explicit attempts to re-organise the brain may be too deliberate to be effective, over-riding our implicit understanding of re-organising it via engaging with the psyche. But we can bear the neurobiological models of the psyche in mind in promoting integration. Does one of the three axes of neural architecture shed light on what the client brings to therapy? What's the polyvagal nature of the therapeutic relationship? Which emotional system is evident, and which is notable by its absence? And so forth.

Neuroscience may enable therapists of different persuasions to speak a common language, encouraging better integration of the many branches of the profession (Cozolino 2017). And a common language may make it easier to go cross-disciplinary and collaborate with other professions. Therapists may even be better placed than neuroscientists to appreciate aspects of brain functioning such as the subtleties of hemispheric conflict and co-operation, thanks to our familiarity with the fine details of inner experience.

Making neuroscience useful to therapists

What do therapists who've learnt some neuroscience do with it in practice? I asked some who've participated in my seminars and discussion group.

A top hit is telling clients who feel stuck in patterns of behaviour and thinking that new neural pathways can develop in their brains, giving them hope that engaging in therapy can lead to change. This may be a sort of placebo effect, and no technical detail is needed to convey the idea – in fact, scientific accuracy has little to do with it!

These therapists say they find it helpful to have a neuroscience perspective on what may be happening in clients' minds and brains, and why. It adds an extra dimension to their reflections on how best to work with a person. They can talk to the client about it so he has more understanding of what ails him and how therapy may help. If they can explain something to a client in emotional pain, he's likely to feel some relief. Some report feeling better equipped to address the challenges that clients present, and when they consequently feel more hopeful, so may the client.

I'm often asked how neuroscience has changed the way I work. It's difficult to answer this question, since I've been studying neuroscience for over 20 years and my learning has been gradual. I never made a conscious decision to change course in how I work. What I do know is that I frequently think about the ideas I've presented in this book, and sometimes offer my clients a brief synopsis of, for example, one of the axes of neural architecture, polyvagal theory, the emotional systems and three levels of emotional control in the brain, or the window of tolerance and cycle of emotional arousal. I feel more confident discussing memory, the nature of 'unconscious' feelings and material, and working with trauma and dissociation. Not everything is instantly crystal clear, but instead of feeling befuddled by strange phenomena, I find it helpful to reflect on those phenomena in the light of my neuroscience understanding as well as the psychological theories lodged in my skull.

The acid test is whether over time therapists find it useful to include neuroscience in their theoretical stance. And, of course, whether their clients find it useful to be fed a little of it. Perhaps, as Cozolino says, the value of neuroscience for therapists is not so much to generate new ways of doing therapy as simply "to help us grasp the neurobiological substrates of the talking cure" (2017: 417). Then we might understand the work better and feel more confident in tackling its difficult aspects.

Training therapists in neuroscience

Neuroscience will only make significant inroads into psychological thinking if there's more basic training in the subject; "psychotherapy training needs to include much more training in neuroscience", says Watt (2003: 112). Although there's increasing reference to neuroscience on training courses, I've yet to hear of any counselling or therapy course attempting a comprehensive inclusion of the subject. Doing this raises questions. What would the syllabus be (perhaps this book could serve as a consultation paper)? How do you strike a balance between neuroscience, psychological theory and experiential learning? Who would teach the neuroscience? Would all the trainers and supervisors need to be trained beforehand in order to provide consistency throughout the different elements of a course? These questions will only be answered by trying it.

Approaching neuroscience with both hemispheres

The left hemisphere wants to use neuroscience to inform therapeutic work ("what does neuroscience say I should do?"). It may rush to try to 'apply' neuroscience in the room, and to formulate methods supposedly 'based in neuroscience'. Nothing wrong here, but let's balance it with the right hemisphere. Let's take our time to allow neuroscience to sink in and wait to see what unfolds in our intuitive minds. Let's be tolerant of each other's different levels of knowledge and gaps in knowledge. Let's talk about neuroscience, allowing for disagreements without abandoning the conversation. And let's start with the big picture view before immersing ourselves in too much detail.

The big evolutionary picture

Psychotherapy and psychiatry are, arguably, the professions most responsible for addressing problems associated with the evolution of the human nervous system. LeDoux states his view unambiguously:

> there is an imperfect set of connections between cognitive and emotional systems in the current stage of evolution of the human brain. This state of affairs is part of the price we pay for having newly evolved cognitive capacities that are not yet fully integrated into our brains.
>
> (2003: 322)

He thinks this is the price we pay for the rapid development of language in the human brain. How fitting then that it should be the 'talking cure' that aims to integrate our cognitive capacities! He gets to the core of the matter:

> Our brain has not evolved to the point where the new systems that make complex thinking possible can easily control the old systems that give rise to our base needs and motives, and emotional reactions ... *Doing* the right thing doesn't always flow naturally from *knowing* what the right thing to do is.
>
> (2003: 323)

Isn't this precisely the conundrum we and our clients face in the therapy room? It implies that we must focus attention on the affective and somatic, as well as the cognitive, aspects of our work if we're to avoid cementing evolutionary imperfections in place.

While therapy requires reflection with the felt sense, the human nervous system is nevertheless still primed for action rather than reflection (Maturana & Varela 1987). Despite all the achievements of the sciences and the arts, despite all the philosophers and spiritual teachers over millennia, despite all the books examining human successes and failures, despite all the psychological research, we remain prone to creating poverty and misery, to resorting to violence and war – and now to destroying the basis for life to flourish, or even continue, on our beautiful blue and white planet. The human nervous system is obviously a work in progress. Understanding it better won't in itself mean we overcome the dangers we've created, but it might help. It seems we must develop our capacity for reflection and for listening to each other.

As Edelman writes, "perhaps when we understand and accept a scientific view of how our mind emerges in the world, a richer view of our nature and more lenient myths will serve us" (1992: 171). If neuroscience can help us be more compassionate towards our human failings, and more effective in addressing them, that would be welcome. Maybe we can play an active role in our evolution.

Glossary

Adrenaline. A hormone released from the adrenal glands during sympathetic arousal.

Amygdala. A subcortical brain area associated with generating stress, anxiety and fear.

Anterior. The front part of something, e.g. a brain area.

Anterior cingulate. A cortical brain area associated with feeling and emotion.

Autonomic. Not under conscious control, i.e. involuntary.

Autonomic nervous system. The part of central and peripheral nervous systems we can't consciously control, e.g. heart rate.

Axon. The single nerve fibre that sends signals from the neuron cell body to synapses.

Basal. Belonging to the bottom layer of an area.

Binding. The brain's capacity to unite the disparate activities of different brain areas into one conscious experience.

Blood-brain barrier. The walls of blood vessels in the brain that protect it from toxic molecules in the blood supply.

Brainstem. A large subcortical brain area where the brain meets the top of the spinal cord, associated with autonomic regulation of the body's vital functions.

Brain waves. Patterns of neural firing across the brain, different rates of firing corresponding with different mental states (alpha, beta, gamma etc.).

Broca's area. An area of the left frontal lobe associated with speaking.

Caudate (caudate nucleus). A subcortical area in the basal ganglia, associated with OCD.

Central nervous system. The brain and the spinal cord.

Cerebellum. A subcortical brain area at the back of the brainstem, associated with co-ordinating movements.

Cingulate. A cortical area overlying the corpus callosum, associated with emotion and the body.

Circuit. A feedback loop of pathways linking groups of neurons.

Columns. A term for the way neurons are arranged in the cortex.

Connective tissue. The tissue that lies between other tissues such as nerves and muscles.

Connectome. The particular set of connections between neurons in an individual brain – a neural version of your genome.

Contralateral. Refers to nerves crossing from one side of the body to the other, e.g. the right hemisphere controls movement in the left side of the body.

Corpus callosum. The band of nerve fibres linking left and right hemispheres.

Cortex. The wrinkly-shaped upper part of the brain.

Cortisol. The most commonly cited stress hormone, a glucocorticoid.

CRH (corticotropin releasing hormone). A stress hormone released by the hypothalamus that leads to cortisol release in the body, sometimes referred to as CRF (corticotropin releasing factor).

Cytokines. Small proteins important in the immune system.

Default mode network. A term for a number of brain areas active when the brain isn't engaged in any particular task.

Dendrite. A nerve branch of one neuron that receives signals from synapses with other neurons.

Dopamine. A neurochemical associated with motivation.

Dorsal. At the top of something, e.g. the frontal lobes.

Dorsal vagus. The branch of the vagus nerve system that generates life threat states.

EEG (electroencephalogram). A device for tracking brain waves.

Endocrine. Related to hormones.

Endorphins. A neuropeptide associated with feeling good – short for 'endogenous morphine', also referred to as 'endogenous opioids'.

Enteric nervous system. The neural system in the intestinal walls.

Epigenetics. Changes to gene expression, as opposed to changes to DNA.

Epinephrine. American for adrenaline.

Excitation. A signal from one neuron to another encouraging it to fire.

Executive functions. The highly evolved functions of the frontal lobes, e.g. decision making, empathy.

Explicit memory. The memory of something we can recall, e.g. an event or a fact.

Firing. The electrochemical signalling of one neuron to another.

fMRI (functional magnetic resonance imaging). A common type of brain scanning by recording changes to blood oxygen levels that correlate with neural activity.

Frontal lobes. The cortical lobes at the front of the brain, associated with highly evolved functions.

GABA (gamma-aminobutyric acid). The inhibitory neurotransmitter.

Glia. Cells in the brain that support and nourish neurons.

Glucocorticoids. The scientific term for stress hormones, e.g. cortisol.
Glutamate. The excitatory neurotransmitter.
Grey matter. Refers to neurons and short axons to neighbouring neurons.
Heart rate variability. The variation in the time between heartbeats.
Hippocampus. A subcortical brain area associated with narrative and spatial memory.
Homeostasis. The way our viscera and internal milieu remain on an even keel.
Hormone. A biochemical produced in the body that enters the bloodstream.
HPA axis. HPA = hypothalamus – pituitary gland – adrenal glands, the biochemical route for triggering stress via a sequence of hormones.
Hypothalamus. A subcortical brain area associated with triggering hormone release.
Images. The dynamic maps the brain makes of everything, usually outside awareness – neural, not visual, images.
Immune system. Cells found all over the body and brain, including white blood cells, that protect us against alien organisms.
Implicit memory. Memory we can't recall, e.g. somatic and affective memory of what happened in infancy.
Inhibition. A signal from one neuron to another, dampening it to make it less likely to fire.
Insula (insular cortex). A cortical brain area close to the cingulate, associated with inner body state and feelings.
Internal milieu. The fluid insides of the body.
Interoception. The sense of the inner state of the body, often outside awareness.
Lateral. At the side of the brain viewed from the front or back.
Lateralisation. Refers to the anatomical and functional division of the brain, especially the hemispheres, to left and right sides.
Limbic system. A subcortical grouping of brain areas above the brainstem, including the amygdala, hippocampus, hypothalamus and thalamus.
Lymph system. The network of vessels alongside blood vessels that carries lymph fluids, part of the immune system.
Maps, mapping. Dynamic patterns of firing in the brain that represent everything the brain deals with.
Medial. In the middle of the brain when viewed from the front or back.
Microbiome. Our gut bacteria.
Monoamines. The group of neuromodulators that includes serotonin, dopamine and noradrenaline.
Motor. Everything to do with movement in, and of, the body, including that of heart and lungs etc.
Motor cortex. The part of the frontal lobes that controls bodily movement.

Myelin. White fatty stuff coating long axons so that signals travel faster.

Neocortex. 'New' cortex – the four cerebral lobes (as opposed to paleocortex).

Nerve bundles. Bunches of nerve fibres.

Nerve fibres. Axons, with a neuron at one end and synapses at the other.

Neuroception. The brain's perception, beneath awareness, of social safety, danger or life threat.

Neurogenesis. The birth of new neurons across the lifespan.

Neuromodulator. A neurochemical that modulates the effects of GABA or glutamate, e.g. dopamine, serotonin, noradrenaline.

Neuron. A brain cell, or cell in the spinal cord or enteric nervous system.

Neuropeptide. Neurochemicals that affect how we feel, e.g. endorphins.

Neuroplasticity. The brain's capacity to change across the lifespan, mainly through changes to synapses.

Neurotransmitter. Neurochemicals that are part of signalling across synapses, especially GABA and glutamate.

Noradrenaline. A neuromodulator associated with mental energy.

Norepinephrine. American for noradrenaline.

Nuclei. Closely connected groups of neurons with similar functions.

Occipital lobes. The cortical lobes at the back of the brain that look after vision.

Orbital. Over the eye sockets.

Orbitomedial prefrontal cortex. The middle part of the frontal lobes above the eye sockets, associated with the social brain.

Oxytocin. A hormone associated with bonding.

PAG (periaqueductal grey). A subcortical brainstem area associated with generating emotion.

Paleocortex. 'Old' cortex that evolved before neocortex – specifically, the cingulate and insula.

Parasympathetic. Refers to the parasympathetic nervous system.

Parasympathetic nervous system. The part of the autonomic nervous system that looks after rest, digestion and growth.

Parietal lobes. Between the occipital and frontal lobes, and above the temporal lobes, associated with bodily and spatial senses.

Peptide. Biochemicals in body and brain that affect how we feel, e.g. endorphins.

Peripheral nervous system. The nerves that lead from the brainstem and spinal cord to every corner of the body.

Peristalsis. The movement of the gut to enable digestion.

Polyvagal theory. The hierarchy of autonomic responses to social situations – safety, danger, life threat – based around the ventral vagus, dorsal vagus, sympathetic and parasympathetic nerves.

Posterior. The back part of something, e.g. a brain area.

Posterior lobes. The three cortical lobes behind the frontal lobes: occipital, temporal and parietal.
Prefrontal cortex. The front (and largest) part of the frontal lobes.
Premotor cortex. In the frontal lobes, for planning movements rather than enacting them.
Prosody. The rhythms and intonation of speaking.
Receptor. Where neurochemicals deliver their message, e.g. on a dendrite.
Reward system. Brain areas and networks that fire when we pursue something 'rewarding'.
Sensorimotor. Aspects of the nervous system involved in both sensing the body and causing it to move.
Sensory. To do with internal and external senses, e.g. interoception, seeing, hearing.
Serotonin. A neuromodulator associated with dampening emotional arousal.
Somatic. Of the body.
Somatic nervous system. The aspect of the peripheral nervous system that links muscles with the central nervous system.
Somatosensory. Concerned with sensing the body, e.g. somatosensory cortex.
Somatotopical. Laid out like a map of the body.
Striatum. A subcortical brain area belonging to the basal ganglia, part of the reward system.
Subcortex. The collection of brain areas underneath the cortex that evolved first.
Sympathetic. Refers to the sympathetic nervous system.
Sympathetic nervous system. The part of the autonomic nervous system that triggers arousal, especially raised blood flow for movement.
Synapse. The minute gap between the axon of one neuron and the dendrite of another where neurochemicals facilitate communication.
Synaptogenesis. The birth of new synapses at any point in the lifespan,
System. A neural network complex enough to enable a particular function e.g. seeing or hearing.
Temporal lobes. Between the occipital and frontal lobes, and below the parietal lobes, associated with hearing, speech and memory.
Thalamus. A subcortical brain area that's a relay station for sensory signals on their way to other brain areas.
Vagus. The main nerve bundle in the parasympathetic nervous system.
Vagal brake. The capacity of the ventral vagus to dampen sympathetic arousal, especially in the heart, in the cause of social engagement.
Vagal tone. The degree to which the social engagement system functions well due to the effect of the ventral vagus.
Vasopressin. A hormone that works alongside oxytocin and testosterone.
Ventral. At the bottom of something, e.g. the frontal lobes.

Ventral vagus. The branch of the vagus nerve system that enables social engagement.
Vestibular. To do with balance.
Viscera. The organs and much of what else sits inside the body.
Visual cortex. Another term for the occipital lobes.
White matter. Long axons coated in myelin for faster signalling.

References

Assagioli, R. (1990) *Psychosynthesis*, London: Mandala.
Baumeister, R. & Tierney, J. (2012) *Willpower*, London: Penguin.
Blackmore, S. (2017) *Seeing Myself*, London: Robinson.
Bloom, F., Nelson, C. & Lazerson, A. (2001) *Brain, Mind and Behaviour*, New York, NY: Worth Publishers.
Bohm, D. (1983) *Wholeness & the Implicate Order*, London: Ark Paperbacks.
Boyesen, G. (2006) "How I Developed Biodynamic Psychotherapy" in J. Corrigall, H. Payne & H. Wilkinson (eds.) *About a Body*, London: Routledge (pp. 132–138).
Bullmore, E. (2018) *The Inflamed Mind*, London: Short Books.
Butler, D. & Moseley, L. (2013) *Explain Pain*, Australia: NOI Group.
Carter, R. (2000) *Mapping the Mind*, London: Orion Books.
Carter, R. (2009) *The Brain Book*, London: Dorling Kindersley.
Carter, S. (2012) "The Healing Power of Love: An Oxytocin Hypothesis", 13th International EABP Congress of Body Psychotherapy seminar, Churchill College, Cambridge.
Claxton, G. (2005) *Wayward Mind*, London: Little, Brown.
Claxton, G. (2015) *Intelligence in the Flesh*, London: Yale University Press.
Cozolino, L. (2006) *The Neuroscience of Human Relationships*, London: Norton.
Cozolino, L. (2010) *The Neuroscience of Psychotherapy* (second edition), London: Norton.
Cozolino, L. (2016) *Why Therapy Works*, London: Norton.
Cozolino, L. (2017) *The Neuroscience of Psychotherapy* (third edition), London: Norton.
Craig, A. (2015) *How Do You Feel?* Woodstock, UK: Princeton University Press.
Damasio, A. (1996) *Descartes' Error*, London: Papermac.
Damasio, A. (1999) *The Feeling of What Happens*, London: Heinemann.
Damasio, A. (2003) *Looking for Spinoza*, London: Heinemann.
Damasio, A. (2010) *Self Comes to Mind*, London: Heinemann.
Damasio, A. (2018) *The Strange Order of Things*, New York, NY: Pantheon Books.
Dennett, D. (1984) *Elbow Room: The Varieties of Free Will Worth Wanting*, Oxford: Clarendon Press.
Doidge, N. (2008) *The Brain That Changes Itself*, London: Penguin.
Edelman, G. (1992) *Bright Air, Brilliant Fire*, New York, NY: Basic Books.
Edelman, G. (2005) *Wider than the Sky*, London: Penguin.

Edelman, G. & Tononi, G. (2000) *A Universe of Consciousness*, New York, NY: Basic Books.
Eiden, B. (2009) "The Roots and Development of the Chiron Approach" in L. Hartley (ed.) *Contemporary Body Psychotherapy*, London: Routledge (pp. 13–30).
Enders, G. (2015) *Gut*, London: Scribe Publications.
Fenwick, P. & Fenwick, E. (2011) *The Truth in the Light*, Guildford, UK: White Crow Books.
Fisher, J. (2017) "Using the Heart to Heal the Mind", Confer seminar "Heart Brain, Gut Brain", London.
Fonagy, P. (2010) "Attachment & Mentalisation as a Common Framework for Therapy", UKCP research conference lecture, London.
Frith, C. (2007) *Making Up the Mind*, Oxford: Blackwell Publishing.
Gallese, V. (2014) "Embodied Empathy and Mirror Neurons", Confer seminar, London.
Gazzaniga, M. (2016) *Tales from Both Sides of the Brain*, New York, NY: Ecco.
Gendlin, E.T. (1964) "A Theory of Personality Change" in P. Worchel & D. Byrne (eds.) *Personality Change*, New York: John Wiley (pp. 102–148).
Gendlin, E.T. (1981) *Focusing*, New York, NY: Bantam.
Gendlin, E.T. (1986) *Let Your Body Interpret Your Dreams*, Willmette, IL: Chiron Publications.
Gendlin, E.T. (1992) "Three Learnings since the Dreambook", *The Folio*, vol. 11 (1), (pp. 25–29), New York, NY: The Focusing Institute.
Gendlin, E.T. (1996) *Focusing-Oriented Psychotherapy*, New York, NY: Guilford Press.
Gerhardt, S. (2015) *Why Love Matters* (second edition), London: Routledge.
Gershon, M. (1999) *The Second Brain*, New York, NY: Harper Perennial.
Glaser, D. (2017) Personal communication.
Goldberg, E. (2009) *The New Executive Brain*, New York, NY: Oxford University Press.
Greenfield, S. (2001) *The Private Life of the Brain*, London: Penguin.
Greenfield, S. (2017) *A Day in the Life of the Brain*, London: Penguin.
House, R. (2013) Letter in "Therapy Today", *BACP Journal*, vol. 24 (6), (p. 42).
James, O. (2016) *Not in Your Genes*, London: Vermilion.
Jarrett, C. (2015) *Great Myths of the Brain*, Chichester, UK: Wiley Blackwell.
Jung, C.G. (1978) *Man and His Symbols*, London: Picador.
Jung, C.G. (1983) *Jung: Selected Writings*, London: Fontana Press.
Jung, C.G. (1986) *Psychological Reflections*, London: Ark Paperbacks.
Jung, C.G. (1995) *Memories, Dreams, Reflections*, London: Fontana Press.
Kalsched, D. (1996) *The Inner World of Trauma*, London: Routledge.
Kandel, E. (2007) *In Search of Memory*, London: Norton.
Kandel, E. & Hawkins, R. (1999) "The Biological Basis of Learning and Individuality" in *The Scientific American Book of the Brain*, Guilford, CT: Lyons Press.
Knox, J. (2011) *Self-Agency in Psychotherapy*, London: Norton.
Kradin, R. (2016) "The Placebo Response & Psychosomatic Disorders", Confer seminar, London.
Lakoff, G. & Johnson, M. (1999) *Philosophy in the Flesh*, New York, NY: Basic Books.

Landale, M. (2009) "Working with Psychosomatic Distress and Developmental Trauma" in L. Hartley (ed.) *Contemporary Body Psychotherapy*, London: Routledge (pp. 151–163).
Lawrence, D.H. (1979) "Letter from D.H. Lawrence to Ernest Collings 17 January 1913" in James T. Boulton (ed.) *The Letters of D.H. Lawrence*, Vol. 1 1901–1913, Cambridge, UK: Cambridge University Press.
LeDoux, J. (1999) *The Emotional Brain*, London: Phoenix.
LeDoux, J. (2003) *Synaptic Self*, London: Penguin.
LeDoux, J. (2015) *Anxious*, London: Oneworld Publications.
Levine, P. (2010) *In an Unspoken Voice*, Berkeley, CA: North Atlantic Books.
Levitin, D. (2015) *The Organised Mind*, London: Penguin.
Lewis, M. (2012) *Memoirs of an Addicted Brain*, New York, NY: PublicAffairs.
MacLean, P. (1990) *The Triune Brain in Evolution*, New York, NY: Plenum Press.
Marsh, H. (2014) *Do No Harm*, London: Weidenfeld & Nicolson.
Maté, G. (2011) *When the Body Says No*, Hoboken, NJ: Wiley.
Maturana, H. & Varela, F. (1987) *The Tree of Knowledge*, Boston, MA: Shambhala.
Mayer, E. (2018) *The Mind-Gut Connection*, New York, NY: Harper Wave.
McCrone, J. (1999) *Going Inside*, London: Faber & Faber.
McGilchrist, I. (2009) *The Master & His Emissary*, London: Yale University Press.
McGilchrist, I. (2010) Personal email communication.
McGilchrist, I. (2013) "The Right Brain, Left Brain Divide", Confer seminar, London.
McGilchrist, I. (2015) Talk at Guildhall, London.
Nataraja, S. (2008) *The Blissful Brain*, London: Gaia.
Ogden, P. (2009) "Emotion, Mindfulness, and Movement" in D. Fosha, D. Siegel & M. Solomon (eds.) *The Healing Power of Emotion*, New York, NY: Norton (pp. 204–231).
Ogden, P., Minton, K. & Pain, C. (2006) *Trauma and the Body*, New York, NY: Norton.
Panksepp, J. (2003) "Damasio's Error" (review of Damasio's *Looking for Spinoza)*, in *Consciousness & Emotion* vol. 4 (1), (pp. 111–134), John Benjamin's Publishing.
Panksepp, J. (2005) *Affective Neuroscience*, New York, NY: Oxford University Press.
Panksepp, J. (2006) "The Core Emotional Systems of the Mammalian Brain" in J. Corrigall, H. Payne & H. Wilkinson (eds.) *About a Body*, London: Routledge (pp. 14–32).
Panksepp, J. (2009) "Brain Emotional Systems and Qualities of Mental Life" in D. Fosha, D. Siegel & M. Solomon (eds.) *The Healing Power of Emotion*, New York, NY: Norton (pp. 1–26).
Panksepp, J. (2012a) Personal email.
Panksepp, J. (2012b) "Neuroplasticity & Emotional Processes of the Brain", Confer seminar, London.
Panksepp, J. & Biven, L. (2012) *The Archaeology of Mind*, New York, NY: Norton.
Perlmutter, D. (2015) *Brain Maker*, London: Yellow Kite.
Pert, C. (1997) *Molecules of Emotion*, London: Simon & Schuster.
Porges, S. (2011) *The Polyvagal Theory*, New York, NY: Norton.
Porges, S. (2012) Personal email.
Porges, S. (2017) *The Pocket Guide to the Polyvagal Theory*, New York, NY: Norton.

Porges, S. (2017a) Personal email.
Ramachandran, V. S. (2005) *Phantoms in the Brain*, London: Harper Collins.
Ramachandran, V. S. (2011) *The Tell Tale Brain*, London: Heinemann.
Rose, S. (2006) *The 21st-Century Brain*, London: Vintage Books.
Rothschild, B. (2000) *The Body Remembers*, New York, NY: Norton.
Sacks, O. (2017) *The River of Consciousness*, New York, NY: Alfred Knopf.
Sapolsky, R. (2004) *Why Zebras Don't Get Ulcers*, New York, NY: Holt Paperbacks.
Sapolsky, R. (2017) *Behave*, London: Bodley Head.
Sapolsky, R. (2017a) Personal email.
Schaible, M. (2009) "Biodynamic Massage as a Body Therapy and as a Tool in Body Psychotherapy" in L. Hartley (ed.) *Contemporary Body Psychotherapy*, London: Routledge (pp. 31–45).
Schore, A. (2003) *Affect Regulation*, New York, NY: Norton.
Schore, A. (2003a) "The Seventh Annual John Bowlby Memorial Lecture" in J. Corrigall & H. Wilkinson (eds.) *Revolutionary Connections*, London: Karnac (pp. 7–51).
Schore, A. (2009) "Right Brain Affect Regulation" in D. Fosha, D. Siegel & M. Solomon (eds.) *The Healing Power of Emotion*, New York: Norton (pp. 112–144).
Schore, A. (2012) *The Science of the Art of Psychotherapy*, New York, NY: Norton.
Schwartz, J. & Begley, S. (2003) *The Mind and the Brain*, New York, NY: Harper Perennial.
Seung, S. (2013) *Connectome*, London: Penguin.
Siegel, D. (1999) *The Developing Mind*, New York, NY: Guilford Press.
Siegel, D. (2007) *The Mindful Brain*, New York, NY: Norton.
Siegel, D. (2010) *Mindsight*, New York, NY: Bantam.
Solms, M. (2015) *The Feeling Brain*, London: Karnac.
Solms, M. & Turnbull, O. (2002) *The Brain and the Inner World*, London: Karnac.
Sperry, R. (1985) "Consciousness, Personal Identity and the Divided Brain" in D. Benson & E. Zaidel (eds.) *The Dual Brain: Hemispheric Specialisation in Humans*, New York, NY: Guilford Press (pp. 11–26).
Stauffer, K. (2010) *Anatomy & Physiology for Psychotherapists*, New York, NY: Norton.
Stern, D. (1998) *The Interpersonal World of the Infant*, London: Karnac.
Timini, S. (2013) Article in *Self & Society*, summer 2013, London: Association for Humanistic Psychology in Britain (pp. 6–11).
Trevarthen, C. (1990) "Growth and Education of the Hemispheres" in C. Trevarthen (ed.) *Brain Circuits and Functions of the Mind*, Cambridge, UK: Cambridge University Press (pp. 334–363).
Trevarthen, C. (2009) "The Functions of Emotion in Infancy" in D. Fosha, D. Siegel & M. Solomon (eds.) *The Healing Power of Emotion*, New York, NY: Norton (pp. 55–85).
Tronick, E. (2009) "Multilevel Meaning Making and Dyadic Expansion of Consciousness Theory" in D. Fosha, D. Siegel & M. Solomon (eds.) *The Healing Power of Emotion*, New York, NY: Norton (pp. 86–111).
van der Kolk, B. (2011) Foreword in S. Porges (ed.) *The Polyvagal Theory*, New York, NY: Norton (pp. XI–XVII).
van der Kolk, B. (2014) *The Body Keeps The Score*, London: Allen Lane.
Varela, F., Thompson, E. & Rosch, E. (1993) *The Embodied Mind*, Cambridge, MA: MIT Press.

Watkins, A. (2017) "Mind Control: Who Is in Charge?", Confer seminar "Gut Brain, Heart Brain", London.

Watt, D. (2003) "Psychotherapy in an Age of Neuroscience" in J. Corrigall & H. Wilkinson (eds.) *Revolutionary Connections*, London: Karnac (pp. 79–115).

Watt, D.F. (2005) "Social Bonds and the Nature of Empathy", *Journal of Consciousness Studies*, vol. 12 (8–10), (pp. 185–209).

Wikipedia. (2017) "Bipolar disorder". Retrieved from https://en.wikipedia.org/wiki/Bipolar_disorder.

Wilkinson, M. (2006) *Coming into Mind*, London: Routledge.

Wilson, R. (2014) *Neuroscience for Counsellors*, London: Jessica Kingsley.

Zajonc, R. (1984) "On the Primacy of Affect" in K. Scherer & P. Ekman (eds.) *Approaches to Emotion*, Hillsdale, NJ: Lawrence Erlbaum (pp. 259–270).

Index

Note: Locators in **bold** refer to tables, and locators in *italics* refer to figures.